Modernist

DONALD DAVIE was born in Barnsley in 1922 and educated at Barnsley Holgate Grammar School and St Catharine's College, Cambridge. During the Second World War he served in the Navy and travelled widely. He was a Fellow of Trinity College, Dublin, lecturer at Dublin University and Fellow of Gonville and Caius College, Cambridge before becoming Professor of English and Pro-Vice-Chancellor at the University of Essex. In 1968 he left England for America to take up a chair at Stanford, and later at Vanderbilt. Donald Davie returned to England in 1988; he died in 1995. Carcanet publish a number of his works, including *Under Briggflatts* (1989), *Slavic Excursions* (1990), *Studies in Ezra Pound* (1991), *With the Grain: Thomas Hardy and Modern British Poetry* (1998), *Two Ways Out of Whitman: American Essays* (2000), *Collected Poems* (2002) and *A Travelling Man* (2003).

CLIVE WILMER is a freelance writer who teaches at Cambridge. He has translated Miklós Radnóti and Gyorgy Petri, and edited essays by Thom Gunn and selections of Ruskin, William Morris and Dante Gabriel Rossetti. Carcanet have published four volumes of his poetry: *The Dwelling Place* (1977), *Devotions* (1982), *Of Earthly Paradise* (1992) and his *Selected Poems* (1995). He edited Donald Davie's *With the Grain* for Carcanet (1998).

Also by Donald Davie from Carcanet

POETRY
Selected Poems
To Scorch or Freeze
Collected Poems
Poems and Melodramas

CRITICISM
Under Briggflatts: a history of poetry
in Great Britain 1960–1985

Slavic Excursions: essays on
Polish and Russian literature

Studies in Ezra Pound

With the Grain: essays on Thomas Hardy
and modern British poetry

Two Ways Out of Whitman:
American essays

A Travelling Man:
eighteenth-century bearings

AUTOBIOGRAPHY
These the Companions

Donald Davie

Modernist Essays
Yeats, Pound, Eliot

edited with an introduction by

Clive Wilmer

CARCANET

First published in Great Britain in 2004 by
Carcanet Press Limited
Alliance House
Cross Street
Manchester M2 7AQ

Essays copyright © the Estate of Donald Davie 2004
Introduction, selection and editorial matter copyright © Clive Wilmer 2004

The right of Clive Wilmer to be identified as the editor
of this work has been asserted by him in accordance with
the Copyright, Designs and Patents Act of 1988

All rights reserved

A CIP catalogue record for this book is available from the British Library

ISBN 1 85754 649 0

The publisher acknowledges financial assistance from Arts Council England

Typeset in Monotype Bembo by XL Publishing Services, Tiverton
Printed and bound by Antony Rowe Ltd, Eastbourne

Contents

Introduction

In his first critical book, *Purity of Diction in English Verse* (1952), Donald Davie wrote: 'there is no denying that modern poetry is obscure and that it would be less so if the poets adhered to the syntax of prose'. Taken out of context, this may surprise those of his readers who think of him as an authority on Modernism, especially as a champion of Ezra Pound. Of course, in the sentence I have quoted he is not exactly condemning the obscurity, but there is an implication that another sort of poetry would be preferable – for instance, the late Augustan verse he explores and celebrates in the book in question. Davie admires such poetry for its lucidity, its verbal restraint ('pure diction') and the attention its language pays to the world of fact. But he is also conscious that literary nostalgia and the kind of critical alertness he practises do not cohabit happily. In 'Homage to William Cowper', a poem of the same period, he calls himself 'A pasticheur of late Augustan styles', but he is all too aware that the committed pasticheur is merely a sentimentalist and that, if poetry is to thrive, it must engage with the reality of the world it is written for and must do so in the language of its time. That reality and that language are the products of historical developments, which for the poet have to include both the Romantic and the Modernist revolutions. In a chapter on Coleridge he records the moment when 'pure diction' is discarded in favour of divine afflatus, to which such purity is alien. The poem ceases to be an object in the world 'out there' and becomes instead a mode of expression. In consequence, the reader is no longer concerned with matters of objective fact but with the unique self of the inspired speaker:

> This is one of the most momentous changes in the history of poetry. It marks the disappearance of the Renaissance conviction about the poem as a made thing, thrown free of its makar, something added to creation and free-standing in its own right. The poet hereafter is legislator, seer, scapegoat and reporter; he is no longer an artificer.

It is therefore no accident that this book on the late Augustans is also concerned with more recent poetry. In particular, it has much to say, most of it sceptical and mildly adverse, about the Modernist masters: about W.B.Yeats, T.S. Eliot and, above all, Ezra Pound. It is important to remember that, though Davie was an academic by profession, he always wrote as a poet. Interesting as literary history might be, the nub of the matter was how good poems are made, and that question is always contemporary. The language of Goldsmith and Cowper could still be learnt from, but the art had moved on since. If modern poets were serious about their art, they could not help but stand in the shadow of T.S. Eliot.

And yet a few years later, in 'T.S. Eliot: The End of an Era' (1956), he comes close to expressing dislike for the third of the *Four Quartets*, preferring instead

> a kind of poetry which stands on its own feet, without my help, as an independent creation, a thing to be walked round, and as satisfying from one standpoint as from another. And so I hope not to be thought lacking in gratitude to Eliot for the *Four Quartets*, nor lacking in respect for the prodigious achievement of that poem, if I say that I hope for quite a different sort of poem in the future, a sort of poem more in harmony with what was written before symbolism was thought of, even (since symbolist procedures are only the logical development of Romantic procedures) before Romanticism was thought of. I am not forgetting the lesson of [Eliot's] 'Tradition and the Individual Talent'. I know that history cannot be unwritten, that there can be no question of putting the clock back; the post-post-symbolist poetry I look for may be more in harmony with pre-Romantic poetry, it can never be the same. There cannot be a conspiracy to pretend that the symbolist revolution never happened.

By 'symbolism' Davie means the late nineteenth-century French poetry that substituted suggestion and association for meaning and argument. The *Symboliste* movement was the point of departure for what we now call Modernism, and Davie's 'post-post-symbolism' is what comes after that. He is referring, in fact, to the poetry of the 1950s: Larkin, Gunn, Amis and himself – the poets of the 'Movement'. As he was later to admit, *Purity of Diction* had been intended as in some sense a Movement manifesto. In the Movement anthology *New Lines*, published in the same year as the essay on Eliot, nine young poets including Davie appeared to repudiate the lessons of Modernism, which, despite the claims of the Modernists themselves, they took to be a product of Romanticism. Instead, they appeared to be aiming for a common language expressing what could be felt as common perceptions, emotions and aspirations. The Movement poem has a social dimension: it is fond of the lubricants of everyday speech and talks of what 'we' feel, in place of the Romantic 'I' or the 'objective correlative' of the supposedly impersonal Modernist. These poets have also returned to a strict understanding of metrical form, giving the poem an objective rhythm and shape. Perhaps most important of all in Davie's view, they follow the syntax and grammar of ordinary prose, with all that that implies about the world beyond the poem.

Modernist poetry, by contrast, is united in '*the assertion or the assumption (most often the latter) that syntax in poetry is wholly different from syntax as understood by logicians and grammarians*'.

The italicized quotation is from Davie's second critical book, *Articulate Energy: An Enquiry into the Syntax of English Poetry* (1955), which, in its critique of Modernism, takes the debate about ordinary language a stage further. But in itemizing the losses entailed in the Modernist disruption of consecutive syntax, Davie brings us closer to the gains they hoped to make. Thus, although Davie firmly announces that the purpose of his argument is 'conservative' – 'it is, I hope, a rational conservatism' – and though he accuses Pound, as many less thoughtful readers have, of 'scrapping the contracts traditionally observed between poet and reader', *Articulate Energy* is more sympathetic to Modernist procedures than its predecessor was. A distance was developing between Davie and his Movement colleagues. Take, for instance, this comment on Pound's *Cantos*. The syntax of the poem, Davie says, seems to be dislocated,

> but in fact of course the *Cantos* are, or are meant to be, articulated most closely. They are articulated, however, by a syntax that is musical, not linguistic, by 'the unifying, all-embracing artifice of rhythm', understood in its widest sense, to mean not only the rhythm that rides through tempo and metre in the verse-paragraph, but also the rhythmical recurrence of ideas hinted at in one canto, picked up in another much later, suspended for many more, and so on.

This is – and was much more strikingly so at the time – a subtle and sympathetic account. One feels it not only in the accuracy of description but in the force and stylistic élan of Davie's prose.

Davie's next major book, one is hardly surprised to learn, was a monograph on Pound. Nevertheless, a period of ten years separates *Ezra Pound: Poet as Sculptor* (1965) from *Articulate Energy*. In the interim, much in Davie's thinking on Pound and Modernism had to develop. This is evident in the title. Pound's poetry is compared to sculpture, a static, rigid and monumental art. The analogy made in *Articulate Energy* was with music, which is abstract, temporal and immaterial. I don't suppose the later Davie would have repudiated the musical analogy, but he would certainly have wanted to modify it, and we can see him doing so in several of these essays, most notably 'The Relation between Syntax and Music in Some Modern Poems in English' (1961) and the extraordinary 'Two Analogies for Poetry' (1962). What happened in broad terms was that, in writing *Articulate Energy*, Davie became preoccupied with the way the English Aesthetes and the French Symbolists tended to compare one art with another. The 'Conclusion' to Walter Pater's *The Renaissance* (1873) was regarded as the manifesto of Aestheticism. There we read that, although each art has … its own specific order of impressions, and an untranslatable charm, while a just apprehension of the ultimate differences of the arts is the beginning of aesthetic criticism; yet it is noticeable that, in its special mode of handling its given material, each art may be observed to pass into the condition of some other art … a partial alienation from its own limitations…

Pater goes on to show how music may be pictorial, architecture poetic, and so on, and then he famously concludes:

All art constantly aspires towards the condition of music. For while in all other kinds of art it is possible to distinguish the matter from the form, and the understanding can always make this distinction, yet it is the constant effort of art to obliterate it.

Symbolist poets such as Mallarmé and Verlaine made similar remarks: 'De la musique', wrote the latter, 'avant toute chose.' Their concern, however, was specifically with poetry. This has nothing to do with melo-dious sound, though of course that is one of the ways in which poetry does resemble music; it is more that a poem is, like a piece of music, what Pound was to call, 'a form cut into time'. The fluidity permitted by time and acoustic sequence gives metamorphic qualities to music and to the poetry that imitates it. For the Symbolists, music provided a model for the kind of poem that seems to be made of pure connotation rather than denotation. Such poetry is deliberately mysterious and therefore tends to that modern obscurity we have seen the young Davie lamenting.

The poetry of Yeats in Ireland, of Valéry in France and of Rilke in Germany begins essentially where the Symbolists left off. Pound and Eliot were also immersed in modern French poetry. In fact, Eliot began writing in his mature manner when, in 1908, he read *The Symbolist Movement in Literature* by Yeats's Paterian friend Arthur Symons. The Symbolist manner is still apparent in *The Waste Land* (1922) and indeed, as Davie was one of the first to notice, in the much less obviously fragmentary *Four Quartets*. When Eliot in *The Waste Land* writes of the *sound* of water where there is no water, he is playing the Symbolist trick of allowing the words to generate meaning when there is no objective fact for the words to point at. As a result of sound and association, our thirsty imaginations are bathed in water, the existence of which is at that very moment denied. The effect is extraordinarily powerful, but it is achieved by dislo-cating language from reality. It is this more than obscurity that Davie is troubled by. He finds it in Yeats as well, particularly in the way Yeats prefers symbols to facts – indeed, only values facts if he can turn them into symbols. He also finds it in Yeats's occasional violations of normal grammar. Pound takes even more liberties with language, fragmenting it and eliding logical connectives, yet in Pound the relation to fact is wholly different. There is in Pound, as Davie increasingly notices, a different analogy, one also indebted to Pater, though it appears in some sense to question the musical one.

Pound was especially conscious of these *fin de siècle* artistic analogies and deliberately developed them further, partly I suspect because he was as interested in the other arts as in poetry and, like John Ruskin before him, thought of them as languages. He therefore developed the concepts of *melopoeia* (poetry when it is most like music), *phanopoeia* (when it is like painting and perhaps sculpture, in other words based on images) and *logopoeia* (which he summed up as 'the dance of the intellect among words', that is, serious verbal play). Pound was conscious of using all three, often all together in one poem, but there could be a predominance and *phanopoeia* provided a rationale for the movement Pound called *Imagisme*. The French name directed the reader to a contrast with *Symbolisme*:

> Imagisme is not symbolism. The symbolists dealt in "association", that is, in a sort of allusion, almost of allegory. They degraded the symbol to the status of a word. They made it a form of metonymy... Moreover one does not want to be called a symbolist, because symbolism has usually been associated with mushy technique.

The fluid suggestiveness of Symbolism was being contrasted with firm evocations of things in the outside world, existing independently of the poet's mind. These things might possess significances, but they were first of all sharply defined facts, resistant to the poet's will. In his 'search for the real' in poetry, Pound tells us, 'I made poems like "The Return", which is an objective reality and has a complicated sort of significance, like Mr Epstein's "Sun God", or Mr Brzeska's "Boy with a Coney"'. In other words, as Davie was the first to demonstrate, he was thinking of sculptures as models for his poems.

I have been quoting from *Gaudier-Brzeska: A Memoir*, Pound's 1916 study of the brilliant young sculptor Henri Gaudier-Brzeska, who had been killed in the First World War. The two men had been close friends. Gaudier had sculpted a magnificent bust of Pound (the Easter-Island-like 'Hieratic Head') and the sculptor, though seven years younger than Pound, had become for the poet a kind of hero, his image of the ideal artist. They had both been involved in the movement known as Vorticism, a notably dynamic development from Imagism which brought Pound into alliance with painters and sculptors: Gaudier, Percy Wyndham Lewis, Edward Wadsworth and, on the fringes of the movement, Gaudier's idol Jacob Epstein. It was Epstein who encouraged Gaudier to practise 'direct carving' in preference to moulding – cutting directly into stone or wood, that is, rather than moulding in clay to cast in bronze. As Davie argues in *Poet as Sculptor*, direct carving gave Pound a model for the kind of verse he wanted: verse that was 'hard' and resistant as stone, not 'soft' and 'muzzy' like the Symbolists (in Pound's view of them, at any rate). In his memoir, Pound quotes a review by Gaudier, which talks of direct carving as an engagement with the real:

> The sculpture I admire is the work of master craftsmen. Every inch of the surface is won at the point of the chisel – every stroke of the hammer is a physical and mental effort. No more arbitrary translations of a design in any material. They are fully aware of the different qualities and possibilities of woods, stones, and metals. Epstein, whom I consider the foremost in the small number of good sculptors in Europe, lays particular stress on this.

In his Preface to the Memorial Exhibition of Gaudier's work, which is incorporated in the memoir, Pound writes in similar terms. 'The sculptor', he says, 'must add to the power of imagining form-combination the physical energy to cut this into an unyielding medium.' In both cases we are asked to think of sculpture as the engagement with a pre-existing material. It is described in heroic terms, but there is no sense that the sculptor triumphs over the material. It is rather the engagement of imagination and physical prowess with a chunk of objective reality. As Pound wrote, 'The key word of vorticist art was Objectivity in the sense that we insisted that the value of a piece of sculpture was dependent on its shape.' 'We' in that sentence means the Vorticists, mostly painters and sculptors, but Pound leaves us in no doubt that their values apply to his poetry as well.

From the mid-1910s Pound is looking for a way of writing that grows from an imaginative engagement with otherness, a 'search for the real'. This involves a complex relationship between artist, subject and medium. Gaudier can raise a fawn, say, from a piece of stone with what may strike us as totemic power, but he does so through respect as much for the stone and its distinctive character as for the animal itself. Thus, respect for one form of otherness, the animal, is dependent on another, the stone. The poet does not deal with matters as unyielding as that, but he can discipline himself to think of his medium, language, as equally resistant and, in doing so, may similarly render justice to nature.

It is often claimed that Pound and Eliot both advocated impersonality. Eliot, in the most famous of his essays, 'Tradition and the Individual Talent', puts forward such a doctrine, which is buttressed (in the essay on *Hamlet*) by his theory of the 'objective correlative'. Davie was never greatly impressed by these essays – for the important reason, as it seems to me, that Eliot's impersonality is designed to *conceal* personality, to diffuse it through a poem from which the reader seems to derive an objective experience of language. Eliot claimed to be a Classicist but, on closer examination, the doctrine of impersonality looks like the ultimate refinement of Romantic subjectivity. In Pound by contrast, Davie would have argued, there is no such concealment. The objective is something out there in the world – a block of stone, a subject, a structure of language – with which the artist engages. The interest in otherness reduces the role of the personal but does not negate it. On the contrary, the work of art is unimaginable without that active and heroic self.

There is no denying that Davie's earlier description of *The Cantos* in musical terms was an accurate one. It is also true, as many more recent critics have shown, that Pound, for propagandistic reasons, exaggerated his distance from Symbolism. Nevertheless, the poet as sculptor now provided Davie with a route out of an impasse. Pound was a poet who valued the non-human and simple matters of fact. Throughout the present collection we find Davie complaining that most modern poetry can find nothing to value in the non-human, unless it can be made to symbolize the human. In his view the poet's task was to know the world and, knowing it, to approach the world beyond it. In 'Two Analogies for Poetry', more than a decade before he recovered his Christian faith, Davie glimpsed the inevitability of a transcendental dimension as the logical outcome of a respect for things. It is a logic already assumed by ordinary language. If words, as Justinian says, 'are the consequences of things', language should be as intransigent as matter. A poet's words are like blocks of stone it is his job to carve. In this way, a poet as inventive and radical as Pound, yet constantly disciplined by material fact, could link the outlook of the Augustans with the innovations of Modernism:

> Pull down thy vanity, it is not man
> Made courage, or made order, or made grace...
> Learn of the green world what can be thy place
> In scaled invention and true artistry...

> (Canto 81)

There were, of course, persistent anxieties. Davie detested Pound's politics and to the end regretted his cavalier treatment of syntax. In *Purity of Diction*, indeed, he had suggested that the two things were connected: that the deliberate abandonment of consecutive language and linear thought would have consequences for civilization at large. It was not an argument he persisted in – the case was almost impossible to prove – but, in spite of welcoming the soubriquet 'Poundian', he maintained a critical distance, especially when in the 1970s he returned to the Christian fold. It could be said that Davie, in trusting the sculptural, threw in his lot with Pound, but that his first objections, though rarely expressed in later years, persisted. The stature of the three great Modernists seemed to him indisputable but, especially in the case of Eliot, he was never quite at peace with them.

In 1991 Davie published his *Studies in Ezra Pound*. The book reprinted *Poet as Sculptor* and added sixteen later essays on Pound. In consequence, the work on Pound I have been free to gather here is relatively slight. I have decided, for historical reasons, to reprint the important essay on *Hugh Selwyn Mauberley*, which Davie twice repudiated (in *Poet as Sculptor* and in the Fontana Modern Masters *Pound* (1975)). I have also included a fine exegetical essay, 'Cypress and Rock-slide', unaccountably left out of the *Studies*. Apart from these there are three memorable book reviews, a late personal reflection on being a 'Poundian', and one of Davie's most beautiful poems, 'Ezra Pound in Pisa'. Indirectly Poundian is the essay on Allen Upward, a largely forgotten writer and thinker, who *inter alia* gave Pound the word 'Vorticism'. The essay on Davie's friend Michael Ayrton, sculptor, novelist and builder of labyrinths, appears with a poem related to it, 'The "Sculpture" of Rhyme'; these are Poundian reflections on the theme of the poet as sculptor.

Pound is the centre of Davie's view of Modernism, so his presence in this book is indispensable. Yeats, though Davie often returns to him, is much less fundamental. All five of the essays I have included are valuable in themselves and all develop issues we find elsewhere in this collection, but their interest is marginal by comparison with the writings on Pound and Eliot. In the earlier ones, Yeats is seen from a Movement-ish perspective. In spite of his persistently Romantic, visionary and post-Christian spirituality – all anathema to the stars of the Movement – Yeats insisted as warmly as they did on the importance of craftsmanship, which made him an important figure for Davie and his associates. In the later essays, Davie looks at those aspects of Yeats which are likely to repel the modern reader – his politics, as odious as Pound's and rather less honestly expressed, and his rhetorical staginess.

But this is much more truly a book about Eliot than either Yeats or Pound. Apart from two historic broadcasts on Modernism, in which Eliot and Pound are ghostly presences ('The Poet in the Imaginary Museum' and 'Two Analogies for Poetry'), there are eight essays on Eliot, and I have also included a curious poem, 'T.S. Eliot – 1928', which I'd expect to puzzle and stimulate in about equal measure. The essays fall into two groups. The four later ones ('Eliot in One Poet's Life', 'Anglican Eliot', 'The Modernist *malgré lui*' and '"The Dry Salvages": A Reconsideration') are personal and retrospective, the last of them revisiting the earliest Eliot essay in the book. The other four ('T.S. Eliot: The End of an Era', 'The Relations between Syntax and Music', 'Mr Eliot' and 'Pound and Eliot: A Distinction') all played a major role, now sadly almost forgotten, in rescuing British readers from the view of Eliot as a poet of fractured narratives or mystico-philosophical reflections. Even if occasionally misguided, as 'The End of an Era' to some extent is – and Davie admits as much in his reconsideration – these essays include some of the most illuminating criticism yet written on Eliot and some of the most useful for anyone learning to read him. They remind me of a sentence in Davie's review of Hugh Kenner's *The Pound Era* ('The Universe of Ezra Pound'). Davie there praises Kenner for showing 'just how the words on the page, and coming off the page, in fact work upon us as we read'. The praise is both just and generous, but it is equally applicable to Davie's best work. No one, not even Kenner, can answer the question 'What does it feel like to read Eliot?' quite as compellingly as Davie does – for instance in his account of the passage from 'Burnt Norton' on pp. 88–93 below. There are critics who never think to raise that question but, for Davie, it is the primary question to ask of great poetry. Criticism that cannot or will not answer it, he would have thought, is simply impertinent.

CLIVE WILMER
Cambridge, 2003

Editorial Note

The essay 'Cypress and Rock-slide' begins with a reference to 'Students of [Pound's] *Thrones*', which is immediately followed by the parenthesis 'students, I'm afraid, rather than simple readers'. Donald Davie was an academic by trade, but he grew to be impatient with the formalities of scholarship. To an editor this is apparent in the sparseness of his footnotes. I have honoured this distaste to a degree, but in certain cases it has seemed to me that some readers − especially those new to Davie and his critical milieu − will want to follow up his reading, particularly when the books concerned have begun to be forgotten. I have therefore silently added and expanded footnotes in what may appear a somewhat random manner. When I have felt it necessary to contribute a footnote of my own − other than these added and expanded citations − I have appended the abbreviation '[Ed.]'.

Davie's impatience with footnotes was also, of course, temperamental. The same could be said for a good deal of worse than casual proof-reading. I have tried to correct errors wherever possible and have mostly done so silently.

C.W.

I The Poet in the Imaginary Museum[1]

1

The imaginary museum in my title is taken from the brilliant book of that name published a few years ago by André Malraux.[2] The central insight of that book is well known and widely accepted as a true and penetrating statement of an element, a basic assumption, common to all the arts in the present century. This perception is at bottom a simple one; and this means – luckily, for my present purposes – that it can be re-stated in summary fashion without being damaged too much. M. Malraux's contention, then, is this: that it is no accident that what we recognize as 'the modern movement' in the arts appears on the historical scene at roughly the same time as certain techniques of reproduction, like gramophone recording in the case of music and colour-photography in the cases of painting, sculpture, and architecture.

The perfection of these techniques – and the long-playing record, which has appeared in the last few years, may be taken to consummate this achievement – means that the modern painter, or sculptor, or architect, or musical composer differs from all his predecessors in one enormously important respect: he has immediately at his disposal, in a way his predecessors had not, the whole achievement of worldwide artistic endeavour over the centuries. In his library of art books or of long-playing gramophone records the modern artist has an imaginary museum infinitely more comprehensive and convenient than even the finest of actual museums and galleries. Where a painter or art-critic less than a hundred years ago – say Baudelaire – would have had to travel across Europe from Madrid to Leningrad in order to compare two paintings by Rembrandt, having to keep in his memory the image of what he had seen in Madrid to set beside what he was going to see in Russia, today such a painter or critic can open his art-book to see the two pictures, both reproduced with unprecedented fidelity, on opposite pages of the one volume.

Moreover he is not limited – as for practical purposes Baudelaire was limited – to the continent of Europe. He can have to hand the sculptures

1   Transcript of two radio talks for the BBC Third Programme, 1957.
2   *Le Musée imaginaire de la sculpture mondiale*, 3 vols (Paris: Pléiade, 1952–4).

of Easter Island or the devil-masks of Nigeria or the rock-paintings of ancient China, no less than Giotto, Rembrandt or Turner. The whole of the artistic past is available to painter, sculptor, architect, musician, as never before. He is free to wander about in the past, to pick and choose from among the styles of the past, in a way his predecessors never dreamed of. And M. Malraux maintains – conclusively, as I think – that this unprecedented attitude to the past – to artistic and cultural 'tradition' in the broadest sense – accounts for and makes inevitable some of the features of modern painting and music in which they differ most strikingly from the painting and music of all other periods and all other cultures.

It is natural to ask: what about the art of literature, or, more narrowly, of poetry? Malraux says nothing of this: and for obvious reasons. For if one thinks about it at all, it is easy to realize that the perfection of techniques of reproduction came, for poetry, five centuries earlier than for music and painting. The invention of printing in the fifteenth century did for poetry what the invention of gramophone recordings did for music, and the invention of colour photography did for painting, only in the last fifty years.

So it would seem, if M. Malraux's contention is correct, that the poet and his reader have been inhabiting the imaginary museum for the past four hundred and fifty years. This reflection – although so obvious – is yet sufficiently arresting. For it seems to mean that poetry is strikingly 'out of step' with the other arts. And it may well be asked whether in our approach to poetry we pay sufficient attention to the special position of this art among the rest. It is commonly assumed, for instance, that 'the modern movement' is something which manifests itself equally in all the arts; that there is, to take one example, a significant connection between the cubist perspective of Picasso and Juan Gris and the exactly contemporary telescoping of historical perspective in the first lines of *The Waste Land*. Or we may recall the symbolist contention, at the start of 'the modern movement', that poetry should 'approach the condition of music'.

Yet if Malraux is right, and modern painting and music owe their modernity to a changed attitude towards the artistic past, then it would seem that poetry, whose attitude towards the past has not been revolutionized by technical inventions, should not share in this 'modernity'. One comes to think that those critics who explain and justify novel features in modern poetry by appeal to what seems to be analogous innovation in the other arts are guilty of an elementary error in historical perspective. Further, since it is indubitable that many poets of our period have conceived themselves to be sharing in a modern movement equally manifest in the other arts, it seems we may have to say that not only those poets' critics, but the poets themselves, have fallen into the error of supposing an affinity where none exists or can exist.

Yet surely, printing had a different and much less far-reaching effect on poetry than colour-reproduction has had on painting. For the medium of painting, like the medium of music, is an international language as the language of poetry is not. After the invention of printing, as before, a poem was written in some one of the languages of the world; whereas pigment and line, a musical chord, the interplay of space and solid in buildings and sculptures – these artistic vocabularies are truly international.

Worse still, we may recall that the literary arts once had such a *lingua franca* which they have now lost. Until only a hundred and fifty years ago, Latin and to a less extent Greek were still international literary languages, in that all but a very few of the serious literary works in all the languages of Europe were written with Latin and Greek models in mind, employing a common vocabulary of Latin and Greek mythology and symbolism. This literary heritage, possessed and exploited by Russian as by Spaniard, by Norwegian as by Greek, constituted something like an international language for poetry. This international language still survives indeed, though it is spoken and understood only by a calamitously depleted number. It fell out of general use ('general' I mean among even the numerically tiny minority that at any given time cares for the arts) at precisely the time when the gramophone and colour photography were being invented.

In other words, at precisely the time when the inherently international media of painting and music were becoming (thanks to the technicians) *effectively* international, the medium of poetry was losing even that degree of international currency which it had enjoyed. At just the time when musician and music-lover, painter and art-enthusiast, are able to leap over the limitations of being born to one nation and one culture rather than another, the poet and his reader find themselves locked more securely than ever before inside one national milieu. This raises the possibility that poetry is and will be 'the odd one out' among the arts in the worst possible way. Poetry becomes ever more parochial and provincial, while painting and music and sculpture become ever more international. Is there not a real danger that poetry will become, among the arts, of only marginal importance?

It is this possibility, surely, which lies behind a remarkable work, Mr Hugh MacDiarmid's *In Memoriam James Joyce*, which appeared a couple of years ago. This enormous poem is itself only an extract from another yet more enormous, to be called *Towards a World Language*. That title in itself explains how this fits in with what I am discussing. Yet, so far as I can see, Mr MacDiarmid throughout this poem is for the moment merely trying to bring home to us the necessity for such an international medium for poetry. He is not trying to create such a language by manifesting it in action.

Another writer has done just that; and I do not mean the writer whom Mr MacDiarmid apparently has in mind, the James Joyce of *Finnegans Wake*. I mean Ezra Pound in his *Cantos*. I do not suppose that Mr Pound had this purpose in mind when, forty years ago, he began his poem. But now, when the poem is almost completed, it seems clear that this is at any rate one of the things this great poem has done. It has created and put into action a language which is literally international, a language to which Chinese, Greek and many other languages have contributed nearly as much as Anglo-American. It becomes clear that, though English is laid under heavier contribution than any other national tongue, yet Pound's *Cantos* cannot properly be described as 'a poem in English'.

I do not pretend that this is the central significance of Pound's poem, and indeed I do not really share Mr MacDiarmid's anxiety about a language for poetry which shall be 'international' in this obvious perhaps superficial sense. But it is only the extreme statement of a problem which is indeed crucial. For if we set aside these two poems, together with the work of Mr Eliot, surely the English poetic scene presents us with just what I foresaw above – a poetry that has committed itself to the status of being no more than a marginal pleasure, a deliberately and self-confessedly *provincial* utterance. I do not mean by this just that Mr Amis, say, or Mr Philip Larkin, does not lard his verse with tags from the Greek or with Chinese characters. We should have every right to be dismayed if they did. But just look at their attitude to what we call the cultural heritage. Here is Mr Kingsley Amis, writing a brief manifesto: 'Nobody wants any more poems about philosophers or paintings or novelists or art galleries or mythology or foreign cities or other poems. At least I hope nobody wants them.' 'Nobody wants any more poems about... foreign cities'. So much for Goethe and Spenser and Du Bellay and Vyacheslav Ivanov and so many other poets down the ages to whom, for instance, the name and the actuality of Rome have been an inspiration, standing for a cultural and moral standard. Or here is Mr Philip Larkin: '[I] have no belief in 'tradition' or a common myth-kitty or casual allusions in poems to other poems or poets, which last I find unpleasantly like the talk of literary understrappers letting you see they know the right people.' 'Tradition' here in Mr Larkin's mouth carries derisive quotation marks, as it does (to take a third example) when Mr D.J. Enright speaks of finding in one of his predecessors: 'The shadow of "Tradition", which apparently takes the form of tasteful quotations from the Greek with an odd nymph or two thrown in: a weary world of 'culture' borne away from the battle-field on one man's shoulders.'[3]

---

3   The three quotations are from D.J. Enright (ed.), *Poets of the 1950s* (Tokyo: Konkyusha, 1955).

Here 'culture' no less than 'tradition' gets inverted commas. And if someone protests that Enright and Larkin only put the quote-marks to show that they mean *fake*-culture, *fake*-tradition, I still demand to be shown what they mean in that case by true 'culture', true 'tradition'. My impression is, from their often admirable poems as from their criticism that there is no place for either concept in their view of the world and of the art which they practise.

These poets are my friends and I think I know perfectly well what makes them, being finely civilized men, pretend to be barbarians; why, though they are humane persons and responsible citizens, they pretend sometimes to be cultural teddy-boys. They are putting the house of English poetry in order: not before time, too. Or rather they are trying to build it afresh, an altogether humbler structure on a far narrower basis. On all sides, our good poets are 'pulling in their horns'. They are getting rid of pretentiousness and cultural window-dressing and arrogant self-expression, by creating an English poetry which is severely limited in its aims, painfully modest in its pretensions, deliberately provincial in its scope. I do not think they would be very offended or even make demur if one added: 'inevitably marginal in importance'.

The problem is: what in the present age should be the poet's attitude to past poetry? There are good reasons why the poet's attitude to the poetry of the past cannot be like the painter's attitude to past painting, or the musician's to past music: because most past poetry is not available to the poet in the same way as all past painting is now available to the painter. By writing as if past poetry did not exist, Mr Amis and Mr Larkin and Mr Enright solve this problem to their own satisfaction. It is one way out, at any rate – but at what a cost!

Yet, why should this be a problem for the poet at all? It seems that the poet has escaped the problem and the opportunity that were presented to the painter by the recent perfecting of the means of reproduction. If that is so, why does the modern poet need to have an attitude to the past any different from Tennyson's attitude or Keats's? To answer this I have had to look at M. Malraux again and to supplement him a little. For he is surely wrong to lay such exclusive stress on the revolution in mechanics of reproduction. The techniques of reproduction – colour photography and musical recording – were discovered, as perhaps all such techniques are discovered, to answer to a need.

This need is the true source of the eclecticism of the modern move-ment, for it came out of an ethnological and anthropological temper of mind, which was then first appearing on the stage of history. This temper of mind was prepared and eager to investigate exotic cultures without prejudice, and from no preconceived position of cultural superiority. The modern sculptor can learn from Polynesian sculptures partly because the corpus of Polynesian sculpture is readily available to him in reproductions, but ultimately he can do so because of a new attitude of humility or anyway open-mindedness towards such supposedly 'primitive' cultures as those of Polynesia. If that attitude had not been inculcated by the first scientific anthropologists, the volumes of reproductions would never have come into existence.

The point is that at this level of attitude, temper, and need, the imaginary museum is as much the habitat of the poet today as of the sculptor. From this point of view, then, the poet finds himself – no less than sculptor, painter and musician – in what we may call 'the imaginary museum situation' but it is the poet's peculiar misfortune that his medium, being so much less international than the media of those other arts, is much less able to cope with the situation.

The modern poet's attitude to the poetic past must differ from Keats's attitude or Tennyson's simply because he has felt the impact, as the painter has, and the sculptor, and the man in the street, of the character-istic temper of scientific anthropology. We have all come to see, thanks to the anthropologist, that the artistic past of the human race is far richer and far more various than Tennyson or any poet before him realized. The masterpieces of the past do not constitute one order, derived from Greece and Rome; nor two orders, Nordic-Gothic on the one hand, classical-mediterranean on the other; nor even three orders or four. There are innumerable orders. We know this to be true of painting, architecture, sculpture, music; it is doubtless true of poetry also – with this awkward difference, that the poet is much less capable than the other artists of facing up to this knowledge and exploiting it. In short, whatever weight we give to the realization that poetry in Europe is chronologically 'out of step' with the other arts – nevertheless, poetry does participate in 'the modern movement' in the arts. As indeed we knew it did – for, after all, it does help to be reminded of cubist perspectives when faced with the first page of *The Waste Land*.

The position, then, is this: that we are not faced with a simple Either/Or. It is not a question of *either* internationalism *or* provincialism, *either* inside *or* outside the museum. Poetry finds itself in an uncomfortable betwixt-and-between; it inherits the imaginary museum and participates in the modern movement to the extent that poets and their readers share a modern sensibility determined and coloured by scientific anthropology and by practice in the other arts; it is outside the imaginary museum and outside the modern movement to the extent that its medium – language – is not international as other artistic media are. In my next talk I shall look from this point of view at the theory and practice of some modern poets.

2

In my last talk I discussed the modern poet's attitude to his art, and in particular to the past history of poetry. The intelligent poet today finds himself in a certain situation *vis-à-vis* poetry and past poetry; and I tried to define this, by asking how the poet's situation differs from the painter's, the sculptor's, and the musical composer's.

The situation in which these practitioners of the other arts find themselves has been defined by M. André Malraux as 'the imaginary museum'. What M. Malraux means is that the modern painter, for instance, differs from painters of all previous ages precisely in his relation to the past achievements of painting. Thanks in the first place to technicians who evolved modern methods of colour-reproduction, but thanks also to modern anthropologists who have shown how many and various are the cultural and artistic traditions of mankind, the painter today has at his immediate disposal virtually the whole corpus of paintings of all ages and localities. The same is true in some degree of the sculptor and, thanks to gramophone recordings, of the musician. All these artists find themselves free to pick and choose among all the artistic styles of the past, in a way their predecessors could not.

The same is not true of the modern poet. For in relation to the art of poetry there has been no technical revolution in the medium of reproduction – nothing since the invention of printing in the fifteenth century. Neither that revolution, nor any other that one can conceive, in the reproduction of poetry, could have effects as far-reaching on poetry as revolutions in techniques of reproduction have had on painting and on music; this is so, because the medium of all the other arts is international as the medium of poetry is not. A poem is written in some one of the languages of the world, and is available (leaving aside the vexed question of poetic translation) only to readers who know that language.

So it comes about that the poet's situation is peculiarly difficult; in so far as poetry shares in 'a modern movement' common to all the arts (and it seems plain that to some extent it does so share, feeling the impact, no less than the other arts, of modern anthropology, for instance), the poet shares with the other artists a new attitude towards the cultural and artistic past of the race, a new freedom in picking and choosing among the styles of the past. Yet in so far as the medium of poetry is not international as the other media are, the poet finds himself less free of the riches of the past than the painter is, if only because most of the poems of the past are in languages he does not understand. Thus the poet stands awkwardly with one foot inside the imaginary museum, and one foot out of it.

It seems to me that you have to grasp this before you can understand the procedures and achievements of the great American, Irish and English poets of this century. First I will look at their theories, then at what is more important, their practice — their styles. Obviously the theories we are after are those that have to do with 'tradition', the theories to be found in Mr Eliot's essay on 'Tradition and the Individual Talent' and Pound's essay *How to Read* and the *A.B.C. of Reading*; and I would like to add Dr Leavis's rejoinder to Pound, his 'How to Teach Reading'.[4] To take the last one first, it seems to me that Dr Leavis's essay has had the effect of swinging academic criticism away from Pound's solution of the problem, away from Pound's understanding of tradition, and behind Mr Eliot's — or rather behind what Dr Leavis took to be Mr Eliot's position, for Mr Eliot's essay is evasive and self-contradictory in the extreme.

Dr Leavis, being like almost all academic critics vowed to the principle and the fact of independent schools of English in our universities, has in effect and perhaps without knowing it committed his followers — which is to say, in varying degrees, nearly all the best critics in these islands — to an extreme provincialism, which assumes (what is in fact wildly improbable) that the poetry extant in our own language affords a paradigm or microcosm of poetry as a whole. As for the evasiveness of Mr Eliot's essay, let me remind you only of the passage quoted *ad nauseam* which says the poet must feel 'that the whole of the literature of Europe from Homer and within it the whole of the literature of his own country has a simultaneous existence and composes a simultaneous order'. There is also that other passage where we learn that 'The poet must be very conscious of the main current, which does not at all flow invariably through the most distinguished reputations'. The thousand-dollar question, as it seems to me, is 'How do you detect a main current through a simultaneous order?'

What is more interesting is to ask why Mr Eliot is so evasive; and I believe the answer is that he is struggling towards a perception of what I have called the betwixt-and-between situation of modern poetry, trying to accommodate a perception of the imaginary museum, of any number of different traditions and different styles all equally available, with the incompatible notion of *one* tradition, a central tradition. Some of his later criticism (for instance 'What is a Classic') shows him solving this deadlock by discriminating between those styles such as Milton's which are usefully available at one period and not at another, and those others such as Dante's and Virgil's which are available at all times and are thereby truly 'classic'.

But this was precisely the position which Pound had reached years before. His *A.B.C. of Reading* shows him as aware as Mr Eliot of how poetry stands with one foot in the museum and one foot out of it. And with admirable directness Pound there specifies, out of all the traditions

4   F.R. Leavis, *How to Teach Reading: A Primer for Ezra Pound* (Cambridge: Minority Press, 1932).

hung on the walls of the museum, which it is absolutely necessary for the modern poet to take account of, which of them are – as Mr Eliot would put it – perpetually available and thereby 'classic'. Pound's list of required reading is not 'out of the question'; it is not 'more than any one man can cope with'. One may cavil at this name or that, supplement the list here or cut it back there, but it is no good turning away with a gibe just because the pedagogue includes in his list one of the traditions of Chinese poetry, and the tradition of Provençal. After all, he is prepared to consider reading in translations, as his critic Dr Leavis (aligning himself with the huffiest academic opinion) is not.

But the poet's attitude to the poetic past, his understanding of what 'tradition' is as a fact of his experience, manifests itself far more certainly in the way he writes, in his style, than in any theoretical formulations. The chief advantage of looking at modern poetry from the point of view of the imaginary museum is that only from this standpoint do poetic styles as various as those of Wallace Stevens and T.S. Eliot, of Ezra Pound and W.B. Yeats, appear as so many different (yet related) answers to one and the same problem – the problem of a radically changed relationship to the poetic past, a relationship which must be different from Tennyson's or Pope's, yet also from that of a Matisse or a Mestrović, a Stravinsky or a Corbusier.

This seems to me the radical problem facing the modern poet. Much has been made of the challenge presented to modern poetry by the new sciences of psychology, for instance, and sociology; but the real challenge is that of anthropology, which underpins those others. Or again one hears of the disadvantage for the poet of having no one coherent system of mythology and symbolism on which to draw and in terms of which to communicate; but this too is only an aspect of the same thing – because the problem for the poet is not that he has no mythology to use, but that he has no one such mythology, in other words, that he has too many mythologies to choose among and nothing to direct him which one to choose in any given case, nothing to tell him which of the innumerable galleries in the imaginary museum are those he should frequent.

Take one example: our still general distaste, as critics, for archaism in poetic diction. If we are asked to justify this aversion of ours, we say that poetry should 'express its age', not escape into some age of the past. And we quote the judgement of Gerard Manley Hopkins that the language of poetry should be 'the current language heightened', based on the spoken language of its time.

Yet if (as Malraux has argued) what is specifically 'modern' about the modern age is its changed attitude to the past, then the modern poet will express his age, express the modern sensibility, precisely by picking and choosing, manipulating and adapting, among the poetic styles of the past. Faced with a work out of the imaginary museum like Ezra Pound's translation (version, imitation, whatever) of the Confucian Classic Anthology of Chinese poetry, our distaste for archaism in diction is worse than useless; for the poet's achievement there is precisely in choosing now this, now that style from the English past in order to convey now this, now that mode of ancient Chinese sensibility. We cannot any more – though we still do, I am afraid – endorse without large qualifications Hopkins's famous manifesto in favour of 'the current language heightened'. We shall have to learn to take this as part of Hopkins's Victorianism, not his 'modernity'; it was a position possible only before the advent of the imaginary museum.

Yet we do not have to relinquish our conviction that there is indeed a sort of archaism in poetic diction which, other things being equal, is 'a bad thing'. Often, still, we encounter poems which we know to be bad just because they advertise, in their diction and style, an elaborate pretence or a mistaken conviction that nothing has changed since the death of Keats. In these cases, what we get, instead of the original poem which the poet thought he was writing, is an unconscious pastiche or sometimes an unconscious parody of poems by Keats. But it is just here that the modern poet can cut in: our objections are silenced as soon as the poet, when he uses a style from the past, makes it plain to the reader that he knows what he is doing – that his is a conscious pastiche or a conscious parody. Pastiche and parody, from this point of view, are matters of degree; and we have to say that there is an element of pastiche or of parody whenever a poet gives the merest indication – as it were a slightly lifted eyebrow – to show that he is well aware, even as he writes Keatsian verse, that a lot of water has flowed under the bridge since Keats wrote as he did. An elementary device of this kind – rather a heavy-handed one – is the use by Ezra Pound, in *Hugh Selwyn Mauberley*, of hovering quotation marks:

> For three years, out of key with his time,
> He strove to resuscitate the dead art
> Of poetry; to maintain 'the sublime'
> In the old sense...

Here the quotation marks about 'the sublime', no less than the phrase 'In the old sense', show the poet is aware that the concept of 'the sublime', once a serious principle informing a poetic style of the past, is no longer viable, though not for that reason to be laughed entirely out of court. Or again, far more deftly and unobtrusively, a modern poet may acknowledge the element of pastiche in his writing after an archaic manner, by carrying his archaic language on a just slightly inappropriate metre. Or, yet again, the poet's awareness of the element of parody may be made as plain as it is by Eliot in the *Four Quartets* when, after a passage in delicately wrought seventeenth-century manner, he begins a new paragraph with

'That was a way of putting it; not very satisfactory'.

But, as that last example should have indicated, the most delicate way of acknowledging an element of parody or pastiche in a passage of writing is simply to set it beside something deliberately incongruous, so that the incongruity effects an ironic detachment from both. When the passages chosen are slightly adapted quotations from specific poems of the past, what we get is a modification of an ancient poetic genre, the *cento*.

But the principle is just the same when the items juxtaposed are not quotations from specific past poems, but careful imitations of specific past styles. By writing in this way the poets acknowledge, on the one hand that, like the painter, they are free to pick and choose as never before among the styles of the past; on the other hand that this unprecedented freedom is bought at a cost – the cost of never feeling entirely at home in any one of the styles they adopt. The modern style in poetry is the arrangement in new patterns of the styles of the past. To try to forge a style independent of the past can only produce poems which are, if not bad, at best minor and provincial achievements, for the good or paradoxical reason that what is specifically modern about the modern age in art is precisely its catholic and uncommitted attitude to all the ages of the past.

I have been doing no more than just glancing over the surface, indicating without really exploring some of the ways in which an apprehension of the imaginary museum situation can be made to serve analysis and evaluation of modern poetic procedures. There are other ways, just as there are other devices than those of Eliot and Pound for acknowledging the element of parody or pastiche; Wallace Stevens, for instance, has perfected a whole range of other most delicate stylistic devices to the same purpose. At some point it might be necessary and I think possible, though difficult, to distinguish parody from pastiche.

Again I throw out the suggestion for what it is worth – I believe it could be shown that whereas English poets younger than Eliot have failed by not realizing that the imaginary museum situation bears on poetry at all, American poets of those generations have mostly failed by accepting the imaginary museum too wholeheartedly, not realizing poetry's partially special position. Or again there is the interesting question of those poets in English – Robert Graves and Edwin Muir are examples – who have taken abundant note of modern anthropological researches; I believe it could be shown that this does not redeem them from provincialism, if only because they have applied themselves to distinguishing one or two archetypal patterns underlying apparent cultural diversity: and this is the sort of thing that older anthropologists, such as Frazer, did, whereas modern anthropology insists, as Malraux insists, on a diversity which is irreducible, of any number of culture-patterns each of them *sui generis*.

There is one more point that is worth making, because it is important –

at least, to some people. If the modern style in poetry is as I have defined
it, one can say of it that it precludes formal perfection. At some point, it
appears, there must always be a flaw in the mirror, a deliberately
contrived maladjustment between content and form; the modern poem
can never speak for itself as completely as, say, a poem by Dryden. The
illusion must, if only for an instant, be broken; the convention at some
point must be deliberately transgressed. The modern poet must always, as
it were, peep round from behind his poem, to advise the reader – if by no
more than a lifted eyebrow or a sidelong glance – that the poem is not to
be trusted all the way, that there are modes of experience or ways of
saying things which the poet is aware of though his poem on its own
account is not.

To be sure this is to understand 'form' in an inadequate, even a rather
mechanical way; for in a more sophisticated understanding of poetic form
the very breaking of illusion and convention, the very flaw of the surface,
is itself a formal artifice of a delicate kind. All the same the point remains
that a poem by Dryden enjoys a kind of formal beauty and completeness
that no poem by Mr Eliot enjoys, that (we have got as far as this) no truly
modern poem *can* enjoy.

If I am right, before the imaginary museum situation arose, poems
could be complete in themselves, self-dependent, cut loose from the poet
who wrote them, in a way no modern poem can be. That sort of pleasure
can be afforded by modern poems only when they are minor, even
provincial achievements. I have sympathy with those poets (such as
Robert Graves, I suspect) who care so much for this kind of poetic pleasure that they choose to write minor poems possessing it, rather than
major poems which must do without it; and equally I sympathize with
those modern readers who for the same reason would rather read the
minor poems of our age than the major ones.

Postscript: The argument pursued in these two broadcasts on the Imaginary
Museum is so disconcerting in its implications, not to say *unnerving*, that I no
less than others have tried to forget about it, or to pretend that somehow,
somewhere, the argument is flawed. Yet no one to my knowledge has
found that flaw. Some have complained – reasonably enough – that at the
end of my argument I use the terms 'major' and 'minor' as if they had
firm and definite meanings, whereas in fact of course they are very
approximate words indeed. It may placate such critics to tell them that, in
the sense I give to 'minor' and in the terms of this argument as a whole,
all the poems I have written myself have to be called, at best, *minor* poems.

The Listener, 11 July and 18 July 1957; reprinted with postscript in *The Poet in the Imaginary
Museum: Essays of Two Decades*, ed. Barry Alpert (Manchester: Carcanet, 1977).

II T.S. Eliot: The End of an Era

1

I find it very surprising that all readers seem to either accept or reject the *Four Quartets* as a whole – and yet not really surprising, since the cleavage comes plainly not along any line of literary fact, but is flagrantly ideological: the religiously inclined applaud the Quartets, the more or less militantly secular and 'humanist' decry them. As simple as that.

At any rate, I find it still surprising (and depressing) that no one should yet have remarked to my knowledge how the third Quartet, 'The Dry Salvages', sticks out among the rest like a sore thumb. At first sight it is not only incongruous with the others, strikingly different in conception and procedure, but different unaccountably and disastrously. One could take it by itself and prove convincingly that it is quite simply *rather a bad poem*. It amazes me that, so far as I know, no one has yet done this; and until very lately I thought I was the person to do it. In fact, I aim to do it here and now – but now with the proviso that all I can say against it is true only so far as it goes, that from another point of view all the vices become virtues and fall into place. It is possible, of course, that all other readers have been clever enough to see the thing aright from the start. But it goes without saying that I don't think so. Here at any rate, to begin with, is my case against 'The Dry Salvages'.

2

Leavis and Rajan have both applauded the opening lines of the poem, and Helen Gardner was so misguided as to choose them for the basis of her claims for Eliot specifically as a manipulator of language:[1]

> I do not know much about gods; but I think that the river
> Is a strong brown god – sullen, untamed and intractable,
> Patient to some degree, at first recognized as a frontier;

---

1 F.R. Leavis, 'Eliot's Later Poetry', *Scrutiny* 11.1 (1942–3); B. Rajan (ed.), *T.S. Eliot: A Study of his Writings by Several Hands* (London: Dobson, 1947); Helen Gardner, *The Art of T.S. Eliot* (London: Cresset, 1949).

Miss Gardner says that the 'strong brown god' is 'a personification which the poet's tone makes no more than a suggestion, a piece of only half-serious myth-making'. But the first line has not sufficiently defined the tone (a single line hardly could) for this to be true; and indeed it is to my ear still too uncertain, eight lines later, to carry the journalistic cliché, 'worshippers of the machine', by giving it the invisible quote-marks which, as Miss Gardner allows, such an inert and faded locution requires. What in any case, we may well ask, is the tone in which we could hear without embarrassment the first line spoken? 'I do not know much about gods' – who could conceivably start a conversation like that without condemning himself from the start as an uncomfortable poseur? Is it not rather like 'Poems are made by fools like me/But only God can make a tree'? What is it but a gaucherie? And yet there *is* a tone in which we have been addressed, which hovers here in the offing, a tone familiar enough but still far from acceptable, a tone which has indeed become a byword as a type of strident uncertainty in the speaker and of correspondingly acute embarrassment in the hearer – it is the tone of Whitman.

But what is Eliot thinking of, that he should talk like Whitman? And our bewilderment deepens:

> Unhonoured, unpropitiated
> By worshippers of the machine, but waiting, watching and waiting,
> His rhythm was present in the nursery bedroom,
> In the rank ailanthus of the April dooryard,
> In the smell of grapes on the autumn table,
> And the evening circle in the winter gaslight.

'Worshippers of the machine'; then the incredibly limp 'watching and waiting'; and finally, limpest of all, 'his rhythm was present'. 'His rhythm was present in the nursery bedroom' – could anything be more vague and woolly? After this statement has been issued, we know not a tittle more about the relation between river and bedroom than we did before. And the poetry is not just bad, but unaccountably so. For 'His rhythm was present in' represents just that bridgework, that filling in and faking of transitions, which Eliot as a post-symbolist poet has always contrived to do without. From first to last his procedure has been the symbolist procedure of 'juxtaposition without copula', the setting down of images side by side with a space between them, a space that does not need to be bridged. There is an example just over the page in 'The Dry Salvages': 'The salt is on the briar rose,/The fog is in the fir trees.' For now, from 'The river is within us' through to the end of the first section, the poetry picks up, the diction becomes distinctively Eliotic and fine; and only an unwonted straightforwardness, the vulnerable stance face to face with the subject, the overtness of the evocation, are there to trouble us with something pre-symbolist and old-fashioned.

But, then, what shall be said of the famous sestina of the second section, which Rajan calls 'as intricately organized as anything Eliot has written'?[2] Shall I be thought laughably naïve for calling attention to the rhymes? In the first sestine comes an extremely beautiful perception:

> The silent withering of autumn flowers
> Dropping their petals and remaining motionless;

The rhymes found to correspond to these in the later sestines are as follows, in order:

> ... the trailing
> Consequence of further days and hours,
> While emotion takes to itself the emotionless
> Years of living among the breakage...

> ... the failing
> Pride or resentment at failing powers,
> The unattached devotion which might pass for devotionless...

> Where is the end of them, the fishermen sailing
> Into the wind's tail, where the fog cowers?
> We cannot think of a time that is oceanless...

> Setting and hauling, while the North East lowers
> Over shallow banks unchanging and erosionless...

> No end to the withering of withered flowers,
> To the movement of pain that is painless and motionless...

Should we not be justified in seeing here a case of sheer incompetence? Is it not plain that the trouvaille at the head of the page, 'Dropping their petals and remaining motionless', gets the poet into more and more patent difficulties (and dishonesties) once the rhyme on it has been taken up as a determining feature of his stanza-form? 'Emotionless' – how? 'Oceanless' – grotesque! 'Erosionless' – does he mean 'uneroded'? And 'movement... pain... painless... motionless' – our confidence in the poet has by this time been so undermined that we cannot, in justice to ourselves, take this as anything but incantatory gibberish. Faced with this, we have to feel a momentary sympathy with the rancour even of a Robert Graves – who, whatever his limitations, would never allow such slapdash inefficiency into his own verses.

The next passage reads:

> It seems, as one becomes older,
> That the past has another pattern, and ceases to be a mere sequence –

---

2   Rajan, *op. cit.*, p. 87.

Or even development: the latter a partial fallacy
Encouraged by superficial notions of evolution,
Which becomes, in the popular mind, a means of disowning the past.

Is this the poet who wove to and fro the close and lively syntax at the beginning of 'East Coker', or the passage from 'Burnt Norton' beginning 'The inner freedom from the practical desire'? How can we explain that the same poet should now proffer, in such stumbling trundling rhythms, these inarticulate ejaculations of reach-me-down phrases, the debased currency of the study circle? And worse is to come – Possum's little joke:

The moments of happiness – not the sense of well-being,
Fruition, fulfilment, security or affection,
Or even a very good dinner...

At the dismal jocularity of that 'very good dinner', we throw in our hands. The tone that Miss Gardner thought established in the very first line can now, we realize, never be established at all. Or else, if we prefer to put it this way – it has been very thoroughly established, as excruciatingly unsettled, off-key. To be sure, the diction now picks up again for a while, though still liable to such upsets as the lame gabble, 'not forgetting/ Something that is probably quite ineffable:...' But section III begins with *Krishna*, which sticks in the throat even of Dr Rajan (who for the most part seems to be reading a different poem): 'Mr Eliot is never happy in "the maze of Oriental metaphysics" and his wanderings this time are uncomfortably sinuous.' And there is, as Rajan further notes, a self-advertising virtuosity, almost Euphuistic, about 'the future is a faded song, a Royal Rose or a lavender spray'.

At this point re-enter Whitman, conspicuously. S. Musgrove, author of *T.S. Eliot and Walt Whitman*, compares with this passage turning on 'Fare forward, travellers', Whitman's 'Song of the Open Road'; and he comments:[3]

Once again, Eliot has employed Whitman's material and manner in order to reject his philosophy. For Whitman, time stretches away in one infinite linear direction, towards a positive and perfect future, in which the possession of something actual, something better than the present, awaits the growing spirit of man. For Eliot, the sense of a direction is illusory; time is an eternal present which can never yield more than is now known, in which the only kind of possession conceivable is one alike in kind to dispossession from the demands of the self...

3   *T.S. Eliot and Walt Whitman* (Wellington: New Zealand University Press, 1952), p. 55.

This is a good deal less than fair to Whitman, who is at pains in 'Song of the Open Road' to make it clear that there is no destination to the voyaging, no end to it, no perfection to be aimed at or achieved except in the process of still and still going on. Thus Eliot, with his 'Fare neither well nor ill, so it be forward' (my words, of course, but a fair summary of Eliot's drift), has dropped from Whitman only his optimism, substituting for it the Chekhovian compassion which strips its objects of all dignity: 'Fare forward, you who think that you are voyaging...' And to be sure, Musgrove talks as if the one unforgivable thing about Whitman, what proves his vulgarity, is precisely his optimism – a good example of that rigid neo-Augustinian temper among Eliot's adherents which very properly enrages a secular liberal like Kathleen Nott.[4] For Whitman's optimism is not by any means the worst thing about him. There is beneath and beside it what Lawrence pointed out – 'Always wanting to merge himself into the womb of something or other'; that is, the drive to 'transcend' the self by losing it in identification with some inhuman process, of which, as Wyndham Lewis pointed out long ago, the process of time is perhaps the most obvious and popular. Moreover, as Lawrence and, following him, Yvor Winters have shown, this drive is especially marked in the American literary tradition, from Emerson and Melville to Hart Crane – its obsessive symbol very frequently, as here in 'The Dry Salvages', the sea. And, sure enough, Rajan comes aptly in once more with the suggestion that section IV, 'Lady, whose shrine stands on the promontory', 'perhaps owes something to the sermon in *Moby Dick*'. Even the Hinduism fits in, if one recalls Yeats's remark about 'those translations of the Upanishads, which it is so much harder to study by the sinking flame of Indian tradition than by the serviceable lamp of Emerson and Walt Whitman'. And yet, when one recalls also Yeats's verdict on Emerson and Whitman, 'writers who have come to seem superficial precisely because they lack the Vision of Evil', one finds it unaccountable that Eliot, the author of the essay on Baudelaire, however American, should have fallen into this trap of ecstatic merging with the process.

The last section begins with an admirable new departure, in the vigour of 'To communicate with Mars, converse with spirits', but then it modulates, through a very beautiful yet again strangely uncritical treatment of the Bergsonian *durée* in music ('but you are the music/While the music lasts'), into the inhuman conclusion that human life for all but the saints is mere purposeless *movement*, scurrying activity, only at fleeting uncontrollable moments elevated into the meaning and dignity of true *action*.

---

4   See Nott, *The Emperor's Clothes* (London: Heinemann, 1953).
5   One traces it as far afield as Berenson, in his remarks on Umbrian space-composition and 'the religious emotion'. See D.H. Lawrence, *Studies in Classic American Literature* (London: Heinemann, 1924) and Yvor Winters, *In Defense of Reason* (Denver: Alan Swallow, 1947).

We realize that the poet indeed meant the shocking 'emotionless' of the sestina; and if that helps to validate the poetry of that passage, it only makes the poet seem even less humane.

3

If we are to turn the force of these various objections we have to go a long way round – and yet in a way we need to go no further than Hugh Kenner's essay on 'Eliot's Moral Dialectic', which relegates to the status of curio every other piece of criticism on the *Quartets*.[6] Kenner there distinguishes the predominant structural principle of this poetry as a diagram in which two terms (life and death, beginning and end) are first opposed, then falsely reconciled in a third term, and then truly reconciled in a fourth term, a metaphysical conception. His examples are section III of 'Burnt Norton', where the opposed terms light and darkness are combined in the parody-reconciliation of the 'flicker' in the twilit murk of London, only to be truly reconciled paradoxically in the metaphysical Dark Night of the Soul; and section III of 'Little Gidding', where the opposing terms attachment and detachment are reconciled in parody in 'indifference', only to be truly reconciled in Love.

Section III of 'East Coker' yields up the same pattern:

> ... So the darkness shall be the light, and the stillness the dancing.
> Whisper of running streams, and winter lightning
> The wild thyme unseen and the wild strawberry,
> The laughter in the garden, echoed ecstasy
> Not lost, but requiring, pointing to the agony
> Of death and birth.
> > You say I am repeating
> Something I have said before. I shall say it again.
> Shall I say it again? In order to arrive there,
> To arrive where you are, to get from where you are not,
> > You must go by a way wherein there is no ecstasy.
> In order to arrive at what you do not know
> > You must go by a way which is the way of ignorance...

Darkness and light, stillness and dancing, are two pairs of opposed terms. They are reconciled in 'the agony/Of death and birth'. Birth, coming from the dark to the light, is a sort of death, for as soon as we are born we begin to die; and death, going from the light to the dark, is a sort of birth – into eternal life. And the stillness of a seizure, the dance of pain, are reconciled in agony. But this is a false reconciliation which is at once abandoned for the true one carried in the borrowings from St John of the Cross. Thus, 'I shall say it again./Shall I say it again?' is an ironical trap. Musgrove suggests an allusion to Whitman's 'Do I contradict myself? Very well, I contradict myself'. This points it up even more; for the point is that Eliot *is* contradicting himself even as he *seems* to repeat himself – inevitably, because it is characteristic of the terms he is thinking in that the false reconciliation, being a parody of the true one, is very hard – all but impossible – to distinguish from it in words, even in words charged to the utmost, as in poetry.

Since the third sections of 'Burnt Norton', 'East Coker' and 'Little Gidding' are thus broadly parallel in structure, one would expect to discern the same structure in section III of 'The Dry Salvages', which is the Whitmanesque passage I have just quoted. But 'The Dry Salvages', as we noted at the start, is the odd one out in all sorts of ways; and though the pattern is there, it is there only with a difference, and is hard to discern. 'And the way up is the way down, the way forward is the way back' – here are the terms opposed, right enough. But we look in vain for the false reconciliation, though the image of the traveller is obviously apt for it – since travelling is the same state whether one travels from here to there, or there to here. But this parody-reconciliation is ruled out of court when the poet jumps at once to his insight (a restatement, as Kenner has noted, of the insight of 'Tradition and the Individual Talent'): 'You cannot face it steadily, but this thing is sure,/That time is no healer: the patient is no longer here.' Yet the parody-reconciliation *is* present in the lines that follow, though never overtly offered – it is there precisely in the shade of Whitman that haunts the passage, the Whitmanesque tone that hovers here as an overtone.

But we can, and must, go further. This diagram that Kenner has brilliantly extricated he does not offer to us merely as the structural principle informing these passages and others like them. He hints that the same diagram informs the *Four Quartets* as a whole. If this is so, then 'The Dry Salvages', the third of them, should appear to be the false reconciliation, the parody. And here it seems we may at last be coming near to understanding, and forgiving, its peculiarities.

It is generally recognized that parody is to be found in the *Four Quartets*, that in 'East Coker', for instance, when the poet says, of the lyric at the start of section II, 'That was a way of putting it – not very satisfactory:/A periphrastic study in a worn-out poetical fashion', we are meant to take this at its face value and to agree that the passage referred to is, therefore, a parody. But when Kenner asks us to compare 'Down the passage which we did not take' at the start of 'Burnt Norton' with the 'cunning passages, contrived corridors' of Gerontion (himself, as Kenner argues, a living parody of the true self-surrender that we find in Simeon), we are advised that we must look for parody elsewhere in the *Four*

Quartets, where it is not explicitly pointed out to us by the poet. For instance, the false reconciliation which I have pointed out in 'East Coker', 'the agony/Of death and birth', while it looks back to the significantly theatrical image, 'With a hollow rumble of wings, with a movement of darkness on darkness', looks forward surely to 'The wounded surgeon plies the steel' and the much-elaborated skull-and-crossbones conceit which occupies the whole of section IV of the poem. Several readers have objected to this as strained and laboured; and since the necrophily which informs it has already been shown as a parody of the true reconciliation between dark and light, should we not take it that the strain and the labouring are deliberate, a conscious forcing of the tone, a *conscious* movement towards self-parody? What is it in fact but what we were warned of in the typically opalescent lines from 'Burnt Norton' – 'The crying shadow in the funeral dance,/The loud lament of the disconsolate chimera?'

It is my argument, then, that in the sense and to the degree in which section IV of 'East Coker' is a parody the whole of 'The Dry Salvages' is a parody. It is hardly too much to say that the whole of this third quartet is spoken by a nameless persona; certainly it is spoken through a mask, spoken *in character*, spoken in character as the American. This, and nothing else, can explain the approximations to Whitmanesque and other pre-symbolist American verse-procedures; and the insistent Americanism, of course, as all the commentators have noted, is a quality also of the locale persistently evoked by the images – of the Mississippi and the New England coast for instance. It is thus that the incompetence turns out to be dazzling virtuosity; and the inhumanity of the conclusion reached turns out to be only a parody of the true conclusion reached in 'Little Gidding', which is thoroughly humane in its insistence that all varieties of human folly and imperfection are the conditions for apprehending perfection, that the world is therefore necessary and to that extent – even the worst of it – good.

4

There remains only one question. Admitting, as we have had to admit, that the *Four Quartets* – and 'The Dry Salvages' no less than every other part – represent a superbly controlled achievement of its kind, what are we to say of that kind? What kind of poetry is this, in which loose and woolly incoherent language can be seen to be – in its place and for special purposes – better than clear and closely-articulated language? This is a question raised not just by the *Quartets* but by Eliot's work as a whole. The opening paragraph of the fifth section of *Ash-Wednesday* is what Leavis says it is – a magnificent acting out in verse-movement and word-play of 'both the agonized effort to seize the unseizable, and the elusive equivocations of the thing grasped.'[7] But it is also, from another point of view, what Max Eastman says it is – an 'oily puddle of emotional noises'.[8] It is easy to say that Leavis's point of view is right, and Eastman's wrong – that any poetic effect can be seen and judged only as it plays its part in the economy of the whole poem, and that any amount of violence done to language, any amount of sheer ugliness, can be justified as means to a justifiable poetic end. But this is to assert that Eastman's pang of angry discomfort, which I suppose is shared by every sensitive reader at least at a first reading, is not a protest against ugliness on behalf of beauty, but only a protest against the functional in favour of the pretty. Are we in fact prepared to waive the claim 'beautiful' which we make for those lines of poetry which move us to applause as surely as the lines from *Ash-Wednesday* move us to rebellion? And are we, moreover (for this too is implied), prepared to waive the claim 'poetry' for those lines we applaud – unless, that is, their engagingness can be seen as functional?

Well, we – you and I, dear reader – may be prepared to waive these claims. What is quite certain is that not only that legendary figure, the common reader, but the enthusiast and the specialist – a person like Dr Rajan – is not prepared to do so; not prepared because he has not realized it is what is required. More, the poet himself – a poet like Robert Graves – is not prepared to do so. And (what perhaps should make us pause) younger poets than either Graves or Eliot *have* realized what is required of them by poetry like Eliot's and have refused – at least where their own writing is concerned – to waive their claims to poetry and to beauty in the old-fashioned pre-symbolist sense.

'Pre-symbolist', yes. For it is pre-eminently symbolist and post-symbolist poetry that waives these claims and insists that the reader waive them also. Eliot waives them when he says, in 'East Coker', 'The poetry does not matter'. The exegetes cushion the shock of this by taking it to mean '*That sort* of poetry doesn't…', the sort which we have just heard called 'A periphrastic study in a worn-out poetical fashion', which we have agreed to consider as parody. Well, that interpretation can be allowed to stand for classroom consumption. But it isn't what Eliot means, or it isn't all that he means. He means what he says: the poetry doesn't matter, the beauty doesn't matter – for no verse can be judged either poetic or beautiful except in so far as it is seen to be expressive; and what it has to express may demand, as it does in 'The Dry Salvages', rather the false note than the true one, the faded and shop-soiled locution rather than the phrase new-minted, the trundling rhythm rather than the cut,

7   F.R. Leavis, *New Bearings in English Poetry*, new edition (London: Chatto and Windus, 1950), p. 128.
8   Max Eastmann, *The Literary Mind* (New York and London: Scribners, 1931), p. 111.

woolliness rather than clarity — 'See now they vanish,/The faces and places, with the self which, as it could, loved them.' Woolliness becomes the only sort of clarity, the wrong note is the right note, and nothing is so beautiful as what is hideous — in certain (not uncommon) poetic circumstances.

If it is true that Kenner's essay has made everything else on the *Quartets* (and not on them only but on Eliot's work in general) seem like literary curiosities, none of these curios is so appealing to me as Anthony Thorlby's essay, 'The Poetry of Four Quartets', which was published after Kenner's but was obviously not written in the light of it.[9] Thorlby is seriously wrong about the *Quartets*; nothing could be further from the truth than his assertion, 'What is remarkable in Mr Eliot's use of imagery is not that it is symbolic or capable of interpretation, but that the interpretation is essential to its poetic coherence.' Or rather, if this is true in one sense, if we take 'interpretation' to mean 'seeing the place of any part in relation to the whole', it is certainly untrue if we take it to mean, as Thorlby does, that each image as we come to it must be construed, like the images of allegory. What is appealing and important about Thorlby's essay is that it represents a man recognizing that the symbolist revolution in poetry has happened, and trying to come to grips with it. To be sure, Thorlby does not acknowledge that the revolution he perceives is the symbolist revolution; indeed, he writes as if it were inaugurated specifically by *Four Quartets*, seemingly unaware that the revolution was over, and successfully over, long before Eliot began to write, and that all Eliot's poems, the earliest as well as the latest, are constructed on that assumption — that the symbolist procedures have arrived and supplanted all others. Then, again, Thorlby's objections to the procedure as he detects it could be easily countered by anyone versed even a little in symbolist theory; for his argument rests upon a hard and fast distinction between 'having an experience' and 'seeing the significance of that experience' — a distinction made untenable by Bergson. Nevertheless, Thorlby at least perceives the essentially post-symbolist nature of the poetry of the *Quartets* — which is more than can be said for most of the commentators — even if he hasn't the label to tie on to it. And he grasps quite a lot of the implications of the symbolist revolution in terms of the revised expectations that the reader must now entertain — a matter of crucial importance which is hardly ever touched upon.

Thus it is very nearly correct — it is entirely correct from most points of view — to say with Thorlby: 'Mr Eliot's poetry is *about* the many forms in which the life of poetry has flourished; which is a very different thing from simply accepting one form and creating within it a poetry of life.'

9   'The Poetry of *Four Quartets*', *Cambridge Journal*, 5.5 (February 1952), pp. 280–99.

And it is entirely correct to say, as he does:

> Mr Eliot, then, is not standing outside his material looking in upon the experience he is writing about, composing it into one form; he is himself at the centre... looking around him upon so many of the problems of today which he hopes to illumine by its light.

This last point is the vital one. If no one has made it before Thorlby, that was (I suspect) for fear of falling foul of the master's own propaganda for impersonality in poetry, on the gap between the man who suffers and the poet who creates. Eliot was always perfectly fair on this, and one can hardly resent his insistence when one finds critics, deaf to all his warnings, reading 'Gerontion' as a *cri de coeur* rather than what it is – the rendering of the state of mind of an imagined persona, from which the poet is wholly detached.[10] From this point of view Eliot is indeed impersonal, standing quite aside and apart from his creation – my diagnosis of 'The Dry Salvages' as parody makes the point all over again. And yet Thorlby is right too: in another sense Eliot is never outside and apart from his poems. No post-symbolist poet can be outside his poems as Milton was outside 'Lycidas', and no post-symbolist poem can ever be as impersonal as 'Lycidas' was for John Crowe Ransom when he called it 'a poem nearly anonymous'. If Eliot enters his poems only disguised as a persona, wearing a mask, at least he enters them. Reading a parody, we are inevitably aware (though as it were at one remove) of the parodist. Perhaps no other kind of poet is so much in evidence in his own poems as the parodist is, the histrionic virtuoso, always tipping the wink. And if Eliot thus enters into his own poems, his reader must do likewise, changing his focus as the poem changes focus, knowing when to give almost full credence to what the poetry says, when to make reservations according as he detects the voice of now one persona, now another parodying the first.

I share Thorlby's preference for a kind of poetry which stands on its own feet, without my help, as an independent creation, a thing to be walked round, and as satisfying from one standpoint as from another. And so I hope not to be thought lacking in gratitude to Eliot for the *Four Quartets*, nor lacking in respect for the prodigious achievement of that poem, if I say that I hope for quite a different sort of poem in the future, a sort of poem more in harmony with what was written in Europe before symbolism was thought of, even (since symbolist procedures are only the logical development of Romantic procedures) before Romanticism was thought of. I am not forgetting the lesson of 'Tradition and the Individual

---

10 This is a particularly good example of Davie's changes of mind. Compare his remarks on 'Gerontion' on pp. 60, 79 and 95 below. [Ed.]

Talent'. I know that history cannot be unwritten, that there can be no question of putting the clock back; the post-post-symbolist poetry I look for may be more in harmony with pre-Romantic poetry, it can never be the same. There cannot be a conspiracy to pretend that the symbolist revolution never happened. (The annoying thing of course is that, because Eliot has been seen by the influential critics most often in the perspective of the specifically English tradition rather than in the perspective of Europe as a whole, it is commonly held that he has done just what I seem to ask for, has re-established continuity with the poetry of the seventeenth and eighteenth centuries. And he has really done so – but only in relatively superficial ways.)

If I hope for a different sort of poetry, that hope is reasonably confident – not because I give much weight to the younger poets of today who, when they think in these terms at all (they seldom do), declare that the post-symbolist tradition is 'worked out'; nor even because the respectable poetry written in England and America by poets younger than Eliot is plainly not written according to his prescription; but simply because the *Four Quartets* represent a stage of such subtlety and intricacy in the post-symbolist tradition that it is impossible to think of its ever being taken a stage further. Surely no poet, unless it be Eliot himself, can elaborate further this procedure in which the true key is never sounded, but exists in the poem only as the norm by which all the voices that speak are heard as delicately off-key, as the voices of parody. It is, at any rate, in this hope and this confidence of something quite different in the offing, that I have written the second half of my title: 'T.S. Eliot: *The End of an Era*'.

Twentieth Century 159.950 (April 1956).

III The Young Yeats

Thomas Davis, whose name and memory we honour in all these lectures,[1] was like Yeats, a poet. A poet; but much else besides. 'Thomas Davis', we say, 'poet and patriot'. And it's unfortunate, perhaps, to have to point out that Yeats sometimes objected to Davis for just that reason. Yeats seems to have suspected that Davis was patriot first, and poet second; at any rate, that in being so many other things besides a poet, Davis wasn't as good a poet as he might have been. We find all this in one of Yeats's essays in autobiography, *The Trembling of the Veil*. There Yeats speaks of a period in the 1890s where he was still under thirty. He had come back to Dublin from London to found 'The National Literary Society'. Already he envisaged the creation of an Irish Theatre – the scheme that years later was to lead to the Abbey Theatre. But first, he thought, the ground must be prepared – not by the raising of funds nor the securing of patronage nor the forming of committees, but by creating a public that could respond to the plays he had in mind. Hence, the National Literary Society – and already in this we see something characteristically Yeatsian: an ultimate aim that might well be dismissed as head-in-the-clouds idealism, combined with the patience that can bide its time, see far ahead, and concentrate to begin with on what is modest and practicable. But the point for the moment is that in his efforts to create a discerning public – through lectures, through a series of shilling books, through provincial libraries – Yeats ran up against the surviving influence of Davis and the Young Ireland movement of thirty or forty years before; and he came to see the prestige of Young Ireland as the biggest obstacle in his path. 'Young Ireland', he says,

> had sought a nation unified by political doctrine alone, a subservient art and letters aiding and abetting. The movement of thought which had, in the 'fifties and 'forties in Paris and London and Boston, filled literature and especially poetical literature, with curiosities about science, about history, about politics, with moral purpose and educational fervour – abstractions all – had created a new instrument for Irish politics, a method of writing that took its poetical style from Campbell, Scott, Macaulay, and Béranger, with certain elements from

1   'The Young Yeats' was Davie's contribution to a series of Thomas Davis Lectures broadcast by Radio Eireann in 1955–6. [Ed.]

Gaelic, its prose style – in John Mitchel, the only Young Ireland prose-writer who had a style at all – from Carlyle. To recommend this method of writing as literature without much reservation and discrimination, I contended, was to be deceived or to practise deception.

What irks Yeats, we notice, is that the Young Irelanders treated literature and the other arts as *subservient* to political doctrine, as an *instrument* for politics. However much Yeats may have approved Davis's politics, however much he approved the politics of the patriots of his own time, he could not agree that the poet's pen was there to serve the cause. Poetry itself is the cause; if in serving the muse the poet also serves his country, well and good. But that is a secondary consideration; perhaps, in the poet's head as he writes, it should not be a consideration at all.

It seems strange, no doubt, and even frivolous, that we should start assessing the services of an Irish patriot by seeing him first in the middle of a squabble about literary value, about just how good some Irish writers had been *as writers*. It seemed strange and frivolous, too, to the people who attended the first meetings of the National Literary Society. But that was just Yeats's point, – that it is not frivolous, that it is the place to start. And it is a point that needs making just as much now as it did then. Now as then people will turn away, saying 'There's no accounting for tastes'; now as then people will raise an amused eyebrow at anyone who sets out, as Yeats did, to 'create a standard of criticism'; now as then people will think there are more important things to do.

If we think ourselves back into Yeats's situation at the time, we can begin to see why Yeats thought it worthwhile making this stand. He moved among politicians as much as among poets; and of course those politicians were *revolutionary* politicians, the politics that he sympathized with were *revolutionary* politics. And yet, in taking his stand against the literature of Young Ireland, Yeats was challenging the principle behind much revolutionary politics, the principle that the end justifies the means. The poets of Young Ireland were noble characters, dedicating themselves to a noble cause. And yet, so Yeats maintained, their own nobility and the nobility of what they aimed at could not justify the ignobility of the means they used, the ignobility of their writings as literature. It was not of course that they chose ignoble subjects. Their writings were ignoble, often enough, just because they failed to respond to noble subjects such as those of the ancient Irish mythology – failed to respond, that is, by failing to write of them in the scrupulous and durable style that such great subjects deserved. This is related to the other objection Yeats has to the Young Irelanders – that they were committed to abstractions. He lists the things they cared about – 'science', 'history', 'politics', 'moral purpose', 'educational fervour'; and then he exclaims, 'Abstractions all'. Yeats's hatred of abstractions lasted throughout his life; and this comes, once again, straight out of his being, first and last, a poet. He cares for the particular, not the general; for the general only when made specific in particular examples. So, instead of talking generally about the level of Irish taste, he jumps at once to an example of that taste, the high value it put on writings that weren't worth it. Poetry itself is an abstraction; what matters are the particular examples, not 'poetry' but poems. So the end to be aimed at, while it is still unattained, is an abstraction; but the means employed to that end – they are particular and concrete, here and now, and they can be judged. So the end can never justify the means – what holds in poetry, holds in politics too.

It was this which excited Yeats when he heard the old Fenian, John O'Leary say, 'There are things a man must not do to save a nation.' And O'Leary indeed, who was Yeats's mentor at this time in everything outside literature, showed how one could be a revolutionary without believing that the end justifies the means. Yeats says of him:

> He had grown up in a European movement when the revolutionist thought that he, above all men, must appeal to the highest motive, be guided by some ideal principle, be a little like Cato or like Brutus, and he had lived to see the change Dostoievsky examined in *The Possessed*. Men who had been of his party – and oftener their sons – preached assassination and the bomb; and, worst of all, the majority of his countrymen followed after constitutional politicians who practised opportunism, and had, as he believed, such low morals that they would lie, or publish private correspondence, if it might advance their cause.

O'Leary, that is, believed with Yeats that the best of causes could not justify ignoble actions; and this was the tie between them. But we must notice that O'Leary judged by moral standards; and it dawns upon us with a shock that Yeats's standards weren't moral but aesthetic. Whether at bottom aesthetic and moral standards are the same – whether, as Keats said, 'Beauty is truth, truth beauty' – that, thank goodness, is something we don't have to go into. Yet we can't help but remember that when Yeats justified the 1916 rising, he justified it on other than moral grounds – 'A terrible beauty is born'. A terrible *beauty*: not a terrible virtue.

Many people will find it shocking – I think I am shocked myself – to find momentous affairs, involving the destinies of whole nations, justified or condemned not according as they are morally right or wrong, but according as they make for beauty or ugliness. It's necessary to say, though, that Yeats didn't mean by 'beauty' what most of us mean by it, a sort of prettiness, a mere grace or charm. And in any case, the standards he judged by had to be aesthetic standards, just because he judged human actions by analogy from the field of action he knew best, the business of poetry.

We see this very clearly in Yeats's judgement of people. Just as he judged a movement in poetry not by its lofty intentions, but in terms of the poems it in fact produced, so he judged a political movement not by its programme but by the sort of people who led it, and the sort of people it attracted. And just as he judged a poem, not by the sentiments it expressed, but by the language used to express them, in a word by the *style*, so too he tended to judge people by their style of living. He looked always for 'personalities', for men and women who expressed themselves fully and fearlessly in manner and bearing. O'Leary was a personality in this sense. But from the 1890s to the end of Yeats's life, one figure stood out above all Irish politicians as the type and ideal of men who lived in a noble style – the figure of Parnell:

> Had Cosgrave eaten Parnell's heart, the land's
> Imagination had been satisfied,
> Or lacking that, government in such hands,
> O'Higgins its sole statesman had not died.[2]

'Imagination had been satisfied' – that was Yeats's conviction that Ireland could never be at peace with itself until the Irish imagination was supplied, out of literary fiction and historical fact, with images to evoke its pride in its own tradition. A poem written in a noble style, a life like Parnell's lived in noble style – they were, from this point of view, equally essential.

It is this aspect of Yeats, his rating of style in living along with style in writing, which accounts for two objections that one sometimes hears made – the first mostly by Irishmen who knew him, the other mostly by Englishmen and Americans who never met him. People who knew him sometimes complain that he was affected and mannered, a *poseur*, and this obviously comes about because he tried himself to live with the style that he detected in Parnell and a few others. It was always, one notices – as in the writing, so in living – the *grand* style; and one can legitimately complain that the grand style is not the only style. Otherwise, the best answer to the charge that he was mannered and a *poseur* is to retort, as I think Yeats would have retorted, that manner and pose are very good things if the manner is a good manner and the pose a good pose, good enough to fire the imagination of those who observe them. The other objection to Yeats that I have in mind is one that is heard less often now than it was twenty years ago – the charge that Yeats was a fascist or (as the phrase goes) a crypto-fascist. Again, it is easy enough to see how the value Yeats placed on a figure like Parnell, on men who dominated a gathering or a group by sheer force of personality, can seem uncomfortably close to

2 'Parnell's Funeral' from *A Full Moon in March.*

the Fascist's surrender of all initiative to an idolized leader. But the answer to this objection is obvious: in choosing a leader to honour, as in choosing poems to honour, it is necessary to have taste.

Which brings us back to the National Literary Society, and the young Yeats dreaming (in his own words) of a 'national literature that made Ireland beautiful in the memory, and yet had been freed from provincialism by an exacting criticism'. The images from literature and from life that were to inhabit the national memory, and satisfy the national imagination when it delved in that memory, had to be worthy of that role — true images, true as poetic fictions are true, that is truly noble and inspiring. Parnell was one such image out of Irish life; Yeats's own 'Countess Cathleen' was another such, perhaps, out of literature. But before any more such images could be given — in particular, before they could be given on the stage — Irish taste had to be trained to recognize them. Yeats accused the Young Ireland leaders — and the last of them, Charles Gavan Duffy, was back in Ireland for Yeats to cross swords with — of having peopled the Irish imagination with images that were unworthy; so that those false images had to be thrown down, if there was ever to be room for the true ones. By the efforts of the Young Irelanders, as Yeats saw it:

> All the past had been turned into a melodrama with Ireland for blameless hero; and poet, novelist and historian had but one object, that we should hiss the villain, and only a minority doubted that the greater the talent the greater the hiss. It was all the harder to substitute for that melodrama a nobler form of art, because there really had been, however different in their form, villain and victim; yet fight that rancour I must, and if I had not made some head against it in 1892 and 1893 it might have silenced in 1907 John Synge, the greatest dramatic genius of Ireland.

Thus, in Yeats's mind as he looked back, his early campaign against a wrong-headed literary nationalism is intimately connected with that period, ten or fifteen years later, when with Lady Gregory and John Synge, he founded a national theatre and a national dramatic movement. And it is this later achievement that we must now consider.

At the outset we run into a difficulty. For if Yeats thought that the images created by the writings of the Young Irelanders were unworthy of the national pride and affection which was demanded for them, are we to suppose that Christy Mahon, Synge's *Playboy of the Western World*, was a worthy image? Is the figure that Synge created to be given the love and admiration that should be denied to the creations of Thomas Davis? As is well known, the Irish public refused to take Synge's creation on these terms; rather they saw in Synge's amoral hero a gratuitous insult to the Irish national genius. And after all one can sympathize with those

Irishmen who protested at this image of themselves, by rioting in the theatre; at any rate *they* were taking Synge's play more seriously than the Dublin theatre-goers of today who laugh uproariously at what they take, in Synge's play, to be the antics of their country cousins. When Synge's play appeared, Yeats perhaps was caught on the wrong foot as surely as the first-night audience. It all came of his confusing 'style' with the grand style, the elevated style, heroic or tragic. Synge wrote with style, and he made his hero live with style – but the style was comic or tragi-comic, a style for which Yeats in his theorizing had made no provision. In writing about it afterwards, Yeats got out of this difficulty very adroitly. In considering his early controversies, once again in the light of what came later, he says:

> I was preparing the way without knowing it for a great satirist and master of irony, for master-works stir vaguely in many before they grow definite in one man's mind, and to help me I had already flitting through my head, jostling other ideas and so not yet established there, a conviction that we should satirize rather than praise, that original virtue arises from the discovery of evil. If we were, as I had dreaded, declamatory, loose, and bragging, we were but the better fitted – that declared and measured – to create unyielding personality, manner at once cold and passionate, daring long-premeditated act...

There, you see, Synge's creation is presented, not as the answer to Ireland's prayer for an image it might love and honour in memory, but as giving a necessary injection of scepticism and irreverence, so that the Irish imagination might learn to see through the false gods to the true ones – to the truly heroic images that would come thereafter, which would survive disillusioned and distrustful scrutiny, and emerge with their heroism unscathed. This detracts nothing from Synge's achievement, and it is a profoundly interesting account of the place of the 'Playboy' in modern Irish literature and life. All the same one cannot help feeling that Yeats is being wise after the event.

I think, therefore, that the reception given to *The Playboy of the Western World* is not quite such a shameful blot on the 'scutcheon as people commonly believe'. Yeats, however, was shocked and enraged – and understandably. For after all his years of campaigning to raise the level of Irish taste, when Irishmen were in fact presented with a masterpiece, they could not recognize it. And even if that masterpiece was not what they had been led to expect – being comic instead of heroic – yet the power and beauty of Synge's creation should have come home to them. This didn't happen. And the reception given to Synge was the first great blow given to Yeats's vision of a literature that should be national yet of the highest artistic quality.

The second blow to Yeats's hopes of public taste was the reception given in 1913 to Sir Hugh Lane's request for a gallery to house his paintings. Lane had loaned these pictures to the Dublin Corporation but demanded that they be well-housed in a gallery to be built over the Liffey by an English architect, Lutyens. Lane threatened he would take away the loaned pictures to London if the money were not quickly raised for the gallery. When the Dublin Corporation temporized, Yeats castigated the philistinism of his countrymen in a series of poems, one of them characteristically addressed to Parnell, and presenting Sir Hugh Lane as another of Parnell's kind.

The contemptuous tone of this poem, and the implied rejection of public or national opinion as in any way an arbiter of taste – this cannot easily be dismissed as the expression of a temporary mood, or as rhetorical exaggeration in the heat of polemic. There are too many such poems at this date (some of them much more bitter), and this note recurs too constantly, in the poems that Yeats wrote up to the time he died. It seems indubitable that from this time on, despite the work he continued to do for the Abbey Theatre, despite the way in which he participated imaginatively in all the events of the Rising and the Troubled Times, despite his conscientious public service as a senator – despite all this, he had in certain important matters lost hope, and he withdrew in the second half of his life, out of the arena of national aspirations into himself, making his magnificent later poetry mainly personal, passionate and subjective.

How often, after all, we hear the question asked, 'Why has the modern artist so little to say to the man in the street?' – or else (the same question from the other end, the artist's end), 'Why does the man in the street not recognize what I am trying to do for him?' Of all modern artists in whatever country, Yeats tried hardest to answer these questions, to answer before they were asked, by establishing an unobstructed avenue of communication between the finest artists and the nation as a whole. He failed. And modern Ireland owes it to him to ponder his failure, to understand it and to act in the light of it. There is no question, as it seems to me, of reviving Yeats's pipe-dream, and trying to create a national literature available equally to the sophisticated and the simple. Yeats himself had to abandon that aspiration – though not before he had worked for many years, doggedly and resourcefully, in an effort to realize it. He failed. He acknowledged that failure, and the inevitability of it. It is open to question whether Ireland as a whole has acknowledged it likewise.

What Yeats had to realize, reluctantly and bitterly, was that Ireland in matters of culture was, and is, not one nation but several. Here, as in England, as in America, there is not one public but several. There is the largest public of all, the mass-public catered for by the so-called mass-media of the commercial cinema, the popular press, radio and (nowadays)

television, and the pulp-literature of magazines and novelettes. Then
there is what is sometimes called the 'middlebrow' public, catered for by
middlebrow culture – which is characteristically a watering down and
reduction to formula of what, two generations back, was truly creative
art. And finally there is, in every country, the tiny public which a writer
like Yeats must address however little he may like it – the discriminating
élite. It is, I believe, Yeats's perception of these nations within the nation,
and of the impossibility of welding them into a whole, which accounts for
his apparent withdrawal in the last twenty years of his life out of the life
of the nation as a whole. Modern Ireland is anxiously aware of the political and religious differences which cut across national unity; it is apparently much less aware of these cultural differences. Yet to anyone who
believes as Yeats believed, as perhaps all practising artists must believe,
that man lives and expresses himself most intimately in the world of the
imagination, these cultural differences must seem more important than
any others. For how can there be national unity in any meaningful sense,
when inside the nation different individuals inhabit entirely different
imaginative worlds?

Yeats would answer, I think, that a kind of national unity is possible in
these circumstances, on the basis of 'live and let live', of acknowledging
these differences, of seeing them indeed very clearly just so as to allow for
them. To be sure, this sort of national unity is a poor second-best, as
compared with the cultural unity Yeats had visualized in his youth. Then
he had written in his essay, 'Ireland and the Arts':

> I would have Ireland recreate the ancient arts, the arts as they were
> understood in Judea, in India, in Scandinavia, in Greece and Rome, in
> every ancient land, as they were understood when they moved a
> whole people, and not a few people who have grown up in a leisured
> class...

And it is this dream of Yeats's that modern Ireland likes to remember,
without acknowledging that the Irish reality destroyed that dream. The
aspiration of a true artist two generations back – the position he took up
with regard to what a national culture was and should be – has been
perverted and reduced to a formula by middlebrow critics of a later
generation. Yeats's concern for a literature that should address the whole
people, not just an élite – this has come to mean demanding of a play or
a poem that it should be immediately intelligible to that stock figure, 'the
tired business man'. Yeats's concern for a literature that should be truly
Irish – this has come to mean that the first question asked of a poem or a
play is not 'How good is it?' but 'How Irish is it?' And it has produced
that species of literary history which admits that George Moore and J.M.
Synge are in one sense better writers than, say, Gerald Griffin and the
Banim brothers, while still contending that because Griffin and the

Banims aren't smeared with the brush of the Ascendancy, they are in some obscure sense the better writers after all.[3]

These are flagrant falsifications of Yeats's position. But in any case that very position, which was tenable when Yeats first formulated it, is not tenable any longer – as Yeats implicitly admitted long before he died. Yeats hoped that in cultural matters Ireland in the twentieth century might be a special case. He had to renounce that hope and to realize that in Ireland as elsewhere in the twentieth century the preservation of cultural standards had to be in the hands of an élite. His service to his country, outside the poems he wrote, will have borne fruit only when the nation reaches the same conclusion and goes on from there.

3   Gerald Griffin (1803–40) was an Irish playwright, novelist and poet. John Banim (1798–1842) and his brother Michael Banim (1796–1874) were Irish novelists and short story writers. [Ed.]

The Shaping of Modern Ireland, ed. Conor Cruise O'Brien (London: Routledge and Kegan Paul, 1960).

IV The Relation between Syntax and Music in Some Modern Poems in English

In this paper I shall try to understand and explore one aspect of the poetic theory of the symbolist movement in European poetry: a movement born in France in the last decades of the nineteenth century, which has no effect on poetry written in English until the twentieth. In 1920 Paul Valéry, last of the French symbolists, indulged his memories of that movement:

> What was baptized *Symbolism* can be very simply described as the common intention of several groups of poets (otherwise mutually inimical) to 'reclaim their own from Music'. The secret of that movement is nothing else. The obscurities and peculiarities with which it was so often reproached; the apparently overintimate relations with English, Slavic, or Germanic literature; the syntactical disorders, the irregular rhythms, the curiosities of vocabulary, the continual images... this is all easily deduced, once the principle is acknowledged. In vain did those who watched these experiments, and even those who put them into practice, attack the poor word *Symbol*. It means only what one wants it to; if someone fastens his own hopes upon it, he will find them there! – But we were nourished on music, and our literary minds dreamed only of extracting from language the same effects, almost, as were produced on our nervous systems by sound alone. Some cherished Wagner, others Schumann. I could as well say that they hated them. In the heat of passionate interest these two states are indistinguishable.[1]

Now, this is not at first sight very promising. We may remember that English poet of the 1890s who decided that the letter 'v' stands for the most beautiful sound in the English language. And we have been schooled by the youthful Mr Eliot so that when we hear of the music of poetry we think first of the drugged insistent rhythms of Swinburne, in

---

1   *The Art of Poetry*, translated by Denise Folliot (London: Routledge and Kegan Paul, 1958), p. 42.

which patterns of sound are elaborated and sustained at the expense of sense. It seems that this isn't, however, what Valéry understands by the music, or the musicality, of poetry. In the essay from which I've just quoted, he acknowledges that some of the symbolist poets tried to meet the Wagnerian challenge this way: 'For some of them colour in sound and the combinative art of alliteration seemed to hold no further secrets; they deliberately transposed the tones of the orchestra to their verse: they were not always wrong.' It is hard to interpret the urbanity of 'they were not always wrong' except by taking Valéry to mean that mostly, of course, they were. But there is firmer evidence, in a foreword which Valéry wrote at the end of his life to some translations from the Latin:

> Latin is, in general, a more compact language than our own. It has no articles; it is chary of auxiliaries (at least during the classical period); it is sparing of prepositions. It can say the same things in fewer words and, moreover, is able to arrange these with an enviable freedom almost completely denied to us. This latitude is most favorable to poetry, which is an *art of continuously constraining language to interest the ear directly* (and through the ear, everything sounds may provoke of themselves) *at least as much as it does the mind*. A *line* is both a succession of syllables and a combination of words; and just as the latter ought to form a *probable meaning*, so the succession of syllables ought to form for the ear a kind of *audible shape*, which, with a special and as it were peculiar compulsion, should impress itself simultaneously on both voice and memory. The poet must therefore constantly fulfill two separate demands, just as the painter must present to the *simple vision* a harmony, but to the understanding a likeness of things or people. It is clear that freedom in arranging the words of a sentence, to which French is curiously hostile, is essential to the game of verse-making. The French poet does what he can within the very narrow bounds of our syntax; the Latin poet, within the much wider bounds of his own, does almost what he will.[2]

Now we must certainly recognize that among the poetic devices 'to interest the ear directly' are all the Swinburnian instruments of alliteration, consonance and assonance, terminal and internal rhyme and chime and half-rhyme; Valéry's own poetry is orchestrated very richly – some have thought, too richly – in these ways. But after all what is Swinburnian is not this array of devices (since they are used by every poet one can think of), but only a degree of coarseness and lack of subtlety in their deployment. And by the time Valéry comes to speak of syntax, especially when he speaks with envy of Latin syntax, of course the English poet who comes to mind is not Swinburne, but Milton. And it is Milton's 'linkèd

2   ibid., pp. 295–6.

sweetness long drawn out', not any Sitwellian or Swinburnian 'vowel-music', which we should bear in mind when we consider Valéry's insistence on the musicality of poetry, on the duty it has to the ear as well as to the intelligence.

For it would be wrong to suppose that Valéry's experiments in poetic syntax are undertaken solely to distort word-order so as to get assonantal or alliterative clusters – as wrong as to explain in the same way the analogous syntactical experiments of Milton. 'Linkèd sweetness long drawn out' – it is the linking and the drawing-out which attracts Milton, just as it attracts the poet who first envisaged his own poem, *La Jeune Parque*, as 'an operatic recitative, à la Gluck: thirty or forty lines in one long phrase almost; and for contralto voice' (*Lettres à quelqu'un*). What they envy music for is its continuity, its sustained fluency, its never stopping but to start again.

This is a most important matter, and it is worth dwelling on some of its implications. In the first place, as the citation from Valéry has shown already, this is an understanding of the musicality of poetry which immediately issues, not in manipulation of vowels and consonants, but in manipulation of syntax. Perhaps the supreme masterpieces of this sort of musicality in English poetry are the two marriage-hymns of Spenser, where the music resides just here – in the draping of the sentences, the syntactical units, over the lines, the metrical units, so that the stops and starts of the grammar are played off, with bewildering and glorious variety, against the stops and starts of metre. Secondly, as the name of Spenser demonstrates, this is a time-honoured aspiration and objective in poetry, stretching back beyond Spenser into the history of the Italian *canzone*, out of which he may have learned it. It is so ancient in fact, and the pleasure of it is (one would have thought) so marked a feature of the experience of enjoying poetry, that it is absurd I should find it necessary to emphasize and define it. That I nevertheless do find it necessary is the third and most alarming implication in the whole matter: how on earth have we got into a position where, if this is indeed still a source of pleasure to us in our reading (and I certainly hope for that at least), yet we look in vain to literary criticism for any examination of it or indeed, much of the time, for any acknowledgement that it exists?

For the most influential criticism of our time in English does not merely ignore this feature of poetry; its whole tendency is to preclude the possibility of it. I have in mind not at all the objections that have been raised to *Paradise Lost* (some of which I find unanswerable), nor the fairly general preference for the rough and broken cadences of Donne over the different music of Spenser and Milton (for that is rather a sign of grace, being an understandable preference for one kind of music over another). I think rather of the critical habit of speaking of a poem as a structure, or as a delimited field in which forces are balanced against each other to set up a tension, of our speaking of planes or levels of meaning, and of, for instance, Professor Wilson Knight's definition of the Shakespearean play as 'an extended metaphor'. When one first encountered this formula, one took it that the extension was an extension in time, in the time taken to see the play acted, or to read it. But no. Professor Knight said, it was extended in space like a carpet, and the pattern of it was not a pattern developing in time but should be seen every part of it at once, like the pattern in a carpet. When Mr John Holloway protested that the play, like it or not, does occupy a duration of time, when he pointed out that there- fore to recognize a reference as harking back to an earlier one is a very different and more obviously legitimate activity than recognizing the first reference as looking forward to the later one, he was making a point as almost foolishly elementary as the point I have just made about syntax and music. It is a point like mine, and related to it. For to see the music of poetry in the way Milton and Valéry see it, as 'linkèd sweetness long drawn out', is to emphasize how poetry, like music, erects its structures in the lapse of time. The experience of reading or hearing a poem, much more than the experience of looking at a painting, goes on; it inhabits a duration. A poem, we see, is a sequence of verbal events, a train of actions, of preparations, crises, dénouements. And this is the truth about poetry which many of the metaphors most favoured nowadays by English and American critics, metaphors taken from geometry or architecture, seem designed to obscure.

Of the stanzas in Spenser's 'Prothalamion', it has been justly said, 'the elaborate *canzone* is sustained by the structure of the sentence'. And indeed a stanza from the poem exemplifies better than anything else in English what I take to be Valéry's ideal of poetic music as a function of poetic syntax – a single sentence seventeen lines long, its grammatical ordering never in doubt, grammatical pause played off against metrical pause with such delicate resourcefulness as always to give the reader time to draw breath just before he needs to. The taking of a new breath – whether actually in reading aloud, or in imagination when reading with the eye – corresponds to the equally unflurried rapid sorting-out by the mind of grammatical relationships, in such a way that the physical act, the drawing of breath, embodies and makes immediate, as an intimate phys- ical sensation, the intellectual act of apprehending a relationship. As the breath launches out upon a new access of rhythm, so the mind launches out upon an added curve of meaning. Yet this is not for sound to echo sense; it would be merely fanciful and arbitrary to pretend to hear in the voice's sweet lapse from line to line the plash and ripple of the Thames or even the breathing of the zephyr-wind. And similarly, though the rhyme comes home so pleasantly and the sounds are such as to delight the ear and the mouth with the various quantities of the vowels, the interplay of fricatives and sibilants in consonants, this orchestration is subdued to the melodic unwinding of the syntax. What is this if it is not all that Valéry asked for? And am I therefore proposing Edmund Spenser as a symbolist *avant la lettre*? Plainly, the specifically symbolist version of this ancient resource is still to be inquired for.

We find it, I think, if we revert to the recognition that poetry conceived of as musical in this way has the merit, particularly to be valued at the present time, of insisting on a poem as an artefact which unrolls in time, imposes its shape on time as a peculiarly meaningful duration. Coming from this direction to a Shakespeare play, we shall cease to see it (as we are now asked to do rather often) as simultaneously present in all its parts, extended in imagined space. On the contrary, common sense is given its way and we remember *Julius Caesar* or *Othello* as a shape cut out of time, occupying the time necessary for its performance.

But we cannot fail to remember also, as soon as we think about it, that *Julius Caesar* or *Othello* on this showing still differs from a symphony or a piece of chamber music in the way it carves itself out of lapsing time, making a duration for itself. For of course the Shakespeare play occupies two distinct times, the time it takes for its performance but also the quite different time of several days or weeks or (in the case of *A Winter's Tale*) of more than twenty years,[3] which we are to imagine as necessary for the sequence of events portrayed. So important, indeed, is this second time, that a measure of the dramatist's skill in creating his illusion is precisely his capacity for making this second imagined time supersede, in our own awareness as spectators, the first time actually elapsing. The rule of the unity of time in neo-classical drama was applied in order to make the gap between these two times as narrow as possible − an objective which nowadays we think not worth the trouble, pointless, not worth any trouble at all. And so it is; for so long as the gap remains, it doesn't matter how wide or narrow it is. But suppose the gap could be eliminated altogether, suppose the two times could be made identical, so that what the actors do on the stage should not 'stand for' certain events but should themselves *be* those events, the only happenings there are. This might indeed be worth doing, and would collapse the two times of literature into the one time of music. This appears to be what the symbolists attempted.

Drama of course is a special case, yet the post-symbolist plays of Yeats are there to show how drama can be made to approach in this way, through ritual and dance, the condition of music. My concern, however, is with non-theatrical verse, in which the only events are verbal events. What if these verbal events could be made not to stand for other imagined events which they tell us about, but should themselves become the only occurrences there are, the succession of words themselves the sequence of events which constitutes the action of the poem? As a matter of fact this has always been a possibility in a kind of poem sometimes called 'the pure lyric', of which indeed Spenser's marriage-hymns might be thought to be especially elaborate examples. But in fact, in the stanza from 'Prothalamion' Spenser is telling a story, the story of what he did; and he did it, of course, in a different time from the time which the poem itself occupies. Most of what passes for lyric verse has a substantial narrative element:

> I wandered lonely as a cloud
> Which floats on high o'er vales and hills,
> When all at once I saw a crowd,
> A host, of golden daffodils

The verb 'saw', coming where it does in the poem, is an event in the sequence of events which is our experience of the poem. But nothing is made of its character as an event in the time-span which is the duration of our reading. On the contrary, the verbal event is at once drained of all its eventfulness by our realizing that it merely 'stands for' an event which is quite other than itself, an event occurring in quite another time, the time that Wordsworth took on the walk he is telling us about. It would regain much of its eventfulness, its character as an event in its own right would be exploited, if it were (in defiance of all the logic governing tense-sequence in prose) put in the present tense, 'When all at once I see a crowd'. And the sudden introduction of a present tense, in defiance of all prosaic logic, is a marked feature of symbolist narration, as here in Mallarmé's 'Prose pour des Esseintes':

> Mais cette soeur sensée et tendre
> Ne porta son regard plus loin
> Que sourire et, comme à l'entendre
> J'occupe mon antique soin.

(But this sensible and tender sister/Did not go farther/Than smile, and as I heard her/I capture my ancient care.) A verb in the present tense necessarily 'stands for' an event which occupies the same time, the present time, as the event of the word's own occurrence in the poem. Thus the event it is is simultaneous with the event it describes; and simultaneity thus achieved, it is a none too difficult task – largely a matter of discreetly ambiguous imagery throughout – to make the two events identical or at least indistinguishable. It's worth noting that to have all the verbs in the present tense, from first to last of a poem, would fail of this effect or at least make the effect much less surely and strongly, because of the well-known phenomenon of 'the historic present', according to which the reader, once he has caught on to the convention, automatically translates every present tense into a past tense even as he apprehends it. It is essential to surprise the reader because surprisingness is a feature of eventfulness. Moreover, it is not a matter of just buying the surprising present tense by an outlay of past tenses; for once the logical sequence of tenses is broken, the sequence itself is compromised, so that the past tenses become immediately suspect also. None of the past tenses thereafter can be trusted. The order of time in which they would make sense is disrupted from within, and quite discredited. And the only order of time which the reader is left with, the only order of time he can trust, is the one time which the tale takes in the telling, the time which the poem takes to be spoken or read. The two times of literary narrative have been collapsed into the one time, the pure duration, of music.

This thoroughly simple trick is an elementary example of the reason why, whatever else symbolist poems may describe or adumbrate, one thing they always describe is themselves, their own way of coming into being, comporting themselves, and coming to an end. Thus Edmund Wilson has to say of a poem by Valéry:

> In such a poem as *Le Cimetière Marin*, there is no simple second meaning: there is a marvellously close reproduction of the very complex and continually changing relation of human consciousness to the things of which it is conscious. The noonday is inorganic Nature, but it is also the absolute in the poet's mind, it is also his twenty years of inaction – and it is also merely the noonday itself, which in a moment will no longer exist, which will be no longer either tranquil or noon. And the sea, which, during those moments of calm, forms a part of that great diamond of nature in which the poet finds himself the single blemish, because the single change, is also the image of the poet's silence, which in a moment, as the wind comes up to lash the sea, will give way to a sudden gust of utterance, the utterance of the poem itself.

And this is why Boris Pasternak, the only post-symbolist poet in Russia, can declare: 'The clearest, most memorable and important fact about art is its conception, and the world's best creations, those which tell of the most diverse things, in reality describe their own birth'. How can it be otherwise, if the events which the poem narrates are the events of its own words occurring in it, one by one?

But it is high time that I gave some examples of this feature of symbolist poetry surviving into English poetry. Look, then, at the sequence of tenses in Yeats's 'Coole Park and Ballylee':

> Under my window-ledge the waters race,
> Otters below and moor-hens on the top,

Run for a mile undimmed in Heaven's face
Then darkening through 'dark' Raftery's 'cellar' drop,
Run underground, rise in a rocky place
In Coole demesne, and there to finish up
Spread to a lake and drop into a hole.
What's water but the generated soul?

Upon the border of that lake's a wood
Now all dry sticks under a wintry sun,
And in a copse of beeches there I stood,
For Nature's pulled her tragic buskin on
And all the rant's a mirror of my mood:
At sudden thunder of the mounting swan
I turned about and looked where branches break
The glittering reaches of the flooded lake.

Another emblem there! That stormy white
But seems a concentration of the sky;
And, like the soul, it sails into the sight
And in the morning's gone, no man knows why;
And is so lovely that it sets to right
What knowledge or its lack had set awry,
So arrogantly pure, a child might think
It can be murdered with a spot of ink.

The bibliographical history of this poem is interesting, in a way which bears upon what I am saying. The present point is sufficiently made by the baffling changes from past to present tense and back again, in the second stanza; and in particular by the outrageous, the impossible sequence of tenses 'a child might think/It can…', instead of 'It could'. The effect of this is that a decisive event has taken place in between the end of the penultimate line and the beginning of the last line. What has happened is concealed behind the cryptic whiteness of that blank space on the page. Yet we know it by its effect, the dislocation it has effected in the tense-sequence; what has happened in that white space is that poet and reader have become the children they began by only talking about, so that what began as a potentiality ('they could') has turned into an actuality by the time it arrives (we 'can'). And of course what arrives, what is actualized, is a word – not the word we expected, its arrival therefore all the more actual, all the more an event.

But it is the use of the white space of the page which is more worth insisting on, for this too figures in symbolist theory, in Mallarmé for instance: 'L'armature intellectuelle du poème se dissimule et tient – a lieu – dans l'espace qui isole les strophes et parmi le blanc du papier: significatif silence qu'il n'est pas moins beau de composer que les vers.'⁴ I am suggesting that this too, so remote as it seems from any matter of poetic syntax, in fact is or at least may be the simple consequence of certain syntactical usages, such as dislocated sequence of tenses. I shall hope to find other examples.

There is, for instance, the opening of 'A Game of Chess', section II of Eliot's *The Waste Land*:

> The Chair she sat in, like a burnished throne,
> Glowed on the marble, where the glass
> Held up by standards wrought with fruited vines
> From which a golden Cupidon peeped out
> (Another hid his eyes behind his wing)
> Doubled the flames of sevenbranched candelabra
> Reflecting light upon the table as
> The glitter of her jewels rose to meet it,
> From satin cases poured in rich profusion.
> In vials of ivory and coloured glass
> Unstoppered, lurked her strange synthetic perfumes,
> Unguent, powdered, or liquid – troubled, confused
> And drowned the sense in odours; stirred by the air
> That freshened from the window, these ascended
> In fattening the prolonged candle-flames,
> Flung their smoke into the laquearia,
> Stirring the pattern on the coffered ceiling.
> Huge sea-wood fed with copper
> Burned green and orange, framed by the coloured stone,
> In which sad light a carvèd dolphin swam.
> Above the antique mantel was displayed
> The change of Philomel, by the barbarous king
> So rudely forced; yet there the nightingale
> Filled all the desert with inviolable voice
> And still she cried, and still the world pursues,
> 'Jug Jug' to dirty ears.

It is necessary to quote the whole passage, so as to illustrate the repeated insistence upon the past tense, and hence the force of the expectation which is denied by the vicious snarl of the present tense 'pursues'. The poem returns to the past tense at once:

---

4   'The intellectual armature of the poem conceals itself and is contained – takes place – in the space which isolates the stanzas and among the white of the paper: a significant silence which is no less beautiful to compose than the verses themselves.' [Ed.]

And other withered stumps of time
Were told upon the walls; staring forms
Leaned out, leaning, hushing the room enclosed.
Footsteps shuffled on the stair.
Under the firelight, under the brush, her hair
Spread out in fiery points
Glowed into words, then would be savagely still.

But the single present tense has done its damage, and it is irremediable. The past tense which to begin with was the vehicle of a rapt if morbid interest in what it recorded, after the interruption is flat and weary, limply recording. And again, surely, there is sense in saying that the momentous event, which transforms the speaker from the fascinated historian *temporis acti* to the jaundiced reporter of *moeurs contemporaines*, takes place nowhere in the verse – not even in 'pursues' itself, shattering event as that is, but somewhere unstated between 'cried' and 'pursues', somewhere in or under 'and still the world', *parmi le blanc du papier*.

Of equal interest in this passage is the wonderfully contrived and sustained ambiguity between the past participle and the past indicative:

In vials of ivory and coloured glass
Unstoppered, lurked her strange synthetic perfumes,
Unguent, powdered, or liquid – troubled, confused
And drowned the sense in odours

Is it fanciful to think that the reader hesitates a moment over 'unstoppered', half taking it for a past indicative because of its juxtaposition with the indeed indicative 'lurked', which is identical in grammatical form? The same could be said of 'powdered', again by infection from 'lurked'. Perhaps these are too ingenious. But there can at least be no question of the ambiguity of 'troubled, confused…', both in the first place surely are taken as adjectival participles like 'powdered'. It is only after swinging round the line-ending and coming upon 'drowned', that the reader realizes them for what they are, past indicatives. Yet of course this is to misstate the situation: what they are is both things at once, participles in the first line, active verbs (retrospectively) when we get to the second. So much we have learned from William Empson, who gives examples of this kind of ambiguity from poetry much older than the symbolist movement – a recognition which may give us pause. But at least I think he never drew from such cases the moral that now seems in order – the observation that such ambiguities as these operate powerfully to drive the reader on from line to line, to force home to him just how poetry moves and must move always forward through time. For it is only by 'going on' with the poem, that the reader can perceive the ambiguity and to that extent resolve it.

This, as I now think, is the appropriate context in which to consider an observation of Valéry's, for which I have in the past, and in another place, created a context quite different:[5]

> ... you have surely noticed the curious fact that a certain *word*, which is perfectly clear when you hear or use it in *everyday* speech, and which presents no difficulty when caught up in the rapidity of an ordinary sentence, becomes mysteriously cumbersome, offers a strange resistance, defeats all efforts at definition, the moment you withdraw it from circulation for separate study and try to find its meaning after taking away its temporary function. It is almost comic to inquire the exact meaning of a term, that one uses constantly with complete satisfaction. For example: I stop the word *Time* in its flight. This word was utterly limpid, precise, honest, and faithful in its service as long as it was part of a remark and was uttered by someone who wished to say something. But here it is, isolated, caught on the wing. It takes its revenge. It makes us believe that it has more meanings than uses. It was only a *means*, and it has become an *end*, the object of a terrible philosophical desire. It turns into an enigma, an abyss, a torment of thought...
>
> It is the same with the word *Life* and all the rest.
>
> This readily observed phenomenon has taken on great critical value for me. Moreover, I have drawn from it an illustration that, for me, nicely conveys this strange property of our verbal material.
>
> Each and every word that enables us to leap so rapidly across the chasm of thought, and to follow the prompting of an idea that constructs its own expression, appears to me like one of those light planks which one throws across a ditch or a mountain crevasse and which will bear a man crossing it rapidly. But he must pass without weighing on it, without stopping – above all, he must not take it into his head to dance on the slender plank to test its resistance!... Otherwise the fragile bridge tips or breaks immediately, and all is hurled into the depths. Consult your own experience; and you will find that we understand each other, and ourselves, only thanks to our *rapid passage over words*. We must not lay stress upon them, or we shall see the clearest discourse dissolve into enigmas and more or less learned illusions.[6]

This, as I understand, is the observation about language which has particularly occupied philosophers of our time who have engaged in linguistic analysis; and, so far as I can see, Valéry proceeds from this observation to

5 See Davie, *Articulate Energy: An Enquiry into the Syntax of English Poetry* (London: Routledge and Kegan Paul, 1955), pp. 103–4.
6 *The Art of Poetry*, pp. 55–6.

much the same conclusion as Wittgenstein and others have come to – that it is of the nature of words that they should be taken on the run, that only when so taken are they serviceable. It's worth saying this in passing, because it has been claimed for some recently written English poetry which offers to supersede the poetry with affinities to symbolism, that in doing so it takes note of philosophers' worryings about how far language can be trusted; yet the symbolist Valéry appears to be thinking much more nearly than any of these newer poets, about the same problems as the philosophers.

But if we may affect for a moment a condescending indifference to the philosophers' dilemmas, what has Valéry said here, that is novel for literary theory and the practice of literary criticism? Is he saying any more than what we all knew already, that in all discourse and pre-eminently in literature a word is defined by its context? I think he is. For again I suspect that when we think of context in this way, we use a spatial image, seeing the context of a word as an ambience surrounding it, a field in which it lies. When Valéry speaks of 'our rapid passage over words', he forces us to realize how a context unrolls in time, successively. In fact, it would be more accurate to say that any word in any discourse has two contexts – first, what leads up to it, second, what leads away from it. And the grammatical ambiguity of Eliot's 'troubled, confused' forces us to the same recognition: in the context of what leads up to them, these words mean one thing, being past participles used adjectivally to qualify 'perfumes'; in the context of what leads away from them, they mean something else, being active verbs describing what the perfumes do to the observer. In their character as the culmination of what leads up to them, what lies behind them in their past, they are one thing; in their character as starting-points of what leads away from them, what is before them in their future, they are something else. And this, which is true of all words everywhere, is forced home on us in respect of these words in particular by the poet's turning to use two accidents, first the paucity of terminal inflections in modern English (which brings it about that the past participle and the past indicative have the same form), and secondly the rhythmical necessity of the line-ending.

Since I have hinted at one cross-reference into philosophy, I will risk another. E.A. Burtt, in his *Metaphysical Foundations of Modern Physical Science*, after demonstrating how it was necessary for scientific thought to abandon the Aristotelean analysis of time in terms of potentiality and actuality, observes that as a result 'We are forced to view the movement of time as passing from the past into the future, the present being merely that moving limit between the two'. Is that not precisely the perception of time's inexorable lapse to which we are compelled by a syntactical ambiguity like Eliot's? If so, we may be brought up with a jolt by Burtt's next sentence, 'Time as something lived we have banished from our metaphysics, hence it constitutes for modern philosophy an unsolved problem'. But it is precisely here that we need to remember Mr Empson's principle that in the case of such ambiguities the words are the two meanings at one and the same time. We need to insist, at whatever cost to logic and prosaic conventions, that the words are *both* participles *and* active verbs. Only by doing so, by refusing to accept an Either/Or, do we force in between 'what the words have meant' and 'what the words are going to mean', the condition in which we appreciate what they do mean, now, as verbal events actually occurring and occupying the present time. We do this when we recognize the ambiguity, or the possibility of it, and hesitate between the two possible meanings or else embrace them both. Thus syntactical manipulations of this sort, at the same time as they make of the present only a moving limit between past and future, also make the present time something to be dwelt upon and dwelt in, something lived. Mrs Susanne Langer has analysed the effect of music in precisely these terms, as something which so shapes time as to make us live its elapsing, its duration, with unusual attention to each present moment.[7]

7   Susanne K. Langer, *Philosophy in a New Key: A Study in the Symbolism of Reason, Rite and Art* (Cambridge, Mass.: Harvard University Press, 1942).

Poetics (The Hague: Mouton, 1961); reprinted in *The Poet in the Imaginary Museum.*

V Two Analogies for Poetry[1]

Poetry is a special kind of verbal discourse; it is also a special kind of art. So we may approach not a definition of poetry, but at least a description of it, in at least two ways. On the one hand we may approach poetic discourse by comparing it with, and distinguishing it from, other kinds of discourse in words – the discourse of the philosopher, of the orator, of the scientist writing in his laboratory book, of the priest in prayer, of the mother murmuring to her child, and so on. On the other hand we can approach the poetic art by comparing it with, and distinguishing it from, other kinds of art or, as we say more naturally, other arts – the art of the painter, of the architect, the sculptor, the choreographer, the musician.

But in this country in the present century it is striking how much more common it has been to approach poetry in the first way, as a special kind of discourse, than in the second way, as a special kind of art. There is the ancient and honourable philosophical discipline of aesthetics which is committed to finding common ground among all the arts, and assumes that poetry is one of these; but aestheticists are not very thick upon the ground, and their speculations and conclusions are by no means common currency among students of poetry. Such 'students' – and by 'students' I mean here simply keen and curious readers – are prompt and at ease with discussions about how a poetic use of language differs from a scientific use of it; they are at a loss – so my experience tells me – with discussions about how a poet's use of his medium, language, differs from a sculptor's use of stone or a painter's use of pigment. Indeed they are not just at a loss; they are at once suspicious and resentful. In the circles I am thinking of – and they are the circles where I find the keenest and most thoughtful readers of poetry – the very word 'art' is a danger-signal. Hackles rise at the very expression 'the art of poetry'. For unsophisticated speakers of current English, 'art' is the name of only one among the arts, that of painting; for sophisticated speakers it is, commonly, a word irremediably tarnished by its association with Walter Pater and Oscar Wilde, a word so tarnished by this (for them) criminal past that they resent it as a confidence-trickster.

I have never understood why this should be so. Even if Walter Pater were such a narrowly eccentric thinker and such a corrupting influence as

---

1   Transcript of a radio talk for the BBC Third Programme, 1962.

these people seem to believe (and surely Pater is neither of these things), this would still not account for the passions which his name arouses. But I am not concerned to vindicate Pater; and in any case I am fairly sure that the prejudice against 'art' in relation to 'poetry' is far too deeply rooted, as well as too passionate, to derive only from prejudice against Pater's aestheticism. But however it may arise, this attitude is exasperating to me personally, and this is what I should like to explain.

For some years now I have found it easiest to set my ideas in order, about the poems I write myself and the poems of others, by thinking of the poet by analogy with other kinds of artist – specifically, by analogy with the musical composer on the one hand, the sculptor on the other. I shall try to explain what this means in practice, but first I want to insist that practice is indeed the only court I appeal to. I find it useful, convenient, personally profitable, to think along these lines, using these ideas. I have no wish to make these ideas prevail, if that means denying that other ways of thinking may be more convenient for others. I do not maintain that thinking along these lines makes one see poetry more truly for what it is, than thinking in other ways about it. I would maintain only that this way of thinking brings one to *part* of the truth about poetry, and to a part which is now generally and misleadingly overlooked. For what is frustrating in my experience is that in the present climate of literary opinion thinking along these lines cannot get a hearing; literary people refuse to think in these terms at all, refuse to those of us who think in this way even the right to participate in the give-and-take of literary discussion.

To make poetry-like-music seems to have been an avowed aim of the French symbolist poets. The last of these, Paul Valéry, insisted that this was the central and distinguishing trait of the whole school; and to wrestle instead with the word 'symbol' could never bring us to the heart of what these French poets were up to. For a succinct and lively image of poetry-like-music we can go to Pasternak, at a point in *Doctor Zhivago* where he is talking about how poetic inspiration came to the poet Zhivago:

> At such moments the correlation of the forces controlling the artist is, as it were, stood on its head. The ascendancy is no longer with the artist or the state of mind which he is trying to express, but with language, his instrument of expression. Language, the home and dwelling of beauty and meaning, itself begins to think and speak for man and turns wholly into music, not in the sense of outward, audible sounds, but by virtue of the power and momentum of its inward flow. Then, like the current of a mighty river polishing stones and turning wheels by its very movement, the flow of speech creates in passing, by the force of its own laws, rhyme and rhythm and countless other forms and formations, still more important and until now undiscovered, unconsidered and unnamed.

A passage such as that is so remote from the vocabulary, or the one or two vocabularies, recognized by English criticism today that I fear, if its author were anyone less illustrious than Pasternak, it would be regarded as a mere flight of dangerous rhetoric. Our poets may know – it is to be hoped they *do* know – the state of affairs in which the creative initiative is no longer with the artist but with his medium, language; but our critics, so far as I can see, have no way of allowing for this state of affairs, of distinguishing it from variously vicious kinds of verbal intoxication and more or less 'automatic writing', or of squaring it with their demands (which are just, so far as they go) that the writer be in control of his experience and of his language. Yet the poetic work in English which by common consent is perhaps the most splendid achievement of the last twenty-five years, Mr Eliot's *Four Quartets*, advertises by its very title that it belongs with poetry-like-music. If our prejudices will not permit us even to entertain speculations about analogies between the arts, how can we appreciate the structure and the meaning of the *Four Quartets*? Indeed, I believe we have not even begun to do this.

Obviously it is meaningful to speak of both poems and pieces of music as having 'structures'. Yet to most of us it will seem, after a moment's thought, that this term can be applied to poetry and music only by drawing an analogy with another art, architecture. It is only in respect of architecture that the term 'structure' has a literal meaning; it is only there that the word is really at home. The interesting thing is that 'structure' is common currency in our literary criticism. Equally is it common form for our critics to speak of planes and levels of meaning, and also of stresses and tensions which are created, balanced, and resolved. The real home for all of these expressions is architecture.

Thus it appears that our literary criticism does proceed, after all, by drawing analogies with other arts – at least with one such art. But it does so in the most perilous way, not realizing what it is doing. When Pasternak speaks, in relation to poetic language, of 'the power and momentum of its inward flow', we cannot come to terms with what he is saying because the model which our critical vocabulary creates for us is of a poem as analogous to a building or an arch, architectural compositions which make no provision for the idea of 'flow'. A poem is necessarily a shape made out of lapsing time, out of the time the poem takes to be read; yet we seem to conceive of a poem by analogy with architectural forms, forms which occupy not time but space.

We are not necessarily wrong to do this. Though all poems are shapes cut out of lapsing time, not all poems exploit this feature of their existence. There are poems, and fine ones, which on the contrary contrive to make us forget the reading time which they occupy. I am thinking of those poems which come full circle, which return upon themselves, of which we feel, when we finish reading them, 'How well the end was foreseen in the beginning'. For these poems, it seems to me, our current vocabulary, devised on an analogy with architecture, is the most useful and illuminating vocabulary possible. On the other hand it is plain that other sorts of poems, those which exploit and emphasize the time they take between first line and last, poems which do not come sweetly home upon themselves but on the contrary are open-ended, can be discussed in our current critical vocabulary only at the price of being certainly distorted and probably undervalued.

It thus appears, first, that we cannot help drawing analogies with the other arts when we discuss poetry: we cannot help it because such analogies are in and behind the very terminology we use, since criticism of any one art necessarily takes in the washing from criticism of the others; and, secondly, precisely because this is so, there can be no question of one among the other arts being the one right analogy for poetry: we have to be prepared to draw our analogies from architecture or painting or music or sculpture, according as the poem we are to deal with lends itself to, or implicitly asks for, one of these analogies rather than the others.

There are some poems which ask for the analogy to be drawn from sculpture. If I were learned enough I dare say I could find that the idea of the poem-as-sculpture has as long a history as the idea of the poem-as-music, or the poem-as-architecture, or (the most ancient of them all) the poem-as-painting. But there is no need to go back further than to the imagist and vorticist movements of less than fifty years ago. Imagism, at least as Ezra Pound conceived of it, opposed to the symbolist ideal of the poem-as-music an ideal of the poem-as-sculpture; and his fullest statement of this position came a few years later when he was fighting under the banner of 'vorticism'. It comes, appropriately enough, in the memoir which Pound wrote for the sculptor Henri Gaudier-Brzeska – a most important document happily made available again, last year, by the Marvell Press.[2]

The first thing to be said about sculpture in this connection is that it comprises two radically different operations: those of carving on the one hand, and of moulding, or modelling, on the other. Pound appears interested chiefly, if not exclusively, in the sculptor as carver, chisel in hand, assaulting the block. According to Michelangelo, at once great sculptor and great poet, the carver feels or persuades himself at such a moment that the form he wants is already present in the marble, and that his own function is to make what is already there reveal itself. This is as far as possible from what the moulder feels, for whom, as he begins, the whole world is infinitely malleable, literally 'like clay in his hands'. The carver's activity enforces humility as surely as the moulder's invites presumption. It is for this reason that the carver's way with his medium attracts and challenges

2   Ezra Pound, *Gaudier-Brzeska: A Memoir* (Hessle: Marvell Press, 1960).

the poet more than the moulder's way. For the moulder's way of making something out of nothing is what the poet can see already from the case of the musician. And poets like the symbolists, who want to make poetry-like-music, are characteristically excited by the degree to which their art can cut loose from the world of nature, creating an alternative world answering only to its own laws. Poetry can never be as 'pure' in this sense, as independent of nature and answerable to its own laws, as music is; it can never equal music in this respect since its medium, language, necessarily refers to the world the poet wishes to be free from. Yet the symbolists went further towards music in this respect than one would have believed possible.

To a poet who is enamoured of the world offered to his senses in all its copious variety, who believes that his mission is not to transform, still less to annihilate, but rather to serve that world – for such poets, of whom Gerard Manley Hopkins might be one example and Ezra Pound another, the analogy with music or with sculpture-as-moulding offers a freedom they do not want, and tempts to an arrogance which they distrust. The analogy with carved sculpture is what their poems demand of the reader who wants to do them justice.

But this poetry-as-carving is divided from our students of poetry by an even wider gulf than poetry-as-music. For what this poetry has to do with is a reality which is as fully and undeniably *out there*, as certainly other than us and confronting us, as is the block of marble where it lies in the quarry before the sculptor. This reality may be physical – in which case this poetry is making a claim which our critics have for the most part abandoned, the claim to be exploring the same reality as the sciences explore, but with different categories and different instruments. Or the reality which poetry-as-carving explores may be metaphysical: in which case it is making a claim which, once again, our mostly agnostic or infidel criticism has agreed to abandon, the claim to be exploring the same reality as religion or ontology. To be sure, many symbolist poets claimed to be exploring a metaphysical reality through their poems, just as many musicians have claimed the same for their music. But in these cases sceptical or materialistic critics find it easy enough to transform the metaphysical reality allegedly *out there* into a psychological reality *in here*, inside the artist's head. The art in these cases constructs a reality independent of the natural world; and the critic need not violate or distort the art-work by taking its world as altogether inside the head of the poet in the first place, and subsequently in the head of the reader. But poetry-as-carving, which claims to have to do with no world but the world of nature, cannot be transformed in this way; the reality it deals with cannot be seen as a reality only in the poet's head.

The great advantage of taking poetry as a special kind of verbal discourse, rather than a special kind of art, is that it evades these ancient and troubling questions about the metaphysical or religious grounds of the poetic activity. To take poetry as a special kind of discourse is to make it a special kind of communication between persons; and thus, it seems, one reality which all poems explore is the social and psychological reality of how we get on together and communicate with each other. This is the reality which the most infidel reader, and the most fervently religious, can be sure that they share.

However, since all poetry is a making no less than a saying, and since some poems offer themselves, not as a way of getting or keeping in touch or practising group-therapy, but as a truthful report on a reality not social at all nor even human, it may be that we sell the pass on poetry from the start by refusing to consider any metaphysical or ontological grounds for the poetic activity. To approach poetry as a special kind of art is to make it difficult, indeed I think impossible, to evade any longer these troublesome but necessary questions.

Postscript: The points made in this piece, written when I had newly arrived at these perceptions, seem to me now, many years later, very important.

The Listener, 5 April 1962; reprinted with postscript in *The Poet in the Imaginary Museum*.

VI *Ezra Pound's* Hugh Selwyn Mauberley

The name of Ezra Pound (born 1885) undoubtedly belongs in the first place to the history of American rather than English poetry. Nevertheless his personality and his activities during at least one phase of his long career, together with the poems he then wrote, cannot be ignored in any survey, however selective, of twentieth-century English poetry. From 1908 until 1920, he made London his headquarters, playing a militant and decisive part in the crucial literary and artistic battles then being fought out on the English scene; in particular over several of these years he acted as at once mentor and sponsor of the youthful T.S. Eliot. Moreover, two of his major works of that period, *Homage to Sextus Propertius* (1917) and *Hugh Selwyn Mauberley* (1920), are explicitly attempts to portray and diagnose the state of British (not at all of American) culture at the historical moment which, for instance, D.H. Lawrence in *Women in Love* similarly took to be for England a tragically momentous turning-point. But the conclusive reason why Pound cannot be ignored is that *Hugh Selwyn Mauberley* at any rate has been accepted into the English poetic tradition, in the sense that every subsequent British poet at all serious about his vocation has found it necessary to come to terms with this work, accepting or else quarrelling with its conclusions about British culture no less than with its revolutionary strategies and methods.

Because Eliot has thrown in his lot with Britain as Pound has not, the British reader will probably come to *Hugh Selwyn Mauberley* only after reading Eliot's poetry up to and including *The Waste Land*. Yet as Eliot has been the first to insist, in respect of many of the poetic methods common to both poets it was Pound who was the pioneer. Moreover, where the poets make use of a device common to both, there is every danger of not realizing that Pound's intention is different from Eliot's in profoundly important ways.

A conspicuous example of this is the strategy which is common to *Hugh Selwyn Mauberley* and to *The Waste Land* – the extensive use of interlarded and unacknowledged quotations from poets and poems of the past, and of more or less devious references and allusions to these sources. When the reader recognizes that in Pound's poem such references are sown more thickly than in *The Waste Land*, and that the allusions are sometimes more devious, it is easy to decide irritably that Pound's use of the device is less serious than Eliot's, and open to objections which Eliot escapes:

> Turned from the 'eau-forte
> Par Jacquemart'
> To the strait head
> Of Messalina:
>
> 'His true Penelope
> Was Flaubert',
> And his tool
> The engraver's.
>
> Firmness,
> Not the full smile,
> His art, but an art
> In profile;
>
> Colourless
> Pier Francesca,
> Pisanello lacking the skill
> To forge Achaia.

A good French dictionary will reveal that 'eau-forte' means an etching; and the context then makes it clear that the fictitious minor poet, Mauberley (whose career we are following as in a biography), is at this point turning in his art from the relatively full and detailed richness of the etcher's rendering of reality to the severely selective art 'In profile' of the engraver of medallions. A very little knowledge of Flaubert will reveal that the French novelist differs from his English contemporaries, at least in intention, in rather the same way, as throwing his emphasis upon selection of the one telling detail rather than on accumulation of many details and instances. And in the art of the Italian Renaissance, the medallist Pisanello can be opposed in just the same way to the painter Piero della Francesca, master of composition and colour. This is entirely and sufficiently intelligible. But the reader may well protest that the point could have been made more directly, without all this 'name-dropping'. It is easy to protest that this is pretentious, a parade of recondite expertise for its own sake — a charge which at one time was often brought against Eliot. In fact, in the course of answering this objection, we not only distinguish Pound's attitude and achievement from Eliot's, we uncover what is uniquely valuable in Pound's work as a whole, and in this poem in particular.

In the first place Pound would say that to talk of 'recondite expertise' begs the whole question: if knowledge of the art of the medallion, of paintings by Piero della Francesca, and of novels by Flaubert, is out-of-the-way knowledge for us, it shouldn't be. For Pound these names represent experiences which should be familiar to any educated man, and he is arguing, in particular, that neither we nor the Americans can see our own cultural traditions in proper perspective except in the context of achievements in other languages or by other cultures. He would be happy if our reading of these lines sent us to the Victoria and Albert Museum, the British Museum and the National Gallery to look at the late Roman or Italian Renaissance coins, and at Italian paintings. Pound in fact, while he shares with Eliot a wish to attain by these vivid juxtapositions an unexampled conciseness of especially ironic expression, has a further intention which Eliot does not share. He has never ceased to be the pedagogue. Just as in his London years he sought to instruct (apparently to good effect) all of his contemporaries whom he respected – Eliot, the novelists Percy Wyndham Lewis and James Joyce, even the much older and already illustrious W.B. Yeats – so in all his writings he is trying to instruct his readers, telling them what buildings and paintings they should look at and what books they ought to read. For instance, concealed behind the cryptic reference to the etching by Jacquemart is the name of the French poet Théophile Gautier, who is pointed to much more explicitly elsewhere in the poem. Pound alludes to Gautier as Eliot does, because Gautier suits his purposes, but also because he is sure he fits ours too, if we only knew it.

In fact Pound is much more interested than Eliot in the spectacle of human events and affairs for their own sake, not merely as somehow reflecting his own predicament. It is this interest which he shares with Robert Browning, whom he has consistently honoured as his own first master; and it is what distinguishes him not only from Eliot but from his other great contemporary and associate, W.B. Yeats. Whereas Eliot's diagnosis of the state of western Christian culture is not of the sort that can be abstracted from *The Waste Land* and argued over, Pound's diagnosis in *Hugh Selwyn Mauberley* asks to be treated, and *can* be treated, in just this way. Pound's view of history is put forward in all seriousness: so in *Hugh Selwyn Mauberley*, if Pound has misgauged the temper of the period he is dealing with, the poem must suffer thereby, as Yeats's poem 'The Second Coming' doesn't suffer for all its very odd view of history. In fact, Pound's reading of English cultural history from about 1860 to 1920 is a wonderfully accurate register of the temper of those times, and squares with the facts as we know them from other sources.

   And yet, so far are we from conceiving of a poetry that asks to be measured against commonly observable reality, that even those readers who recognize and applaud Pound's historical insight will not rest content with this, but probe further to find in *Hugh Selwyn Mauberley* a diagnosis by the poet of his own state of mind and his own predicament.

Though Pound has said, 'Of course I'm no more Mauberley than Eliot is Prufrock',[1] the poem is commonly read as if H.S. Mauberley, the fictitious poet whose representative biography the poem presents, is no more than a transparent disguise for Pound himself. Yet Mauberley, as the poem presents him, an apprehensive and diffident aesthete, all too tremulously aware of the various artistic achievements of the past (herein, incidentally, another reason – a dramatic one – for the 'name-dropping' in the poem) and of niceties of nuance in social encounters, ever less capable (as the poem proceeds) of coming to terms with the vulgarity of his age, and therefore defensively withdrawing into an always more restricted world of exquisite private perceptions – what has this figure in common with Pound, the poet, who alone among his associates and contemporaries had Browning's (or Chaucer's) zestful appetite for the multifarious variety of human personality and human activity?

The misreading arises from the first five stanzas of the poem. For this poem about Mauberley begins with a section not about Mauberley, but about E.P., that is, Pound himself ('E.P. Ode pour l'élection de son sépulchre'):

> For three years, out of key with his time,
> He strove to resuscitate the dead art
> Of poetry; to maintain 'the sublime'
> In the old sense. Wrong from the start –
>
> No, hardly, but seeing he had been born
> In a half-savage country, out of date;
> Bent resolutely on wringing lilies from the acorn;
> Capaneus; trout for factitious bait;
>
> Ἴδμεν γάρ τοι πανθ οσ ενì Τροìη
> Caught in the unstopped ear;
> Giving the rocks small lee-way
> The chopped seas held him, therefore, that year.
>
> His true Penelope was Flaubert,
> He fished by obstinate isles;
> Observed the elegance of Circe's hair
> Rather than the mottoes on sun-dials.
>
> Unaffected by 'the march of events',
> He passed from men's memory in *l'an trentuniesme*
> *De son eage*; the case presents
> No adjunct to the Muses' diadem.

---

1   *The Letters of Ezra Pound, 1907–1941*, ed. D.D. Paige (London: Faber, 1951), p. 248.

This has been taken as Pound's judgement upon himself, but in fact it presents Pound as he knows he must appear to some others. It was the French poet of the Middle Ages, François Villon, a most distinguished 'adjunct to the Muses' diadem', who in the first line of his *Grand Testament* described himself as passing from sight in his thirtieth year, 'l'an de mon trentiesme eage'; Pound, in his ironic and entirely characteristic use of this inserted quotation, is deriding, in effect, the confidence with which the speaker so conclusively consigns him also to oblivion. Similarly, the earlier reference to Pound's native America as 'a half-savage country' is an example of the Englishman's misplaced condescension. All the same, this fictitious Englishman is no fool. By introducing the line from Homer's *Odyssey*, 'For we know all the things that are in Troy', the speaker of this poem wittily makes Odysseus's own story of Troy into the siren-song which Pound heard and was seduced by. And in fact Pound had already started his version of the story of Odysseus, the long epic poem which has occupied him ever since. In the speaker's view, Circe, representing Pound's epic aspirations, had beguiled him from pursuing his voyage home to his faithful wife, Penelope, to his true objective, which was Flaubertian. The irony of this famous line 'His true Penelope was Flaubert' (which is echoed, as we have seen, in a later section) has been well disentangled by a transatlantic critic. For Pound, he says,

> Flaubert represents the ideal of disciplined self-immolation from which English poetry has been too long estranged, only to be rejoined by apparently circuitous voyaging. For the writer of the epitaph, on the other hand, Flaubert is conceded to be E.P.'s 'true' (=equivalent) Penelope only in deprecation: Flaubert being for the English literary mind of the first quarter of the present century a foreign, feminine, rather comically earnest indulger in quite un-British preciosity;... a suitable Penelope for this energetic American.[2]

Thus the speaker of the poem says what is true while meaning to say (in identical words) what is false.

Pound has lately said, of commentators on *Hugh Selwyn Mauberley*, 'The worst muddle they make is in failing to see that Mauberley buries E.P. in the first poem; gets rid of all his troublesome energies.'[3] But though we have been obtuse if we suppose that the speaker of this epitaph is Pound himself, there is no way of knowing that the speaker in fact is Mauberley. Moreover Pound's comment implies, what it is not easy to discover within the poetry itself, that subsequent sections of the poem are also to be understood as spoken not by Pound himself but by the imaginary Mauberley. This is indicated by further examples of the same stilted

2   Hugh Kenner, *The Poetry of Ezra Pound* (London: Faber, 1951), pp. 170–1.
3. See Thomas E. Connolly, in *Accent* (Winter 1956).

and precious diction as 'the case presents/No adjunct to the Muses' diadem'. (The model for this sort of language, incidentally, is another Frenchman, Jules Laforgue.) Section III, for instance, is written in this style and expresses the views of Walter Pater in one place and of Swinburne in others, more wholeheartedly than Pound himself might choose to do. But this mannered language can be taken, and has been taken, as indicating a degree of ironical detachment in the poet, without supposing that the detachment goes so far as to require another speaker altogether. Again, section V, the beautiful and bitter comment on the First World War, reduces the value of European civilization to 'two gross of broken statues', in a way that doubtless Pound would not endorse, though he might sympathize with the anger at waste and loss which thus expresses itself. But from a lyric one doesn't anyway expect considered judgements; so that the dramatic fiction, Mauberley, isn't necessary here, either. The section where it is essential to realize that Mauberley and not Pound is speaking is section II, where Mauberley acknowledges that if Pound's epic pretensions were not what 'The age demanded', still less does it demand his own 'Attic grace', his 'inward gaze', his 'classics in paraphrase'. Having talked of how Pound is out of step with his age, he now talks of how he himself is out of step with it, though in a quite different way. If readers have found themselves incapable of this rapid change of stance (preferring instead an impossible compound poet, of epic and sublime pretensions in section I yet vowed in section II to Attic grace and Gautier's '"sculpture" of rhyme'), the poet is partly to blame; he is trying to make ironical detachment and slight shifts of tone do more than they can do, by way of directing and redirecting the reader's attention.

The admirable sixth and seventh sections, entitled respectively 'Yeux Glauques' and (a line from Dante) 'Siena mi fe'; disfecemi Maremma', are those which provide a tart and yet indulgent capsulated history of late-Victorian literary culture. 'Yeux Glauques' establishes the milieu of, for instance, D.G. Rossetti, in the 1870s:

> The Burne-Jones cartons
> Have preserved her eyes;
> Still, at the Tate, they teach
> Cophetua to rhapsodize;
>
> Thin like brook-water,
> With a vacant gaze.
> The English Rubaiyat was still-born
> In those days.

The masterly compression here is all a matter of punctuation and grammar played against the structure of the quatrain. Grammar makes

'Thin like brook-water,/With a vacant gaze' refer to the distinctively
Pre-Raphaelite ideal of feminine beauty, as embodied in several women
(the most famous is Rossetti's Elizabeth Siddal) who were at once these
painters' models and their mistresses, but embodied also in the paintings
of the school, of which one of the most famous is 'King Cophetua and the
Beggar Maid'. But metre and rhyme make 'Thin like brook-water' refer
also, in defiance of grammar, to Edward Fitzgerald's translation of Omar
Khayyám's *Rubaiyat*, which went unnoticed for years until discovered by
Rossetti, remaindered on a bookstall. Such ('Thin like brook-water') is
Mauberley's view of the Pre-Raphaelite ideals, of the painting and poetry
in which those ideals were embodied, and of the public taste which indis-
criminately overlooked or applauded them. In the next poem, the focus
has shifted to the later literary generation of 'the nineties', and it covers
the same ground as the chapter 'The Tragic Generation' from *The
Trembling of the Veil*, among Yeats's *Autobiographies*; Pound's immediate
source is a more obscure book, *Ernest Dowson* by Victor Gustave Plarr,
who is concealed in the poem under the fictitious name, 'Monsieur
Verog'. To read these two poems as spoken by Mauberley rather than
Pound turns the edge of the otherwise weighty objections[4] that Pound's
irony here is of the unfocused kind which enables him to have it both
ways, so that the tartness and the indulgence, the mockery and the affection, lie side by side without modifying each other. If Mauberley is the
speaker, however, this unresolved attitude is dramatically appropriate and
effective, and helps to account for his own subsequent failure.

After this sketch of a historical development comes a survey of the
state of affairs it produced, concentrated into five acrid portraits – of
'Brennbaum' (perhaps Max Beerbohm); of 'Mr Nixon', the successful
best-seller (perhaps Arnold Bennett); of 'the stylist'; of modern woman;
and of the patron, 'The Lady Valentine'. Again Mauberley is speaking, for
in section XII the speaker, waiting upon the Lady Valentine, describes
himself in terms more appropriate to Eliot's Prufrock than to the ebullient
and assertive Pound. The first stanza of this poem is another splendid
example of Pound's witty compactness:

> 'Daphne with her thighs in bark
> Stretches toward me her leafy hands,' –
> Subjectively. In the stuffed-satin drawing-room
> I await The Lady Valentine's commands.

The quotation marks are Pound's acknowledgement that the first two
lines are an adaptation from *Le Château du souvenir* by Gautier. But the
borrowing is made utterly Poundian by the deflating word 'Subjectively',
which meets the reader as he swings around the line-ending, thus

4   See Yvor Winters, *In Defense of Reason* (Chicago: Alan Swallow, 1947), p. 68.

achieving the maximum surprise and shock. In the Greek legend the river-nymph Daphne was saved from ravishment by the amorous god Apollo, when her father, the river-deity, transformed her on the instant into a laurel-tree. The sexual connotation is present here, as in other episodes of Mauberley's career. But more important is the allegorical meaning by which Apollo the god of poetry figures, sensationally diminished, as the poet waiting humbly upon his patroness. What the poet wants from her is the traditional acknowledgement of poetic prowess, the laurel-wreath; but when she seems to hold this out to him ('her leafy hands') he reminds himself that she does so only 'subjectively', only in his private fantasy, for in objective fact she represents no such respectable body or principle of taste as could permit the poet to value her approval. It would require nothing less than a divine miracle to metamorphose her in this way, from a false patroness to a true one!

We have to say that this whole sequence of twelve short poems reads better, that several difficulties are ironed out, if they are taken as spoken by the fictional Mauberley. Yet many of them can be read as if spoken directly by Pound. The limitation involved here is inherent in any use of a created character standing between the poet and the reader. This device, by which the poet speaks in an assumed character, was first exploited consistently by Browning in his dramatic monologues. What Pound called the 'persona' and what Yeats called the 'mask' are refinements upon Browning's model. Eliot's Prufrock and Gerontion, and his Tiresias who speaks *The Waste Land*, correspond to Pound's Mauberley, and so (though with certain important differences) do Yeats's Michael Robartes, his Ribh and his Crazy Jane. To all three poets the device recommended itself because it helped them to what, at different times and perhaps for different reasons, they all desired, the effect of impersonality. But the device appears to work only if the persona is sufficiently differentiated from the poet himself – otherwise the irony lapses, and the reader overlooks the presence of the persona. If this happens with Pound's Mauberley, it seems to me to happen too, and more calamitously, with Eliot's Gerontion.

How closely at this period Pound and Eliot were working in concert can be seen from a comment made by Pound many years later:[5]

> at a particular time in a particular room, two authors, neither engaged in picking the other's pocket, decided that the dilutation of *vers libre*... had gone too far and that some counter-current must be set going. Parallel situation years ago in China. Remedy prescribed '*Emaux et Camées*' (or the Bay State Hymn Book). Rhyme and regular strophes.
>
> Results: Poems in Mr Eliot's *second* volume, not contained in his first... also H.S. Mauberley.

5   Ezra Pound, 'Harold Monro', *The Criterion*, 11.45 (July 1932), p. 590.

Pound the pedagogue is characteristically evident. But the central point is clear: Pound and Eliot, the two poets who had done most to familiarize free verse in English, had seen the necessity, at least as early as 1918, to revert to writing in rhyming stanzas, and if necessary to find their models in something so unfashionable as a provincial hymn-book. The model they adopted (Gautier, author of *Emaux et Camées*) was not much less unfashionable.

To be sure, there could be no question of simply putting the clock back. The large-scale rhythms of free verse, with its roving stresses, inform Pound's quatrains, which cannot be scanned by traditional principles, and similarly the rhymes are only approximate rhymes much of the time; still, the pattern of the rhyming stanza imposes itself, and the result is, to the ear, a peculiarly pleasant one – powerful surges of expansive rhythm never quite given their head, but reined back and cut short. On the other hand, there are quite different patterns, as in one of the sections on the Great War:

> These fought in any case
> and some believing,
> > pro domo, in any case...
>
> Some quick to arm,
> some for adventure,
> some from fear of weakness,
> some from fear of censure,
> some for love of slaughter, in imagination,
> learning later...
> some in fear, learning love of slaughter...

This may look like free verse; in fact it is a learned imitation of the measures of the late-Greek pastoral poet, Bion.

On the list of contents in the first English and American printings of *Hugh Selwyn Mauberley*, the first and much the longer part of the poem, specifically sub-titled 'Part I', consists of the pieces we have so far considered. Standing on its own, between Part I and Part II, is the poem headed 'Envoi (1919)'. This is one place where there is no doubt who is speaking. It is Pound himself, suddenly stepping from behind the wavering figure of Mauberley and all the veils of irony, to speak out personally, even confessionally, into a situation which he had seemed to contrive just so as not to speak in his own person at all. This wonderfully dramatic moment is signalized by the sudden appearance of a wholly unexpected metre and style, flowing, plangent and *cantabile*, so wholly traditional in every respect that the voice of the poet seems to be the anonymous voice of the tradition of English song:

Go, dumb-born book,
Tell her that sang me once that song of Lawes:
Hadst thou but song
As thou hast subjects known,
Then were there cause in thee that should condone
Even my faults that heavy upon me lie,
And build her glories their longevity.

The tradition that here utters itself is the tradition that is invoked in the name of Henry Lawes, who composed the music for Milton's *Comus*; it is the tradition not of English poetry, but of English song, English poetry for singing.

Tell her that sheds
Such treasure in the air,
Recking naught else but that her graces give
Life to the moment,
I would bid them live
As roses might, in magic amber laid,
Red overwrought with orange and all made
One substance and one colour
Braving time.

We are now enough acclimatized to this unexpected, poignantly archaic convention, to perceive that in its different way it is still dealing with matters that the earlier sections, out of their chilly smiling poise, have already canvassed. The last section of Part I, for instance, spoke of 'Fleet St where/Dr Johnson flourished', and remarked:

Beside this thoroughfare
The sale of half-hose has
Long since superseded the cultivation
Of Pierian roses.

These Pierian roses have become the roses which, if sealed in amber, would be 'Red overwrought with orange' and saved from the ravages of time. Thus, the 'she' whom the book must address is surely the England that Pound is preparing to leave. In an American edition of *Hugh Selwyn Mauberley*, the title-page carried a note, reading, 'The sequence is so distinctly a farewell to London that the reader who chooses to regard this as an exclusively American edition may as well omit it...' It seems plain that this second stanza of the 'Envoi' conveys with beautiful tenderness Pound's ambiguous attitude to an England which he sees as full of poetic beauties yet regardless of them:

Tell her that goes
With song upon her lips
But sings not out the song, nor knows

The maker of it, some other mouth,
May be as fair as hers,
Might, in new ages, gain her worshippers,
When our two dusts with Waller's shall be laid,
Siftings on siftings in oblivion,
Till change hath broken down
All things save Beauty alone.

It is impossible to read this, if one is an Englishman, without real distress. Only Lawrence, in letters written about this time, registers the death of England as a live cultural tradition with such sorrow and with the added poignancy that comes of being English. (Nearly thirty years later, in Canto LXXX written in the Pisan prison-camp, Pound reverts to the theme, using the same imagery, in three beautiful quatrains beginning, 'Tudor indeed is gone and every rose...') The name of Waller locks in with that of Lawes, as one who wrote words for the other's music. The 'two dusts' that will lie with Waller's are those of the poet and of his book. And the 'other mouth' than England's, which may in new ages gain England new worshippers, may well be the mouth of the English-speaking nations in North America. The ambitious and poignant perspectives which have been opened before us underline the irony by which the poet who was so conclusively dismissed at the end of the 'Ode pour l'élection de son sépulchre' is the same who, twelve poems later, here recaptures the tradition of English song at its most sonorous and plangent.

Only now, with Part II, does Mauberley, the titular hero of the whole work, emerge for our scrutiny, his emergence signalized by a new cross-heading 'Mauberley (1920)'. As with Eliot's Prufrock, so with Mauberley, the inability to come to grips with the world for the sake of art is symbolized in the inability to meet the sexual challenge, to 'force the moment to its crisis'. Mauberley, like (apparently) Prufrock, allows the moment of choice to drift by without recognizing it, and is left with 'mandate/Of Eros, a retrospect.' The last stanza of this section – about 'The still stone dogs' – is a reference to a story from Ovid's *Metamorphoses*, but for once this doesn't matter, since the biting mouths immobilized in stone are an obviously apt metaphor for impotence which is partly but not exclusively sexual.

Sections III and IV of Part II trace Mauberley's degeneration, his gradual withdrawal into an ever more private world, until he becomes

Incapable of the least utterance or composition,
Emendation, conservation of the 'better tradition',
Refinement of medium, elimination of superfluities,
August attraction or concentration.

Nothing, in brief, but maudlin confession,
Irresponse to human aggression,

Amid the precipitation, down-float
Of insubstantial manna,
Lifting the faint susurrus
Of his subjective hosannah.

As Mauberley in the very first section of the poem damned Pound
with compassionate condescension as Flaubertian, and used Homeric
parallels to do it with, so here Pound takes his revenge. The Simoon and
'the juridical Flamingoes' (that epithet a Flaubertian *mot juste*) are taken
from Flaubert's exotic novel *Salammbô*, and used (with lordly disregard
for geography, which would protest that they are inappropriate to the
Moluccas) to stand as metaphors from the physical world for the spiritual
state of abstracted passivity which is now Mauberley's condition. As for
Homer:

Coracle of Pacific voyages,
The unforecasted beach;
Then on an oar
Read this:

'I was
And I no more exist;
Here drifted
An hedonist.'

In the *Odyssey* one of Odysseus's ship-mates, Elpenor, killed by accident,
is buried on the seashore, and his oar is set in the sand to mark his grave,
with a noble inscription which Pound, in Canto I, renders as 'a man of no
fortune, and with a name to come'. The contrast with Mauberley's
epitaph is clear and damning.

The troublesome question of who is to be imagined as the speaker
does not arise with these first four poems of section II. It crops up again,
however, in respect of the last section of the whole poem. Since we have
learned that Mauberley, at a relatively early stage of his disastrous career,
attempted in poetry something analogous to the severe and limited art of
the medallist, the title 'Medallion' given to these last quatrains must mean
that here again Mauberley is speaking, that this is one of his poems,
closing the sequence just as another of his poems opened it. The poem is
symptomatic of Mauberley's degeneration in its externality, its fixity and
rhythmical inertness. It shows too how Pound was aware of just these
dangers in a too unqualified acceptance of the Flaubertian doctrine of '*le
mot juste*', as also in the programmes of the Imagists. The poem is not
without distinction; it shows exactness of observation, clarity of order,
and compact economy in the phrasing. For Mauberley is no fool, as we
realized from the first; he is a man of principle, as well as a man of true
poetic ability. The judgement is all the more damning: his principles and

his abilities go for nothing because they are not informed by any vitality. All his scrupulous search for *le mot juste* to describe the braids of hair only transforms the hair with all its organic expressiveness into the inertness of metal. Venus Anadyomene, the mythological expression of how sexual and other vitality is renewed, hardens under Mauberley's hand into the glazed frontispiece to a book on Comparative Religion. (We note that it is the head which, for Mauberley, is rising Venus-like from the sea, not the breasts or the loins.) And not just the 'amber' but also the 'clear soprano' invite a damning comparison with the 'Envoi', a poem just as formal, but with a formality expressive of vital response. Mauberley's deficiencies as a writer are identical with his deficiencies as a human being. For there appears no reason to doubt that the woman here described is the same figure whose challenge earlier Mauberley could only evade. Everything that is hard, metallic and ominous in Mauberley's description of her as an image in a poem symbolizes his fear of her as a person, and his inability to meet her with any sort of human response.

But the most chastening reflection for a British reader is what Pound implies very plainly, that in a culture so riddled with commercialism and false values as English culture is (or was, in 1920), no English artist is likely to do any better than Mauberley did.

Postscript: This essay was commissioned by Boris Ford for *The Modern Age*, the last volume of the *Pelican Guide to English Literature* – a commission which I actively sought, for fear that otherwise Pound's achievement would go unremarked. Accordingly it envisages a reader less well informed than the reader addressed in most of my other pieces. I have changed my mind about *Hugh Selwyn Mauberley* over the years, and my revised opinions may be found in *Ezra Pound: Poet as Sculptor* (1964) and in the Fontana Modern Masters *Pound* (1975). In particular I no longer stand over the account given above of the concluding section, 'Medallion'. In the case of a work of such authority as *Hugh Selwyn Mauberley*, and yet so ambiguous (with an ambiguity that I now believe to be ultimately insoluble), a change of mind is not anything that I think calls for excuse, though I'm aware of many who think it irritating, if not indeed unpardonable. Though I've required that the essay be dropped from future reprintings of *The Modern Age*, I'm glad and impenitent about having it given a new lease of life in print because on balance I think it still a great deal more right than wrong. Pound's poem is so memorable, and speaks still with such authority, that I by no means preclude the possibility that, after three attempts to give an account of it, I may yet some time venture on a fourth!

The Pelican Guide to English Literature, vol. 7, 'The Modern Age', ed. Boris Ford (Harmondsworth: Penguin, 1961); reprinted with postscript in *The Poet in the Imaginary Museum*.

VII The 'Sculpture' of Rhyme

Potter nor iron-founder
Nor caster of bronze will he cherish,
But the monumental mason;

As if his higher stake
Than the impregnable spiders
Of self-defended music

Procured him mandibles
To chisel honey from the saxifrage,
And a mouth to graze on feldspar.

New and Selected Poems (Middletown, Connecticut: Wesleyan University Press, 1961).

VIII *Michael Ayrton's*
The Maze Maker

The flux, the endless malleability of life – have there been people in every age to whom this was the nightmare that it is for many of us today? Doubtless every age can show them, persons hungry for rigid certainties, just as every age throws up their opposites, the people for whom flux is excitement and freedom. But what is clear, surely, is that in the present century the rigidifiers are on the defensive as never before, frustrated and unsatisfied as never before; whereas the melters down, the moulders and manipulators, the apostles of the fluid, are now in the ascendant and in the saddle. Freedom itself – not the fact of it, but the unchallengeable prestige of it as a slogan and a rallying cry that no one can afford not to rally to – is one card in the hand of the melter-down which by itself sweeps the board; once freedom is invoked, the rigidifier has to throw in his hand at once. And everything in the nature of our age conspires in the same direction; the unprecedented speed of change (technological in the first place, demanding moral and psychological change thereafter) compels anyone who has even a minimal grasp of the actual to acknowledge that the only feasible policy for him as for all others must be fluid, plastic, experimental, provisional. Yet there are people for whom this goes against the grain, who are by temperament drawn to the rigid, the hard, the resistant. For such people the present is a very hard time to live in; and the correspondence columns of any local newspaper show them protesting, crying out in pain, seeking ever more hysterical and irrational ways to break out from the impasse in which they find themselves. The more they become hysterical, as their plight forces them to envisage ever more patently foredoomed false alternatives, the more they play into their opponents' hands; and the more plausible becomes the allegation which those opponents contemptuously throw at them – that they are stupid as well as afraid, that a yearning for the rigid and the certain is to be found in any age only among the unintelligent.

Yet this is surely not the case. In another age than ours those who now seek the rigid would have settled for the stable; they would have been conservatives rather than reactionaries. For stability, in the physical and the moral universes alike, might be defined as a controllable proportion between rigid elements and fluid elements, between the persistent and the

unprecedented. Nowadays what drives the naturally intelligent conservative into reactionary postures is the way in which the fluid has totally
overborne the rigid, the impossibility of finding grounds for thinking that
any persistent element in his life is other than an anachronistic survival, a
removable impediment. Changeability seems to be total, as universal
law; not only the tempo of change, but the scope of it, appears to be
uncontrollable because illimitable. And in this case, the man who is stupid
is not he who, however vainly, tries to resist change, but rather the
many pragmatists among the apostles of change, those who think that
they can ride with the wave only to that point in the future where they
can stop it rolling, can alight, and can rigidify life in the momentary shape
it will then have taken, a shape which conforms to their interests or their
principles.

What provokes me to these reflections is thinking about sculpture.
And sculpture has led others who are not sculptors into thinking along the
same lines. Théophile Gautier, for instance:

> *Tout passe. − L'art robuste*
> *Seul à l'éternité;*
> *   Le buste*
> *Survit à la cité.*
>
> *Et la médaille austère*
> *Que trouve un laboureur*
> *   Sous terre*
> *Révèle un empereur.*
>
> *Les dieux eux-mêmes meurent.*
> *Mais les vers souverains*
> *   Demeurent*
> *Plus fort que les airains.*
>
> *Sculpte, lime, cisèle;*
> *Que ton rêve flottant*
> *   Se scelle*
> *Dans le bloc résistant!*

For Shakespeare and many another poet before Gautier, sculptors' work
in brass or bronze seemed in this way the token and the guarantee that art
at any rate, the poet's no less than the sculptor's, could stem and survive
the flux; that art was one element of life which persisted, changing its
forms only within controllable limits, answerable to controls which were
its own and embodied in its traditions. In the century since Gautier
wrote, this ancient conviction has been battered and eroded; and the
progressives, enamoured of the flux, have been at pains to show that art
forms, like all forms, are expendable, and must be thought of hencefor-

ward as provisional merely. In Michael Ayrton's novel *The Maze Maker*, the traditional assurances are given to the young sculptor Daedalus by his master:

> Another time he said to me that we were the keepers of memory. 'Our work will live when the warriors lie in their tombs and our work lies with them,' he said. 'They will be dust and what we make will lie among their bones as whole as when we made it.'

But it is not clear, by the end of the astonishing narrative which Michael Ayrton puts into Daedalus' mouth, whether this assurance has been vindicated. It is not what Michael Ayrton is centrally concerned with. And for that matter, there are good reasons why he subtitles his book, as it were defiantly, 'a novel'. For a fable may have one 'central concern', but a novel does not, though it sometimes helps the critic to pretend that it has. And in this respect *The Maze Maker* is a true novel; it repeatedly seems to be on the point of thinning out and streamlining itself into a fable, but always in the end it sidesteps and dances away. And it is this capriciousness which keeps us reading. It is the urgency of our own concerns which makes us want to schematize it, to make an intricately rigid model out of what is tantalizingly protean.

So it is at least, if one is of those who hanker for the rigid in a world of flux. Gautier was such a one. Another was Ezra Pound, notably in a famous essay, 'The Hard and the Soft in French Poetry', in which, fifty years ago, he explicitly aligned himself with Gautier. And it should be clear by now that I am another of the same kind, if I can diagnose myself. Pound is the most instructive, the exemplary case, and this for all sorts of reasons. In the first place his career demonstrates all too neatly how a liking and a need for the rigid, for what he calls 'the hard', may nourish at the present day extremely authoritarian, indeed Fascist, politics. Less obvious, but more intriguing, is the seeming paradox by which this poet, enamoured of the hard, devotes his major poem the *Cantos* to celebrating a world of metamorphosis. Like his master Ovid, Pound, at the times when he is in control of his material in the *Cantos*, combines maximum hardness in the execution with maximum fluidity in the conception. For the world that he renders is above all things protean, malleable, in process, ceaselessly metamorphic.

And yet there is no paradox. Or if there is paradox it is one that is the very raison d'être of one kind of art – the art that Michael Ayrton, in his book as in his own sculptures, has chiefly been concerned with: the art of casting bronze. For those cast bronzes which Gautier and Pound respond to so eagerly, as showing how art can be durable and rigid, in fact are fashioned out of the most fluid material; the molten bronze is *poured* into the mould. The rigidity and hardness of the end product is in direct proportion to the fluid malleability in the process of production. For a carving in stone is usually softer than cast bronze. Moreover, in both cases the process of artistic creation mimics a process of natural creation. For if on the one hand natural elements of frost and water and sand-laden wind can carve a cliff-face, on the other hand nature is a moulder also. The poet Valéry, a more patient and scrupulous thinker than either Gautier or Pound, had his own art in mind when he wrote that '"living nature" is unable to fashion solid bodies directly':

> Suppose the problem is to produce a lasting object of invariant shape — a prop, a lever, a rod, a buckler; to produce a tree-trunk, a femur, a tooth or a shield, a skull or a shell, nature always makes the same detour: it uses the liquid or fluid state of which every living substance is constituted, and strains off the solid elements of its construction. All that lives or lived results from the properties and changes of certain liquids. Besides, every solid has passed through a liquid phase, melted or in solution.

And yet Valéry goes on to insist that, if in this way an art such as bronze casting mimics nature, on the other hand it surpasses her:

> But 'living nature' does not take to the high temperatures which enable us to work 'pure bodies', and give to glass, bronze or iron in liquid or plastic states the forms desired, and which cooling will make permanent. Life, to model its solid organs, is limited to the use of solutions, suspensions or emulsions.

And it is this tension in the very nature of metal-working which stretches Daedalus on the rack throughout the narrative which Michael Ayrton gives him. The drama and the significance of his condition are precisely this: that to pursue his vocation he has to deal both with the divine Mother, Gaia, whose womb and bowels supply the metals he is to work, but also with the sun, Apollo, from whom he must filch or wheedle the heat that he needs in his kilns before the metals can be worked. The Mother can be propitiated; but the need for a more than earthly heat is of its essence presumptuous, and so Apollo harries and persecutes Daedalus throughout, and none of the artificer's propitiatory services suffice to deflect the sky god's malice for long.

Stone carving involves no such hubris. And Daedalus of course, as a complete sculptor, can cut stone, though apparently it interests him little compared with his metal-working. We hear of two Cretan apprentices of his who applied themselves to the carving of life-sized marble figures; and Apollo, so Daedalus learns after the apprentices have left him, favours them both and punishes communities which treat them badly. Daedalus comments:

> I am proud of this story. It shows how high in reputation my pupils

have become and that although I taught them only the rudiments of marble carving while they were with me at Knossos, they so far persevered as to obtain the approval of Apollo himself. I am by no means certain that I can say as much. He does not seem to approve of me: but then again he may have preferred Dipoinos and Skyllis as part of his relentless persecution of me. If he did so to make me jealous, he has failed.

If we persisted in pressing a fable out of what is nothing of the sort, it seems we might draw the moral: 'Moderation in all things. Seek to emulate Nature, not to surpass her. Make things as hard as nature, but no harder; as soft, but no softer. If you would work metal, take the carver's way only, as Gaudier-Brzeska did, assaulting brass with a cold chisel.' But this will not do – not only because it is quite plainly wide of the mark that Michael Ayrton is aiming at, but for reasons that have nothing to do with his intentions. For if we believe that an art is more than a rhetoric, more than a compassing of certain effects by whatever means; if we believe that on the contrary the morality of art has everything to do with a congruence between process and product, between means and ends – then we must argue that for the rendering of metamorphic flux as a profound reality, nothing will serve but an art that itself comprehends metamorphosis centrally in its processes. And bronze casting is such an art, whereas stone carving is not.

This consideration is more than ever in place when we remember the author that we are dealing with. Readers of Ayrton's *Testament of Daedalus*, which in 1962 was (we now realize) a pilot project for *The Maze Maker* of 1967, will recognize in the latter, at the point where Daedalus describes the suicidal flight of Icarus towards the sun, a passage which differs only in details from what appeared in the earlier book:

His trunk splayed out expanding and the jointed projections of his limbs became the vectors of his energy written white upon the now blackened sky. His proportions altered and the physical structure of his body dissolved and reassembled. The cage of ribs passed through the ribs of wing, each performing an identical function, each affirming the ascent implicit in the descent. The wings of his pelvis spread out from the spine and in their bowl the duration of his flight was contained like a liquid. Time turned in on him so that the sequence of modifications to which he was subject appeared simultaneous. A compact projectile and yet spread across the sky, he evolved in the instant a sequence of related anatomies each designed to succeed and doomed to fail. In these anatomies, the embryo coexisted with the fish, the lizard with the bird and at the apex, where he joined his god, he combined the disintegration of ultimate fatigue with a jolting orgasm compacted of the will to birth.

This is not the second but the third time that Ayrton has rendered this metamorphosis. The first time the rendering was not in words, but in bronze. And even those who have not seen the bronze, who envisage what it must be like from the verbal description of it, can surely concede that it would be an abomination in cut stone; that nothing but bronze, poured molten and allowed to cool, is the appropriate medium for the monstrous conception.

Ayrton has made a series of small bronzes which ought to come to mind when he describes how Deiphobe, the Cumaean sibyl, is entered by Apollo, her divine lover:

> In the basin of the cauldron there was no woman. There was a brazen, extended throat rising from a drum which had become part of the tripod cauldron. It was an entity, boneless as a snake but rigid as metal standing upright on tripod tongs. This image, topped by a head as featureless as an axeblade, spoke in words condensed from scalding steam.

Ayrton has for years thanklessly maintained that it is, as it has always been, normal for literature to programme the arts of painting and sculpture, in just the way (we may suppose) that these sentences 'programme' a bronze sculpture he has yet to execute. The writer can only be grateful and flattered; and he ought to return the compliment by recognizing that the verbal programming of a sculpture is in no way a substitute for that sculpture. One of the improvements made between *The Testament of Daedalus* and *The Maze Maker* is, I should like to think, that Ayrton realizes more clearly than before how words in verse are at least as inappropriate a medium for rendering metamorphosis as carved stone is. All but one of the poems of Icarus have been expunged; and the one that is retained is printed, deprecatingly, as prose. The prose that describes the metamorphosis of Icarus, with its nice distinctions and antitheses ('A compact projectile *and yet…*'), is very plainly announcing its own inadequacy; very insistently a programming only, a description, not a rendering. For the truth is of course that language, whether in prose or verse, is necessarily sequential and cumulative; the thing it cannot render, which is of the essence of metamorphosis, is simultaneity. What happens when language is constrained to carry this inappropriate burden appears if we continue the quotation about the metamorphosis of the Cumaean sibyl:

> Each word came sibilant. The pythoness was whispering. Then her speech thickened and the words stuck mollusc in a mass of sound. Words came from her that rang, others that fell plummeting like stones, and through it all the serpent hissing breathed through the sense.
>
> I do not to this day know exactly what she meant, for I think she

spoke of my future in your time and of another coming of Icarus and of great peril to man, but I do not know this for certain. What she meant I must leave to you, but this is what she said:

> My speech is split, suck at my thistle speech
> My spittle swells to sweeten surety
> See where my mouth is eyed and sees in smoke
> Your summit sky in sallow solstice speak…

I break off there, after the first of four unrhymed quatrains thus spoken by the Sibyl. For the point is sufficiently made. 'Her speech thickened' – it did, indeed; as much in the prose ('the words stuck mollusc in a mass of sound'), as in the verse ('… my thistle speech/My spittle swells…'). The random associations of sound, between 'stuck' and 'mollusc', between 'thistle' and 'spittle', clog the rapid onwardness of successive meanings; they coagulate in muddy eddies which ape the simultaneity they cannot achieve. Dylan Thomas wrote thus, and it cannot be long before Thomas comes in for a revival, his opportunistic variant of the Joycean pun seeming to deny what Marshall McLuhan rightly asserts – that the electronic overload of simultaneous information discharged upon us is more than the printed word, condemned to linear sequentiality, can ever hope to cope with. Ezra Pound never defined that 'hardness' which he so much esteemed in Gautier; but we may define it by its contrary, as the opposite of writing like this in which words run together like so many dabs of iridescent Plasticine nudged together by an indifferent thumb. It is not a question of the experience being meaningless, but of words being pointed towards a meaning which, by their very nature, words cannot compass. At the point where time itself becomes plastic, words fail us – as clay and bronze do not.

Words fail the Sibyl, as Ayrton realizes; and in fact of course oracular utterance must always be pushing language beyond its capacities, the signal emerging mutilated and only half-comprehensible from behind the mush and crackle of electrical overload. This is one good reason for resisting the ancient notion that oracular utterance and poetic utterance are akin. Soft poetry trades on this alleged kinship; hard, sequential poetry denies it. If Daedalus were a devotee of the hard, he would be irritated by the oracular farrago; instead he is bemused respectfully – as apparently the ancient world habitually was. On the other hand he is certainly irritated by the not dissimilar farrago of his son. And yet he comes to think that he should have been respectful in that case too:

> I think I am a fool to hope, but I have not been enough a fool for most of my life and perhaps it is time. My son was a fool.

That son, Icarus, in *The Maze Maker* as five years ago in *The Testament of Daedalus*, is identified with the type of the poet:

I am not impious nor insensitive to the visions of poets and other sacred persons, but in general they are less observant than they think, suffering as they do from revelation, which blinds them. I accept that poets celebrate important things such as honour and beauty and birth and valour and man's relations with the gods but, when you come down to it, what they most celebrate are heroes, which is not surprising. Poets have much in common with heroes. They are neither of them aware of the world, of its true appearance nor its real consequence, its structure nor its marvellous imperfection. They are blind to that and because my methods of gaining experience have been observation, deduction and experiment, I have been no worse off and much better instructed than any poets or heroes known to me. In fact since I am not beset by my own personality I am better off. I prefer cognition to revelation and in my view the valiant act is to live as long and as fully as possible, but then I make things which take time. Honour lasts longer if it is gained by patience rather than by some noble gesture rapidly made.

I am involved in matters which I do not wish disturbed nor interrupted by eloquent activities, the facile assumption of power, speculation on immeasurable phenomena, nor any apotheosis. What I make exists.

I find myself wanting to protest that cognition rather than revelation is the business of much poetry, that patience rather than rapid gestures is the stratagem of many poets and the value extolled in their poetry; in short, that the poetry which I most admire may be called, in the Nietzschean scheme of things though probably not in Ayrton's, an *Apollonian* activity. Indeed, it follows from what I have said about the nature of language as a medium that my image of the admirable poem has more to do with sunlight on carved stone than with Icarus's suicidal heroism. One knows of course the sort of poet – Dylan Thomas again, or Mayakovsky – that Daedalus and Ayrton have in mind; but I want to protest that this type is not, and cannot be, the norm.

To be sure, Ayrton may reply that Daedalus' idea of the poet – as *vates*, as 'sacred person' – is deliberately archaic, the poet as conceived of by Plato. And it is similarly true to ancient history that Daedalus should resent the much higher status given by the ancient world to the poet, as compared with other kinds of image-makers. But when Ayrton the metal-worker writes of Daedalus the ancient metal-worker, he must be probing the essential nature of working metal now as in the ancient world; and he has a sort of duty to deal equally with the complementary or antithetical image of the poet. Accordingly I suspect he has more patience with the Icarus-poet, as the type is met with in the here and now, than I have.

At this point in the narrative Daedalus is set up against the poet, not as one kind of artist confronting another who works another medium, but primarily and indeed insistently as *scientist*, working by 'observation, deduction and experiment'. It is this which makes Daedalus, in Ayrton's treatment of him, such a rich figure. In his own image of himself he is always the anti-hero; but he changes about, more than he himself realizes, in his ideas of what form his anti-heroism takes. If he is here the anti-hero as scientist, elsewhere he is the anti-hero as technician (a term he applies to himself), as technologist, as artist, and as artificer. In one of the most brilliantly inventive and entertaining of all Ayrton's enterprises in alle-gory, his treatment of the Myrmidons who erect for Daedalus the Cumaean shrine to Apollo which he has prefabricated in the galleries of the Cumaean hill, Daedalus figures not as technician nor technologist, but as *technocrat*, for Ayrton here invents for the Ancient World an analogue to the industrial organization of modern times. Technician, technologist, technocrat; artist, artificer, artisan; artful, artistic, arty, artificial – these are the word-clusters which continually spiral and divide and re-form in the reader's mind. And heaven knows, it is a salutary and pertinent exercise. For our confusion about and among these related terms, our blurring of distinctions among them, or our making of distinctions where none exist – this surely is near to the heart of our inability to get our own twentieth-century experience into focus, even when we are concerned with fields of experience that seem to have nothing to do with Art at all.

Our salutary puzzlements as we read the book are complicated, or rather they are compounded, by the fact that what we deal with all the time is one man's image of himself. And that man, Daedalus, though he is very intelligent as well as highly self-conscious, is capable of deceiving himself. For instance, within the narrative as a whole, Daedalus' protesta-tions to himself that he is simply a technician come to seem, even to him as well as to us, attempts to evade the more perilous and ambiguous destiny that is laid upon him – that of the artist. More than once it seems to him that the underground labyrinths which he constructs, as it were compulsively, are so many refuges into which he burrows to escape the eye of Apollo's sunlight; and we may legitimately decode this to mean that he absorbs himself in the minutiae of his craft or his trade, in his tech-niques, to lose sight of the presumptuous and frightening purpose which his techniques are meant to serve, that of artistic creation. While he is still a youth, his kinsman Lycus puts the issue starkly before him:

> If you were destined simply to become a fine craftsman, welcome in any house to work the metals from the storeroom, you might have a good and fruitful life even if you were occasionally mocked as Hephaistos is mocked on Olympus. But you have already made another choice which the gods will resent. They will see it as a chal-

lenge to their divinity, as hubris. Creation... is more painful and more hated than murder, if only because it is less common. I envy you in some ways but I am glad I am not in your shoes.

Nothing that happens later in Daedalus' story contradicts this clair-voyance.

However, this does not exhaust the meaning for Ayrton of the symbol which he picks out in his title. The maze, the labyrinth, is meant to have a more inclusive significance; one which is announced on the second page – 'Each man's life is a labyrinth at the centre of which lies his death...' This we have heard before. It is traditional. And being tradi-tional, undoubtedly it comprehends a truth. Yet, finding it announced so early, I must confess to a sinking at the heart. For is it the whole truth – that man, and the artist in particular, can explore nothing beyond the confines of his own personality? For that is what it means surely: that the artist explores, *cognizes*, not Nature but only his own nature; that the truths he discovers are neither physical nor metaphysical, but merely, when you come down to it, psychological. Of course in any age perhaps, certainly in our own age, this is what most people believe. It is on this understanding that the arts are tolerated, by those who are not artists – on the understanding that physical Nature is investigated by scientists; meta-physical Nature by priests; the nature of man in society by politicians, administrators, and social scientists; psychological nature by psychologists and artists. Only the artists themselves have sometimes rejected this neat distribution of labour, refusing (not as private citizens, but in their capacity as artists) to render unto Caesar that which is Caesar's, and unto the priest that which is God's. I should be sorry to think that Michael Ayrton is not this sort of artist.

Of course it is he himself, Ayrton, who as a sculptor knows how it feels to work metals and to work stone. He speaks therefore with authority. And it may be indeed that metal-working is so different from stone-carving, *feels* so different to the sculptor in the act, that there is something misleading about comprising the two activities under the one rubric, *sculpture*. Thus it may be, what seems to be implied by Daedalus if not by Ayrton behind him, that throughout the early stages of fashioning a bronze, the sculptor is operating wholly as a metallurgist. What seems to be true of the stone-carver on the other hand, if we may trust testimonies left by some of them, is that their knowledge of stone is different from the geologist's knowledge; that they apprehend the different natures of Parian and Istrian and Carraran marble, not by the scientist's method, but by their own faculty of *feeling*. If so, they are examples of the artist refusing to relin-quish to the scientist the responsibility for investigating physical Nature.

However, what Ayrton's narrative throws up most insistently is the artist's relation to not the physical, but the metaphysical. What Ayrton's

wit and invention are engaged upon most often is the translating of
Daedalus' experience out of the metaphysical terms of antique mythology
into psychological terms. He triumphs time and again, sometimes
convincingly, always with entertaining ingenuity. Yet there are one or
two instances in which he offers no explanation that is not metaphysical.
The most striking and significant case is in the first pages of Part II, when
Daedalus, after the flight from Crete in which he saw Icarus fly into the
sun, comes down at Cumae and is compelled to enter that honeycombed
hill, there to live in the subterranean galleries which are the guts of
Mother Earth. What is the nature of that compulsion? Psychological
factors contribute to it – the emotional tumult of having witnessed Icarus'
hubris, and his punishment. And there are physical factors also – the
exhaustion of Daedalus, and the overpowering heat of the sun. Yet these
factors do not account for what is ultimately supernatural – 'I was caught
and sucked into the rock by a wind as fierce and burning as that which
had flung me out from beneath Knossos.' If this event is indeed supernatural, what are we to conclude? If the maze which an artist constructs
about him is in the end only the maze of his own personality, we must
conclude that there is a metaphysical realm, supernatural and religious,
but that this is closed to the artist as to any other man; that his art gives
him no access to it, nor any means of exploring it. Daedalus is, or wants
to think that he is, a rationalist. And the joke is on him for thinking so,
since he has experiences which his rationalism cannot comprehend. Yet
Daedalus acknowledges the existence of the supernatural. Do we? If not,
the joke is on us even more than on him. No one can blame Ayrton, or
any other twentieth-century man, for not having decided how wide a
margin we ought to leave for the supernatural in our experience. But as I
read the pages which tell of Daedalus' scramble up the hill at Cumae, and
his being sucked into the belly of that hill, I find the prose at this point
unwontedly strained, effortful, and portentous.

   It is the man I have called the rigidifier, the devotee of the hard, the
seeker after the certain and the unchanging, who most resists the notion
that the artist is imprisoned within the maze of his own personality, from
which he can never break out to explore any nature other than his own.
For we do not need Freud or Jung to tell us that, however the individual
psyche may be in the last analysis rigidly determined by heredity or in
infancy, it is, as we experience it by introspection, a realm above all
protean and malleable, a world of metamorphosis, of merging and self-
transforming shapes and fluid contours. Not in those subterranean wynds
and galleries, nor in the kneaded wax and the poured bronze which seem
their natural concomitants, shall we find that which some of us will
always want more than anything else – the resistant and persisting, the
rigid and the hard, everything that poets have yearned for naïvely in the
image of the stone that resists the chisel and confronts the sunlight.

What we want to resist, and to have resisted, is always the same thing: time, especially time in its most appalling aspect, as death. 'Only through time, time is conquered,' wrote the poet Eliot. It is thus conquered whenever, once the labyrinth that is a man's work in time is complete, his death is seen to be at the heart of it. An art like sculpture which embodies simultaneity will present an image of the maze with death at the heart of it. Arts like music and literature, which embody time's lapse in their procedures, will chart the building of the maze, stage by stage, and death will be at the end of the work, not in its midst. But what happens when time itself seems to have become so plastic that, as we are told in *The Maze Maker*, the Cumaean sibyl Deiphobe is both the Pasiphae that was and the Pasiphae that will be, the pythoness of Delphi both past and future? The literary mind boggles, and cannot conceive how an art so masterfully plastic as this, imposing this degree of simultaneity, can be one of 'the keepers of memory'. For if all significant events are simultaneously and eternally present, how can it be the function of art to preserve from the past any one event or train of events, and carry it forward into the future? But I dare say this is a riddle only for the literary mind which persists, and has to persist, in seeing time as a line; not as a spiral or (Ayrton's word) a helix.

Southern Review, new series, 5.3 (Summer 1969).
Much of this essay was later incorporated in the 'Conclusion' to Davie's *Thomas Hardy and British Poetry* (1972). See Davie, *With the Grain: Essays on Thomas Hardy and Modern British Poetry*, ed. Clive Wilmer (Manchester: Carcanet, 1998), pp. 158–61.

IX Mr Eliot

In 1928, introducing Pound's *Selected Poems*, Mr Eliot protested against 'Those who expect that any good poet should proceed by turning out a series of masterpieces, each similar to the last, only more developed *in every way*.' On the contrary, he went on, though 'it may be only once in five or ten years that experience accumulates to form a new whole and finds its appropriate expression', yet, to be ready for these accumulations when they come, the poet has to keep in training 'by good workmanship on a level possible for some hours' work every week of his life'. And the implication is that the poet has the right to publish some of these practice pieces. Pound has taken advantage of this right perhaps outrageously; Mr Eliot seems not to have taken advantage of it at all.

What is striking all over again, leafing through his poems,[1] is how little he needs to enter the plea. Not that each of his poems is a masterpiece, nor that he has advanced simultaneously on every front. The second collection, *Poems* (1920), advances beyond the 'Prufrock' volume of 1917 in very few ways, and in many ways is a falling-off. 'A Cooking Egg', for instance, deserves nothing much better than the fate which has come upon it – of being the occasion for a protracted critical wrangle; and in 'Gerontion' the relation between poet and persona is far more fluctuating and frustratingly evasive than in 'The Love Song of J. Alfred Prufrock'. All the same, if we think of Mr Eliot putting in a few hours' work each week of his life, we boggle, appalled, at the sheaf on sheaf that must have been destroyed, and at the austere self-control which decided time and again what, and how little, should be preserved.

The extraordinary fact is, surely, that Mr Eliot has published between hard covers not a single poem which he now needs to blush about reprinting. This is a fantastic achievement; an achievement not of poetry (for greater poets have not proceeded like this and we don't think any worse of them), but of judgement, taste, self-knowledge, self-control. We are not prepared for this rigour of self-criticism in poets. In *Poems 1909–1935*, and again now, Mr Eliot consigns to the austere category, 'Minor Poems', such exquisite pieces as 'Cape Ann' and 'Rannoch, by Glencoe'; and one's admiration for them quails and stammers before the conclusiveness of his deprecation. And in the new collection, which

---

1   T.S. Eliot, *Collected Poems, 1909–1962* (London: Faber and Faber, 1963).

gathers into the major canon only the belated Ariel poem, 'The Cultivation of Christmas Trees', I similarly want to rescue 'A Note on War Poetry' from the rubric, 'Occasional Verses', which stands over five uncollected poems of wartime and since. If, reluctantly, we set aside the poems herded into these carefully subordinated categories (one is called, explicitly, 'Five-Finger Exercises'), what we have from Mr Eliot is pretty much what he said in 1928 that we could not expect from anyone – the accumulations of five or ten years at a time, conclusively discharged in one considered poem or group of poems with no near-misses, no ranging shots, no labour-pains, no afterbirths.

What's particularly remarkable is the way in which the poems and the critical essays are sealed off from each other. The variously cock-eyed or idiosyncratic readings of cultural history which in Pound lay waste whole areas of the Cantos, which in Yeats infect past redemption a poem like 'The Statues' – these appear in Mr Eliot's essays without once spilling into his poetry. Now that many of the essays, having served their vast polemical purpose, seem dated or out-dated, the poems soar on completely undamaged. The criticism never fitted the poems anyhow. And more and more it looks as if it couldn't fit because it tried to assemble, using only English products, a reader's kit which needed, to be serviceable, many tools of foreign and especially French manufacture. From 'Prufrock' to 'Little Gidding' is a movement from Laforgue to Valéry; the body of poetic theory which illuminates and explains it is not in Mr Eliot's essays nor anywhere else in English, but in French. Comically, of recent years we've been detecting in this professed classicist, this admirer of Donne and Dryden and Johnson, elements which we call Tennysonian. Is this to find Mr Eliot out? Hardly. His is a late-Romantic sensibility, and the poems are late-Romantic poems. Written when they were, how could they be anything else? In particular, how could they have escaped the late-Romantic ambition, which according to Valéry over-rode all else in French *symbolisme*, the will to make poetry approach the condition of music? They did not escape this ambition, in the end they realized it – as the title, *Four Quartets*, triumphantly declares.

Normally literature lives in two times at once. 'I wandered lonely as a cloud' lives in the time which we take to speak it, rhythmically shaping that time as we read; but it lives also in the imagined time which Wordsworth took on the walk he is telling us about. Music on the contrary lives in only one time, the time it takes for its performance, time which it shapes as we listen. One way to make poetry into music is to collapse the two times of literature into the one time of music, by making the poem refer to no time except the time it takes in the reading; and this means making the only events in the poem be the happening of its constituent words as one by one they rise and explode on our consciousness. Thus, in 'The Love Song of J. Alfred Prufrock':

Shall I say, I have gone at dusk through narrow streets
And watched the smoke that rises from the pipes
Of lonely men in shirt-sleeves, leaning out of windows?...

I should have been a pair of ragged claws
Scuttling across the floors of silent seas.

This is Prufrock's poem; everything he says before or after this in Eliot's poem isn't Prufrock's poem but only talk about it, mostly about the impossibility of writing it. This is Prufrock's poem, or as much of it as he was able to stammer out. He got even so far with it only because he took himself by surprise. 'Shall I say...' what? And of course in saying what he has to say, he says it. The eventfulness of language is on him before he is prepared, the future tense ('Shall I say') is overtaken by the present tense of verbal happenings, much too fast for him to control. Suddenly language is happening through him. And before he can gather his wits (which is to say, his crippling self-consciousness), the language carries him beyond what he meant to say, into saying what he didn't know he wanted to say, didn't know he had it in him to say: 'And watched the smoke that rises from the pipes/Of lonely men in shirt-sleeves, leaning out of windows...'

For this moment Prufrock, as he steps cat-like but with mounting apprehension through the 'certain half-deserted streets' of the poem's own maundering development, is suddenly carried out of himself, to feel that others exist besides himself, to pity the loneliness of others even as he pities his own loneliness. This is the moment when the Ancient Mariner, seeing the sea-serpents, 'blessed them unaware' – but with this difference, that the unawareness isn't stated but takes place before us, as a verbal event. Just because, in asking, 'Shall I say such a thing?' such a thing gets said, language can take us unawares, blurting out precisely what we were wondering about perhaps not saying at all. To compare that moment in Coleridge's poem with this moment in Eliot's is to compare Romantic poetry with late-Romantic or *symboliste* poetry, poetry like music with poetry that aspires to *be* music.

An effect like this appears to correspond to what Mallarmé demanded, in translation by Symons:

> The pure work implies the elocutionary disappearance of the poet, who yields place to the words, immobilized by the shock of their inequality; they take light from mutual reflection... replacing the old lyrical afflatus or the enthusiastic personal direction of the phrase.

It is language which happens through the speaker, not the speaker who expresses himself through language. And this seems to have been what Mr Eliot was groping for when he talked about impersonality in his essay, 'Tradition and the Individual Talent'. If so, he made a bad botch of it, for instead of talking about impersonality as a poetic effect, a valuable illusion, he talked about the psychology of artistic creation, and has rightly been taken to task for seeming to advance the quite unbelievable proposition that the quality of an artist's products has nothing to do with the richness or poverty of the artist's emotional life at times when he isn't composing.

Yeats also knew this tag of Mallarmé and echoes it in early essays. But as soon as he decided that actor and orator were nearer to the poet than the musician could be (and this he did explicitly in his Abbey Theatre years), Yeats was committed to precisely that 'enthusiastic personal direction of the phrase' which Mallarmé condemned. And this is why, later, Donne could be a strong immediate influence on Yeats as he could not be on Mr Eliot. It means too, so far as I can see, that Yeats's connection with French *symboliste* poetry had to be altogether looser and more remote than Mr Eliot's.

It is only with *Four Quartets* that we reach the logical conclusion of this line of speculation and experiment. There, just as the only happenings in the poem are the occurrences of its own words, so the poetry talks about nothing but itself, continually gnawing its own vitals – though, language being what it is, it can be argued that poems which talk only about their own language by that token talk about everything else. How this can be we see foreshadowed in many places in *The Waste Land*. For instance:

At the violet hour, when the eyes and back
Turn upward from the desk, when the human engine waits
Like a taxi throbbing waiting,
I Tiresias, though blind, throbbing between two lives,
Old man with wrinkled female breasts, can see
At the violet hour, the evening hour that strives
Homeward, and brings the sailor home from sea,
The typist home at teatime, clears her breakfast, lights
Her stove, and lays out food in tins.

This is a sentence, grammatically flawless, which is nevertheless designed to trap the reader more than once. 'I Tiresias... can see (at the violet hour, that is to say, the evening hour...) the typist.' But in this case, there is no subject for the next verbs, no one left to clear the breakfast, light the stove, lay out tins. So, when we get to 'clears her breakfast', we make a rapid retrospective revision, and pretend that what we read from the first was 'I Tiresias... can see... *the evening hour*.' In this way we get a subject for the later verbs because we make it the evening hour which, besides striving homeward etc., also clears breakfasts, lights stoves, lays out tins. But of course 'clears' and 'lights' follow 'the typist' too closely for us not to think that it's still she who does the clearing, the lighting, the laying out. Because in this way we have to revise our expectations continually as the sentence unfolds, the effect is that the typist is both an object of two distinct verbs (of Tiresias's seeing and the evening hour's bringing) and also the subject of 'clears her breakfast'.

When we turn the page and come upon her pathetically squalid seduction, we see the point of all this: for she has not chosen to surrender, but has permitted time and the circumstances to make the choice for her. It is, indeed, the evening hour that has done everything, even to seducing her. And (this is the point) we are made to feel that it is in the very structure of language that this should be so. This is why the syntax has to be flawlessly correct. When we had to revise our notions of how the sentence was going, we also, and by that very token, revised our notion of how people are free agents. It is language that trapped us into our wrong notions, and it is language that makes us put them (dejectedly) right. It is language that does this, not the speaker manipulating language to his own purposes. (Tiresias helps because, being bi-sexual, he is as a speaker unimaginable.)

In an important sense, we, the poets of now, have nothing to learn from Mr Eliot. There is no following him down the roads he has taken because he has been right to the end of them himself, once and for all. As Dryden said of Shakespeare, he has laid waste his whole territory simply by occupying it so conclusively. We can learn from a poet so different as Yeats, and a poet so imperfect as Pound, in a way we cannot learn from Mr Eliot. The one lesson he might teach us – of inhuman accuracy and self-control in publishing only those poems we need never be sorry for – this we shall never learn because the lesson is too hard.

Postscript. I apologize for repeating here things I said a few pages back, in 'The Relation between Syntax and Music in Some Modern Poems in English' – the latter, incidentally, a paper delivered at an international conference on 'stylistics' in Warsaw.

New Statesman, 11 October 1963; reprinted with postscript in *The Poet in the Imaginary Museum*.

X Pound and Eliot: A Distinction

Reviewing Yeats's *Responsibilities* in *Poetry* for May 1914, Pound envisaged a reader who asked, 'Is Mr Yeats an Imagiste?' And Pound replied:
'No, Mr Yeats is a symbolist, but he has written *des Images* as have many
good poets before him...' Later in the review, after quoting the first five
lines of 'The Magi', Pound remarked: 'Of course a passage like that, a
passage of *imagisme*, may occur in a poem not otherwise *imagiste*, in the
same way that a lyrical passage may occur in a narrative, or in some poem
not otherwise lyrical.'[1]

It is hard for us to recover the state of literary opinion in which the
first, most urgent question to be asked about Yeats is 'Is he an Imagiste?'
The literary historian can be called upon to show, by appeal to the historical record, that this state of opinion once existed. It might be thought
that to the literary critic, however, these echoes of battles long ago are of
no consequence; and, indeed, this is how our critics have proceeded,
using for instance 'Imagism' and 'Symbolism' as interchangeable terms. I
am sure that this is wrong: for Imagism as Pound promulgated it, or as he
later elaborated it into 'Vorticism', is not a variant upon Symbolism but
an alternative to it; and this forking of the ways confronts the poet hardly
less challengingly in 1970 than it did in 1914.

This is not to say, however, that Pound was in the right of it, that fifty
years ago he had laid hold of a distinction which we have since lost sight
of, much to our disadvantage. He was right to think that there was a
distinction, and a crucial one, but he surely failed to trace the line of
cleavage accurately. Except very intermittently, and then in a highly idiosyncratic way, Yeats was surely not a symbolist poet, even though
Edmund Wilson in *Axel's Castle* and many another commentator have,
like Pound, asserted that he was. Similarly, Pound never to my knowledge
asked whether Eliot was an Imagist or a Symbolist. And yet, I maintain,
it is in relation to Eliot, not Yeats, that the question is a momentous one.
Depending on the answer we give to it, we shall either succeed or fail in
uncovering the structure of the Eliotic poem. For as I read Eliot he is the
one poet writing in English who is centrally in the *symboliste* tradition.
What Eliot puts into his poems is determined preponderantly by his being

---

1 'The Later Yeats', *Literary Essays of Ezra Pound*, ed. T.S. Eliot (London: Faber, 1954),
pp. 378–81.

an American; how he structures his poems is determined preponderantly by his sitting at the feet of the French, in the first place (as is generally acknowledged, and as he testified himself) at the feet of Jules Laforgue. Four decades of commentary and explication have been largely wasted, because of the refusal of commentators to explore either the American or the French backgrounds. Instead, the attempt has been made over and over again to come to terms with Eliot without going outside the narrowly English tradition. In this endeavour, Tennyson and Beddoes have lately supplanted Webster and Donne as the most appropriate and useful points of reference; and this is a gain, but a necessarily limited one. The urgent question to ask is: 'Was the late Mr Eliot an Imagiste?' And the right answer is the answer which Pound gave, wrongly, when the question was asked about Yeats: 'No, the late Mr Eliot was a symbolist, though he has written *des Images* as have many good poets before him.'

In this section of my essay I take the relatively obvious and easy case of the late poems.

It is notable that, as Eliot got older, he could be seen in his critical writings to give steadily more attention to symbolist poetry, narrowly considered. The crucial name is that of Valéry. Eliot's long and important introduction to what is called *The Art of Poetry*, a volume out of the scheduled complete translation of Valéry's prose into English, was only the last of several considerations, always absorbed and respectful, of what Valéry stands for in the landscape of twentieth-century poetry. If Laforgue was the presiding genius of Eliot's earlier poems, no figure presided more insistently over the later ones than Valéry, deliberately Mallarmé's disciple, and like his master as much high-priest of symbolist theory as a writer of symbolist poems.

We cannot but suppose, therefore, that it is Valéry, bringing with him the whole symbolist endeavour to make poetry approximate to music, who stands behind the title − *Four Quartets* − by which Eliot explicitly indicates a musical analogy for the work which crowns his maturity. And we shall not be surprised to find that 'Burnt Norton', the first of the Quartets, is a poem very much à la Valéry − a poem in the first place about itself and about the writing of poetry, even (more narrowly) about poetry and music and the specifically close relation between these two arts among the others.

Just as 'The Love Song of J. Alfred Prufrock' and 'A Cooking Egg' are generally considered (wrongly) as stories told in verse with some of the chapters left out, just as 'Mr Eliot's Sunday Morning Service' has been considered (wrongly) as the setting of a scene with certain items of description left out (and impaired by others that bulge out of the frame), just as *The Waste Land* has been misconceived by Cleanth Brooks and numberless others as a cryptic allegory with some of the links in the argu-

ment deliberately omitted, so *Four Quartets* is generally misread as a philosophical disquisition or a treatise of Christian apologetics with, again,
large and deliberate lacunae. But, if the musical analogy is taken seriously
at all, just as the structure of 'A Cooking Egg' cannot be narrative structure (however much disguised and fiddled with), just as the structure of
'Mr Eliot's Sunday Morning Service' cannot be scenic, and just as the
structure of *The Waste Land* (at least up to the last two sections, where the
poet perhaps loses his way) cannot be allegorical, so the structure of *Four
Quartets* cannot be logical, discursive. We should not come to *Four
Quartets* with those expectations, we should not give it that sort of attention, we should not try to understand it in that way. And, since it is 'in
that way' that we nowadays conceive of what understanding is, it
becomes almost true to say that we should not try to 'understand' these
poems at all. Consider:

> What might have been is an abstraction
> Remaining a perpetual possibility
> Only in a world of speculation.
> What might have been and what has been
> Point to one end, which is always present.
> Footfalls echo in the memory
> Down the passage which we did not take
> Towards the door we never opened
> Into the rose-garden. My words echo
> Thus, in your mind...

'Thus'! Thus? How? What is the connection, the resemblance, thus
confidently asserted? Words spoken one by one are like footsteps – well,
yes; the argumentative mind can see that in certain circumstances the
comparison might be just. But it turns out that the footsteps never
happened, for they are footsteps in a direction which was never taken. So
it appears that the poet's words dropping into the silence are like, not any
actual footsteps, but only his thoughts of those footsteps. To be sure it
isn't the sound of the words that is like the sounds of footsteps, but the
words themselves (sounds plus meanings) that are like footsteps, perhaps
figurative ones like footsteps in an argument. But then, that argument, it
seems, was never embarked upon. It is easy enough – we are too ready
perhaps – to see words spoken as identical with stages in an argument: we
say the right word and thereby we advance one stage in the argument.
But words that are specifically not stages in an argument, but only like
such stages – this is harder to conceive of. Yet we can corroborate it
readily enough from experience – 'It all sounds very fine', we say, 'but in
fact when you look at what he's saying, it doesn't hang together at all.'
This is something that we might want to say in fact about what might
have been and what has been pointing to one end, which is always

present. 'It sounds very fine but…' And, if that was what we may have wanted to say, suddenly it turns out that we were right: we ought to have said it. For the poet himself is pointing out that that is just the effect he was after and attained. Anyone who sits down and tries to worry out what these lines mean, as a proposition in a treatise, is flying in the face of just what the poet tells him a few lines later: that his labour is wasted, that meaning of that sort isn't there. Yet the warning goes unheeded; the devout exegeses continue.

It would be just as wrong to fly to the other extreme, and to suppose that because we can't understand 'What might have been and what has been/Point to one end, which is always present' these lines are meaning-less. They add up to something, they amount to something; as we know from the very fact that the something they amount to can be talked about. We can say, for instance, as the poet says for us, that this something is like remembering how we didn't go down a passage to a rose garden. At the very least we can say that the experience of not understanding them is more like the experience of not understanding a book of mystical theology than it is like the experience of not understanding the drunken confidence of a stranger met in a bar.

'Burnt Norton' opens in precisely the same way as 'The Love Song of J. Alfred Prufrock'. There, 'something' ('Oh, do not ask, "What is it?"') was, we remember, like going 'through certain half-deserted streets,/The murmuring retreats/Of restless nights in one-night cheap hotels/And sawdust restaurants with oyster shells…' This is different from going or not going down a passage to a rose-garden, if only in this respect – that an encounter with a garrulous drunk is much more of a possibility. In both poems, we have hardly begun reading before we find the poem talking about itself, appealing to the reader with the question: 'So far as you've gone the experience of reading this poem is rather like this, isn't it?'

Put like this, the procedure seems to be no more than a gimmick. And of course that is all it is, in itself. But it can be made to work. In the present case for instance, after six lines of the poem we accept it as self-evidently true that 'What might have been is an abstraction/Remaining a perpetual possibility/Only in a world of speculation'. But nine lines later we ought to have changed our minds. For 'what might have been' (we might have been reading a treatise of mystical theology instead of a poem) has now been presented to us not as an abstract possibility in a world of speculation, but – extraordinary though this seems – as a manifested actuality in a world of lived experience, the experience of language.

These are vistas to set the clearest head spinning. The same possibili-ties are opened up, but in a more manageable way, by a passage later in the poem:

Words move, music moves
Only in time; but that which is only living
Can only die. Words, after speech, reach
Into the silence. Only by the form, the pattern,
Can words or music reach
The stillness, as a Chinese jar still
Moves perpetually in its stillness.
Not the stillness of the violin, while the note lasts,
Not that only, but the co-existence,
Or say that the end precedes the beginning,
And the end and the beginning were always there
Before the beginning and after the end.
And all is always now. Words strain,
Crack and sometimes break, under the burden,
Under the tension, slip, slide, perish,
Decay with imprecision, will not stay in place,
Will not stay still. Shrieking voices
Scolding, mocking, or merely chattering,
Always assail them. The Word in the desert
Is most attacked by voices of temptation,
The crying shadow in the funeral dance,
The loud lament of the disconsolate chimera.

Helen Gardner comments on this, intelligently enough: 'The word itself, like the note in music, has meaning only in relation to other words. It exists in time and in usage; and since contexts and usages change, the life of a word is a continual death.'[2] Certainly the semantic history of word-usages is being alluded to here, though less memorably than in a related passage from 'East Coker'. But the emphasis surely falls much less on the historical time, in which contexts and usages alter, than on the time which a musical composition takes to be performed or a literary compo-sition to be read. And though Miss Gardner acknowledges this she hardly makes it salient enough. For the perceptions at work in these lines are those which lie at the heart of symbolist poetic theory. In Eliot's verse as in Valéry's prose, the first thing to be said about poetry is that it works, it unfolds, only in duration, in lapsing time: 'Words move, music moves/Only in time...' Unlike 'What might have been and what has been/Point to one end, which is always present', the statement 'Words move, music moves/Only in time' does not just sound as if it made sense; it makes sense. Yet we must still beware of supposing that this passage

2   Helen Gardner, *The Art of T.S. Eliot* (London: Cresset, 1949), p. 7.

therefore, unlike that first one, is consecutive argument. For all the prim-
ness of punctuation and the earnest dryness of the vocabulary, this passage
too *is* what it talks about: its structure is musical, not logical. Consider, for
instance, the force of 'but' in what follows – 'but that which is only
living/Can only die'. This means, first, 'Words which live in time as we
do, must die as we do'; *but* also 'We on the other hand, because we are
living as words aren't, must die as they needn't.' At the point where the
semi-colon comes, something has been left out which in normal prose
discourse would limit what follows to one or other of these meanings.
The poet, wanting to have both meanings at once, constructs around the
semi-colon a meaningful silence, a blank place on the paper, where the
clause that would have settled the question is felt by us as present, as a
'might-have-been'. And the next sentence makes room for yet another
meaning.

> but that which is only living
> Can only die. Words, after speech, reach
> Into the silence.

Wondering, as the rhythm carries us over the full-stop, what cluster of
mutually incompatible logical links lies concealed in the silent space
which that punctuation creates (it could be 'And so', it could be 'And
yet'), we realize, as 'Words, after speech, reach' (we reach also, for the
next line) another sense in which words can be said to die, the sense in
which they may compose a dying fall, a cadence which prolongs itself
into the silence after the voice has stopped. This is an effect which poetry
shares with music: 'the stillness of the violin, while the note lasts…' The
fiddle and the bow are motionless, while the note which their movements created still sounds in the air about them.

It's just as well to insist on this because otherwise it will seem as if the
poem here (and elsewhere) is discontented with its own medium,
language, because that medium, like the musical medium, by locking it
into the dimension of time, makes it incapable of rising to the simultaneity, the stillness, of the plastic art which produces the Chinese jar.
And indeed many interpretations of *Four Quartets* as a whole, especially
those conducted from the standpoint of Christian piety, invite us to see
the poems as yearning always for some impossible stasis, 'the timeless
moment'. Certainly the poet, by introducing quotations from St John of
the Cross and other mystics, invites us to set over against the 'time' which
he talks of so constantly the concept of 'eternity'. And so the terminology
of mysticism is undoubtedly useful for coming to grips with the poem.
Still, in this very poem, it is said, 'Only through time time is conquered.'
And for readers of other temperaments and interests it may be useful to
see not time as opposed to eternity, but musical time as opposed to picto-

rial or sculptural space;[3] and to think, when they read, for instance, 'And all is always now', not of the mystic's contemplative trance, but of the perpetual present tense which is the tense of a symbolist poem, where words do not stand for events but *are* those events. Because the very first page of 'Burnt Norton' established it as a poem in the symbolist tradition, a poem which describes and discusses itself, this sort of meaning for 'time' and 'present' and 'now' should be, while certainly not the one meaning they will bear, at least the first meaning to be brought to them.

'Burnt Norton', which stands last in *Collected Poems 1909–1935*, employs just the same devices as the poem which stands first, 'The Love Song of J. Alfred Prufrock'. Like 'The Love Song', 'Burnt Norton' continually feeds upon itself, gnaws its own vitals, postures before its own glass. As in 'The Love Song', in 'Burnt Norton' much that is most crucial and affecting is 'between the lines'; in both poems the syntax of what is said serves to hint at what is unsaid, to frame the meaningful silences which may be gaps between blocks of lines but may equally well, in both poems, be the pregnant stillnesses around colons or semi-colons or full stops.[4] And there are other resemblances. In 'The Love Song', there is a point where the syntax ceases to be that of written prose or studied conversation and becomes, with a sudden access of earnestness and anxiety, the dishevelled syntax of speech: 'It is impossible to say just what I mean!/But as if a magic lantern threw the nerves in patterns on a screen.' The same thing occurs in *Four Quartets*, as here:

> Only by the form, the pattern,
> Can words or music reach
> The stillness, as a Chinese jar still
> Moves perpetually in its stillness.
> Not the stillness of the violin, while the note lasts,
> Not that only, but the co-existence,
> Or say that the end precedes the beginning,

---

3   Pound, in the review which I have quoted from, distinguishes between 'the sort of poetry which seems to be music just forcing itself into articulate speech, and secondly, that sort of poetry which seems as if sculpture or painting were just forced or forcing itself into words'. In *Gaudier-Brzeska: A Memoir* (1917), Pound made the same distinction in almost identical words (see Marvell Press reprint [Hessle, 1960], p. 82). In the *Memoir*, Pound is fairly plainly vowing himself to poetry of the second sort: imagist or vorticist poetry which works by analogy with sculpture. Symbolist poetry on the other hand works by analogy with the art of music. And according to Valéry this analogy is more important to Symbolism than whatever may be gathered from worrying over what is meant by 'symbol'.

4   Cf. Mallarmé: 'L'armature intellectuelle du poème se dissimule et tient – a lieu – dans l'espace qui isole les strophes et parmi le blanc du papier: significatif silence qu'il n'est pas moins beau de composer que les vers.' [The intellectual armature of the poem conceals itself and is contained – takes place – in the space which isolates the stanzas and among the whiteness of the paper: a significant silence which is no less beautiful to compose than the verses themselves.' (Ed.)]

And the end and the beginning were always there
Before the beginning and after the end.
And all is always now.

One looks with impatience, among all the exegeses, for a little literary criticism, which would examine, for instance, the points at which, and purposes for which, Eliot switches from written to spoken syntax, a criticism which would note how in the sentence about the Chinese jar there is the inversion – 'Only by the form... Can...' – so as to point up its written quality, precisely so that the spoken syntax which follows can come with all the greater desperation. And again, what of 'J. Alfred Prufrock' himself, those syllables which have no reference at all except the phantasmal one which they conjure up for themselves? This, too, occurs in *Four Quartets*. When we read in 'East Coker', 'On the edge of a grimpen, where is no secure foothold', we all know what a grimpen is, yet we shall look in vain for any dictionary to confirm us in our knowledge. For 'Grimpen' occurs elsewhere only once, as a place-name in Arthur Conan Doyle's *Hound of the Baskervilles*. It may not be so clear that much the same thing happens here, in 'Burnt Norton'. Yet:

> The Word in the desert
> Is most attacked by voices of temptation,
> The crying shadow in the funeral dance,
> The loud lament of the disconsolate chimera.

And, if we ignore the capital letter on 'Word', then it must seem that the temptations to which the word is exposed, the vices of language, are not so much described as exemplified, in that last opalescent couplet where the shell of Augustan antithetical balance, as it might be in Dryden, holds no kernel of sense but only the vast suggestiveness of a most un-Augustan sonority.

Still, 'Word' does get its capital letter; and very important it is. It permits us, and obliges us, to face up to a restive objection which I dare say we have had more and more difficulty in suppressing, the further we have penetrated through the looking-glass: the exasperated protest that poetry which has for its subject only itself cannot be other than trivial, the narrowness of its scope and focus a damning indictment of the men who write it. What have we been saying, if not that there are no real typists in Eliot's Waste Land, no real flowers and birds in his Burnt Norton, but only the names of these things? If it may be objected to Yeats that in his poems swans are not really swans but stand-ins ('Another emblem there!'), how much more heavily must not the same charge be levelled at Eliot? The ancient and arcane doctrine of the Logos – 'In the beginning was the Word, and the Word was with God, and the Word was God' – provides Eliot, as it sometimes provided Mallarmé himself, with an answer to this comprehensive indictment.

The non-Christian reader, while he may acknowledge that this doctrine, so central as it is to twenty centuries of European thought, somehow carries more weight than the more eccentric ideas of Yeats, may yet feel that the doctrine of the Logos is no less remote than the Yeatsian doctrines from his own lived experience. He may object, though respectfully, perhaps regretfully, that however far the poet may have been from seeing in this no more than a pun it is impossible for him, the reader, to take it as other than a pun or a historical curiosity. Yet in fact the doctrine of the Logos — or at least some aspects of it — can be readily translated into secular quite unmystical terms which no one can afford to ignore. Metalinguistics seems to have established, by thoroughly verifiable methods, that the language we speak determines not only how we communicate to others our sense of the truth, but how we communicate to ourselves; the categories which we find in nature or impose on nature, in order to understand it, are (it now appears) linguistic categories. The speaker of English and the speaker of Chinese will not merely arrange nature differently in order to speak of it, but will arrange it differently in order even to think about it. The syntax of our language determines all our ways of seeing the world and of coming to terms with it. To a personality like Pound's, convinced above all of the plenitude, the variety and multiplicity of experience, this realization will carry the implication, as it did for Pico della Mirandola, that a poem is in duty bound to deal with experience in terms of as many linguistic moulds as possible. But it is equally possible to believe that all the languages move towards the same point by different methods, that the language anyone speaks provides the method, the form or mould, precisely fitted for him to explore reality. This is to believe that the secret answers are concealed in the very structure of the language one uses. This is one way of understanding that 'the Word was with God, and the Word was God'; and on this showing a poem which examines only the structure of its own language by that very token examines everything else, everything there is to examine. And so when Eliot goes on in 'Burnt Norton', from talking about the poem as a form like a Chinese jar and yet as a process, a sequence of events in time, to talking of Love as 'itself unmoving' yet issuing in Desire which moves continually, he is not 'changing the subject'; he is not even making a witty or fanciful analogy (Poem as achieved form=Love; poem as process=Desire), but simply changing the one discussion into other terms and a new key.

Metaphysicians appear to have pursued the same logic. After retiring in confusion before critics who pointed out that the questions they discussed could not be asked in languages with a different structure from their own, who accused them therefore of being tricked by language into dilemmas which were merely verbal, they now take heart and ask why 'verbal' must be '*merely* verbal' and whether, if language tricks them, it does not trick them for their own good and to some purpose. Once the structure of language is taken to be the structure of reality, then merely verbal dilemmas are seen to be the most real of all dilemmas; and the hoary topics of metaphysics, having suffered a sea-change, present themselves as no less worthy of attention than they ever were. Let God be called 'Reality'; and then meta-linguists and metaphysicians alike appear to agree that 'the Word was with God, and the Word was God'.

Some French theorists have divided all men, in their dealings with language, into 'terrorists' and 'rhetoricians'. The terms when translated into English are misleading. The French mean by 'terrorist' the man who is suspicious of language, who takes it for granted that language is always trying to trap us into saying what we don't mean, that every word we use must therefore be scrutinized with a sort of baleful resentment. England in the present century has been full of 'terrorists' of this sort, and our poetry reflects the pressures they have brought to bear. It is only lately, and even so very grudgingly and fearfully, that English poets and philosophers and theorists of language have come to see the strength of the alternative position, that of the 'rhetorician' who trusts language to do his thinking for him, who casts himself trustingly into the sea of language, confident that its currents will carry him to better purpose than if he insisted on swimming against them. If we had not resisted and evaded for so long the challenge of symbolist theory and practice – particular phases of that resistance are signalized by the names of I.A. Richards and F.R. Leavis – we might not have needed to learn the hard way. Eliot to be sure is not to be herded conclusively into either camp; he seems to believe that in the act of successful composition the poet's dealings with language somehow comprehend both attitudes, both suspicious vigilance and trustful surrender. But, as compared with Pound, Eliot presents himself as pre-eminently a rhetorician, a man who serves language, who waits for language to present him with its revelations; Pound by contrast would master language, instead of serving language he would make it serve – it must serve the shining and sounding world which continually throws up new forms which language must strain itself to register. Either all the forms of reality are hidden in language and will be revealed by language if we only trust it sufficiently; or else nature is inexhaustibly prodigal of new forms, for ever outrunning language, which must be repeatedly constrained to keep in the chase.

In what remains of this essay, I shall attempt to show how the principles which operate in *Four Quartets* operate also in earlier poems by Eliot. In particular I shall try to justify my coat-trailing about two of those earlier poems: 'A Cooking Egg' and 'Mr Eliot's Sunday Morning Service'.

Reading some famous lines in which Prufrock compares the activities of a fog to the activities of a cat, sturdy common sense, whose voice, alas, is so seldom heard in Eliot-land, would protest: 'It isn't so. I am not convinced. He can talk for as long as he likes, but he doesn't persuade me that a fog behaves as a cat behaves.' Similarly, even earlier in the poem, reading, 'When the evening is spread out against the sky/Like a patient etherised upon a table', common sense will retort, once again and quite simply, 'I don't believe it.' Instead of the voice of common sense, the voice of the critic (in this case F.O. Matthiessen) protests that the comparison of the evening with the etherized patient is 'too intellectually manipulated, not sufficiently felt'.[5] And this is the very reverse of the truth. For common sense is right: the comparison has no substance at all for intellection to worry out of it, no justification at all in terms of logic and/or sense-perception. To the normal mind, fogs and cats, evening skies and operating-tables have nothing in common whatever. And this is just the point of these comparisons; it is precisely because to a normal mind they are absurd, that we are led or forced to conceive of the abnormal mind, or the abnormal state of mind, to which these comparisons are not absurd but exact. The truth is the opposite of what Matthiessen says: if the comparison has any validity at all, it is in terms of feeling – of the feeling of the observer, projected so intensely upon these disparate objects as to deceive him into thinking them similar; the comparison has no 'intellectual' substance whatever.

The moral is so obvious that I blush to draw it. On all sides we have been told, and are still told, that in Eliot's early poetry the influences of French Symbolists and of English 'metaphysicals' intersect. The case of F.O. Matthiessen shows that if the two traditions *do* intersect, if they *can* intersect (and Rosemond Tuve will tell us that they can't), the point of intersection is easy to mistake. A reader who comes to Prufrock from Webster and Donne, will, like Matthiessen, read these comparisons as if they were conceits, and the poem will fall to pieces in his hands before he has got through the first three lines of it.

When Donne compares lovers with compasses he presents two images (that is to say, two human experiences – of love and of mathematics) which are normally regarded as belonging to widely different kinds or orders of human experience as a whole. We may say, then, that to begin with there is a wide gap between them. And the poem exerts itself to close this gap. But when Eliot compares a fog with a cat, or an evening sky with an etherized patient, the object of the exercise, for him, is to leave the gap wide open. Only in this way can he incite the reader to close the gap for himself, by deducing from the two terms given the third term which is missing, the state of mind of the observer, Prufrock, who

5   F.O. Matthiessen, *The Achievement of T.S. Eliot* (London: Oxford University Press, 1935), p. 29.

sees a similarity where none exists.[6] The poetry isn't a riddle: why are fogs like cats? It is a puzzle: puzzle – find Prufrock. There is left between the images a gap which the reader has to fill for himself; sometimes the gap, the meaningful silence of Mallarmé, exists as a space of blank white paper on the printed page, whereas in the cases we are considering the gap is papered over by what looks like normal syntax. But of course it isn't normal syntax, but the symbolist syntax which is working upon us in ways which have nothing to do with the perception of logical patterns.

This is the view of symbolist procedure which was expressed by one critic when he said that in poems in the symbolist tradition 'images or symbols are ranged about, and the meaning flowers out of the space between them'. But as it turns out this formulation does not get us very far, for it seems to leave the reader free to fill in the gaps with whatever materials he pleases, according to whatever may be the idiosyncratic bent of his own interests. This emerged very clearly from a discussion a few years ago of Eliot's poem, 'A Cooking Egg', from his second collection, *Poems* (1920). This rather trivial poem does not deserve all the attention that has been lavished on it; and indeed in most ways Eliot's second collection as a whole cannot measure up to the first. (This is true, I think, even of the most ambitious poem, which stands first in the collection, the famous 'Gerontion'; for Eliot seems to identify himself with this *persona*, unwittingly, far more than he did with Prufrock.) But this only means that 'A Cooking Egg' perhaps deserves nothing much better than the fate which has come upon it – to be the occasion of a sustained critical wrangle. The discussion will be found in the quarterly *Essays in Criticism* for July 1953 and January 1954. The spectacle it affords, of several distinguished critics falling out about what the poem means, is instructive and rather shocking, and unfortunately, at the time, it gave a handle to the philistines to pluck up heart and exult, 'I told you so; it's nothing but gibberish.' However the discussion was not so pointless as has been made out. Real progress had been made when at the end of it I.A. Richards could ask, 'perhaps it is a current conception of interpretation which is out of focus, at least for such a poem?'[7]

However, the most instructive contribution was F.W. Bateson's. For he began by quoting the formulation already offered – 'Images or symbols are ranged about, and the meaning flowers out of the space between them.'[8] But the problem then became, for Mr Bateson, how the reader was to supply the links which the poet had left out; and he supplied them

---

6   It is true, of course, that if the reading of Eliot has been distorted by a gravitational pull in the reader's mind towards Donne, the reading of Donne has been distorted by the presence of Eliot. We are asked to read Donne's poems as if the interest in them were the mind we deduce from them.

7   '"A Cooking Egg": Final Scramble', *Essays in Criticism*, 4.1 (January 1954), p. 104.

8   ibid., p. 106.

by making up a story about a love-affair between Pipit, the central figure in the poem, and the narrator. That is to say, he treated the poem not after all as a symbolist poem or a poem in the symbolist tradition, but as if it were a narrative with every other chapter left out. The critics found themselves solemnly debating whether Pipit was a little girl or a grown-up or (agreeable lunacy!) perhaps the poet's nannie. And they posed each other such unanswerable conundrums as: did the narrator when he was an undergraduate buy for his old nannie, *Views of Oxford Colleges*? This, of course, is a question on a par with 'How many children had Lady Macbeth?' – and even less relevant to Eliot's poem than the question of the children is to Shakespeare's. The whole procedure is ludicrous. For what spaces are left in the poem, for meanings to flower in, when Mr Bateson has busily paved the whole area with fictions of his own devising? The poet leaves spaces, and he wants them left. If the riddles could be solved, why didn't the poet solve them, for himself and for us? A range of possible answers can be found, and a vast range of other answers can be ruled out as impossible. But if there were one clear and conclusive answer, one key which, when found, broke the poet's code, the whole poetic procedure would lose its justification and its point. It's just here, in fact, that we make room for what at first may look like the most disreputable feature of symbolist poetic theory – the value it places upon a deliberate vagueness, and upon the suggestive hint rather than the plain statement. What it amounts to, on this showing, is the never treating any issue as entirely closed.

We narrow the range of possible answers, and close the gap so far as is proper, not by constructing impressive fictions of our own, but by attending to the developing shape of the whole poem, and above all by noticing in particular the tone of voice where it leaves off before the gap and where it picks up again afterwards. In 'A Cooking Egg' tone is determined above all by rhyme and by verse-movement:

> Pipit sate upright in her chair
>   Some distance from where I was sitting;
> *Views of Oxford Colleges*
>   Lay on the table, with the knitting.

The silly archaism 'sate', and the rhyme on 'sitting'/'knitting' (worthy of Mr Cyril Fletcher) define the tone as detached and a trifle sourly amused and rule out at once the shame and disgust that some of the contributors to *Essays in Criticism* wanted to impart to the lines. Similarly,

> I shall not want Honour in Heaven
>   For I shall meet Sir Philip Sidney
> And have talk with Coriolanus
>   And other heroes of that kidney.

I shall not want Capital in Heaven
    For I shall meet Sir Alfred Mond.
We two shall lie together, lapt
    In a five per cent Exchequer Bond.

It is the fatuous rhyme of 'Sidney' with 'kidney', and of 'Mond' with
'Bond', together with the very heterogeneity of the proper names, which
makes it certain that the unspoken refrain in the space between these
stanzas is something of the nature of ('I shall meet Sir Philip Sidney') 'Like
Hell I shall', or else (the poet's voice placing perhaps the anonymous
speaker), 'Like Hell you will'.

The poem is in three sections marked off by rows of dots, and I.A.
Richards, who alone among the contributors to the discussion was sensitive to tone, rightly perceived that verse-movement dictates a wholly
new tone in the last section:

But where is the penny world I bought
    To eat with Pipit behind the screen?
The red-eyed scavengers are creeping
    From Kentish Town and Golder's Green;

Where are the eagles and the trumpets?

    Buried beneath some snow-deep Alps.
Over buttered scones and crumpets
    Weeping, weeping multitudes
Droop in a hundred A.B.C.'s.

In the first quatrain, as the verse-movement changes, the tone becomes,
for the first and last time, serious and engaged. A real loss is being really
lamented. And this holds over to the line printed by itself. The trumpet
echoes through the blank space which follows like the horn of Roland
carrying from Roncesvaux the last signal of a noble order doomed. But a
trumpet after all is not a horn (the horn sounding through the forest –
stock image of European romance) and if we have forgotten – as up to
this point we are meant to do, meant to make fools of ourselves – that a
trumpet is brassy at best and may be a child's toy, we are made unavoidably aware of it, and of our own stoop to self-indulgent folly, with the
conclusively deflating rhyme, 'crumpets'. This changes the tone again, so
that when we look back at the space after 'the eagles and the trumpets', a
space so lately brimming with our own romantic melancholia, we now
hear a voice saying mockingly into the silence, 'It's a shame, so it is.' In
fact, that whole line about the eagles and the trumpets forces home the
recognition that every word and every poetic line has two contexts, what
leads up to it and what leads away from it, and that the second context
may spring (here by a cruelly delayed-action mechanism) a trap laid for us

by the first. This is language as music, exploiting to the full, as music does, the lapse of time in which it has its being and its operation.

Yet it's essential to realize, even as we begin to recognize how nicely in these ways the range of possible readings can be narrowed, that the range is never narrowed so far as to provide only one right reading. One of the possible readings of 'A Cooking Egg' would begin by dwelling on the title. An egg once fresh now stale; hence (perhaps) a hope once entertained now abandoned. It would read out of the first two stanzas, noting their tone as defined by rhyme and archaism, English upper-class security, continuity and assurance. Oxford (if we remember the date) and Pipit (the excruciating coyness of the name) define class; 'Oxford' means English; 'grandfather and great great aunts' means continuity; sitting upright ('Pipit sate upright') means assurance, even dignity; *Invitation to the Dance* means sentimental philistinism in the arts. And so much for the first section. The middle section shows (through a speaker who either mocks himself or is mocked from the wings by the poet) a ruling class no longer assured of its right to various good things, no longer assured that its own monumental figures (Sir Alfred Mond, Madame Blavatsky) are equal to the great figures of other cultures, like Sidney, the Borgias or Coriolanus; or else, in so far as the class does retain this assurance, its claims are laughed out of court. We may permit ourselves the self-righteous reflection that, in so far as this assurance was insufferable complacency, it is good to see it go. But, says the last section in effect, the loss of security is another matter from the loss of assurance, a real loss and one which may be mourned – which may be mourned, but only a little; for, try to inflate it to a tragedy, and the rhyme on 'crumpets' brings out all the brassiness of the trumpet and the inadequacy of the occasion for the tears being spilled about it. This reading of the poem may seem all the more plausible if we remember that the author was at this time in close alliance with Ezra Pound, another American poet who at just this time was writing a similar mocking threnody on the British imperial twilight, in his *Homage to Sextus Propertius*.

At the bottom of the symbolist method, it has been said, is the discovery that words may have meanings though they have no referents. And most of the misreadings of Eliot derive from a failure, less frequently from a refusal, to recognize this fact about the way language works: 'But where is the penny world I bought/To eat with Pipit behind the screen?' The mind that thinks that looking for a word's meaning is looking for its referent will ask: What is a 'penny world'? And gravely observing that worlds cannot be eaten, it decides that 'penny world' cannot mean what it says, and that 'world' must be a fanciful way of referring to something else, something that is edible, perhaps a bun. 'Penny world' thus revised to become 'penny bun', it asks what sort of a person penny buns may be eaten with, and so comes up with the answer that Pipit must be a nursery playmate, or else a nannie. Its next question is: In what conditions are penny buns eaten, with or without dear little girls or dear old nannies, *behind a screen*? And with that little poser before him, this dogged reader may be abandoned. For enough has been said to show that in symbolist poetry a word always means what it says — always, because what it says is always only itself. 'Art is as realistic as activity and as symbolic as fact,' declared Pasternak. In the world of symbolist poetry worlds can be bought for a penny, and they can be eaten. 'Penny' and 'world' are verbal events occurring rapidly one after the other, the cheapness and littleness of 'penny' crammed up against the vastness of 'world'. The penny, the world, the eating, and the screen are here brought into an arrangement which need not correspond to any possible or likely arrangement of these items in the life which we observe about us. This arrangement of them is possible in language and therefore in the mind of the speaker and thereafter, if the poem is successful, in the mind of the reader. The penny and the world and the screen are in just the same case as the fog and the cat, or the evening sky and the etherized patient, in 'Prufrock'. In every case what seems to be asserted is a relationship between items which is impossible or highly unlikely in the world we observe; and in every case, as a result, we have to realize that the items are arranged thus, not in the world observed but in the mind of the observer. For of course there are dreams and other mental phenomena to tell us that the laws of space and time, which operate outside the mind, do not obtain inside it.

In a brilliant and momentous essay, H.M. McLuhan has traced, over the past two centuries of poetic effort, the logic which led the poets to this startling discovery, that they had been observing, in the stories and pictures they created, laws of temporal and spatial arrangement which in fact did not bear upon their activities at all. In this article, called 'Tennyson and Picturesque Poetry', McLuhan credits James Thomson, author of *The Seasons*, with the original discovery: that there could be maintained in poetry a constant relationship between external events or appearances described, and the state of the mind which first observed and then described them. Thomson is described in the Literary Histories as the poet who first made description of 'nature' (i.e. for the most part, of landscape and weather) self-sufficient matter for poems. It seems an unexciting, a dubiously useful innovation. Thomson is a much more startling innovator if, as McLuhan suggests, what he discovered was not verse-description as such, but verse-description of such a kind that, in offering and seeming to describe the landscape and weather of the observable world, it described equally the landscape of the observer's mind, the weather in the observer's soul. Whether this claim for Thomson can be allowed, is not here the question; in any case it must be allowed that the discovery was repeatedly made, if not originally by Thomson, certainly by his successors in this mode, Cowper, Wordsworth occasionally, Keats and Tennyson certainly. Who can doubt – who has ever doubted – that Keats's 'Ode to Autumn', offering to describe a season of the year, describes at least equally a season in the spiritual life of the poet, a landscape or climate of the human mind? By Keats's time, the psychological fact of this possible correspondence between inner and outer was already almost a commonplace, and built into the poetic theories of, for instance, William Hazlitt and Arthur Hallam. Are we saying, then, that the 'Ode to Autumn' is already a symbolist poem? Not at all. For Keats and Tennyson are still, like Wordsworth, Cowper and Thomson before them, dependent upon nature to present them with the landscape and the weather that will, because they correspond to a state of mind, permit them to express that state. The symbolist poet, on the other hand, has realized that he can do better than wait patiently upon nature until she provides what he wants. Knowing the state of mind he wants to express, he can construct the landscape he wants, so as to make it correspond. And with that recognition comes another: being thus free of nature's caprice, the poet when he creates a landscape is under no obligation to make it observe all the laws which govern nature's landscapes. In Mr McLuhan's words:

> The romantic and picturesque artists had to take advantage of accidents. After Baudelaire there is no need for such accidents. The picturesque artists saw the wider range of experience that could be managed by discontinuity and planned irregularity, but they kept to the picturelike single perspective. The interior landscape, however, moves naturally towards the principle of multiple perspectives as in the first two lines of *The Waste Land* where the Christian Chaucer, Sir James Frazer and Jessie Weston are simultaneously present. This is 'cubist perspective' which renders, at once, a diversity of views with the spectator always in the centre of the picture, whereas in picturesque art the spectator is always outside. The cubist perspective of interior landscape typically permits an immediacy, a variety and solidity of experience denied to the picturesque and to Tennyson.[9]

The change, I suspect, was hardly such sheer gain all round as Mr McLuhan suggests; the intent and patient waiting upon nature which is the constant discipline of a Coleridge, a Ruskin, a Turner or a Hopkins (and I would add, a Pound) – this may induce a religious apprehension of the spiritual in nature, which it is not worth losing just for the sake of a more streamlined poetic method. Nevertheless, McLuhan sufficiently explains the fatuity of asking, about those lines in 'A Cooking Egg': When, in what sort of room, under what circumstances, does one eat behind a screen? To attempt to visualize the scene like this is as woefully

---

9   *Essays in Criticism*, 1.3 (July 1951), pp. 281–2. [H.M. McLuhan is now more widely remembered as Marshall McLuhan, the commentator on mass media. (Ed)]

wide of the mark as to object to Picasso that he disregards the laws of perspective as conceived by Raphael. Yet this is a not uncommon way of misreading Eliot: having taken from *Essays in Criticism* one example of how–not–to–do–it, I will go there for another, Ernest Schanzer's reading of the poem called 'Mr Eliot's Sunday Morning Service'.

Another exegesis would be tedious. 'The poem's setting,' Mr Schanzer begins, 'is indicated by its title,' and in this setting the narrative (which, like Mr Bateson, Mr Schanzer assumes to exist, waiting for him to recon-struct it) 'is supplied by the wandering eye and mind of Mr Eliot.'[10] If, because of the title, we are led to imagine the speaker at a church-service such as we know from observation, we shall start wondering, as early as stanza three, what sort of church Mr Eliot can attend that has an Umbrian easel-painting inside it. Mr Schanzer becomes indignant when the last stanza presents Sweeney in his bath. For even his imagination cannot accommodate in his mental image of Eliot's church an Umbrian easel-painting and an inhabited bathtub. It is hard not to sympathize: Mr Schanzer wants to know if he is in a church or in a bathroom, and all we can tell him is that he is in a poem. The structure of the poem is neither pictorial nor narrative, though Mr Schanzer assumes it is both; it is sustained on the two axes of reference presented in the epigraph ('Look, look, master, here comes two religious caterpillars') by the last phrase, 'religious caterpillars'. The caterpillars announce the flies of the first stanza, and the bees of the sixth, while 'religious' looks forward to the church fathers of stanza two, to the Umbrian painting, and the presbyters. Throughout, these two sets of images interact, particularly in terms of sexual fertility, sometimes very plainly as in 'epicene' (stanza seven), sometimes subtly as in the half-echo, 'pustular'/'pistillate'; but the inter-action is not at all so reducible to the one right and clear reading as would be 'the satiric focus' which Mr Schanzer asks for and thinks he half finds. One begins to misread the poem in Mr Schanzer's way, as soon as one assumes, for instance, that the window-panes of the third line are window-panes which Mr Eliot can see from his pew. In these poems the images are ranged about not according to the laws of space nor (in the case of narrative images, actions and events) according to the laws of time, but simply as they are ranged about in the poet's head.

The plain directive to the reader was given once and for all in the poem which stands first in the *Collected Poems*: 'It is impossible to say just what I mean!/But as if a magic lantern threw the nerves in patterns on a screen.' The magic lantern is somewhere at the back of the poet's skull. Throwing its beams forward through the meshes of the poet's sensibility, it illumines at last the world which faces him; but he is interested, and his readers should be interested, not in that world itself at all, but only in that

10 *Essays in Criticism*, 5.2 (April 1955), p. 153.

world as a screen, on to which are projected 'the nerves in patterns', that is to say, the shape and character of the observer's sensibility.

Postscript: This essay, I am aware, is not easy reading. And I sympathize with the reader who should protest that the reading of poetry ought not to be such a strenuous activity. One way of answering him is to say that, however it may be with other poetry, with T.S. Eliot's the challenge thrown down is indeed as exacting as I make it seem. But a better answer is that this essay presents a model not of 'how to read', but rather (a very different matter) of how to understand what happens to us *as* we read.

Eliot in Perspective, ed. Graham Martin (London: Macmillan, 1970); reprinted with postscript in *The Poet in the Imaginary Museum*.

XI T.S. Eliot – 1928

'Peut-être qu'une fois de plus la couronne d'or nous serait présentée comme elle le fut à César.'

(Maurras, *L'avenir de l'intelligence*)

L'avenir de l'intelligence
Was where? Was in whose head? Jefferson's?
Has Calvin Coolidge heard of it? We go back
To the second President, his term aborted,
President Adams whom the young Republic
Put out of office when he would have taught
Uses for emulation. It is Spring.
Beyond the Mississippi the snow melts
At last, and at the edges of small towns
As the chill sun westers in the silence, streets
Are streets of lake-pavilions, where the shadows
In the long yards are water or else like water.

And that would have been the time for it, before
The open door and the squalid openings westward
Postponed, dissolved, and obviated. Spring!
When the Atlantic states were all the states,
Their Cincinnatus, Washington. When Adams
Writes of the laticlave, angusticlave
And praetext; and the chairs of ivory;
Also the civil and the mural crowns
Of gold; of ivory; of flowers; of
Herbs; of laurel branches; and of oak leaves,
Adams and Washington are the names of streets
Where one rides by, his eyes indifferent, watchful...
'He that has power to hurt and will do none.'

John Adams quoted Shakespeare, and that's much.
One gropes to a theory of the potentate
As cynosure. The dog's tail wags the dog
'Whose worth's unknown although his height be taken.'

Was ever better use made of the passion
For consideration than the Romans made?
Adams asked, thinking of stone and bronze.
Consideration (or to be of note)
Is it a passion? Adams said it was,
And universal. Not in England. There
To be distinguished is a kind of horror
For the many whose strength is union.

And whose hand shot McKinley? If the realm
Is all a spectacle, the North Star even
(Called 'cynosure', that's 'dog's tail', in the Greek),
Assassin is a civic dignity.

Columbian Minerva! See the purchased
Scholars and wits of the Old World perform
Gladiatorial for your famished young!
In a Republic no one knows his place.

Encounter, 26.2 (February 1966).

XII Yeats, The Master of a Trade

On 21 April 1930, Robert Bridges, the Poet Laureate, died. On 7 May, Yeats wrote a letter of condolence to Mrs Bridges. This is what he wrote:

> Dear Mrs Bridges, May I, despite the slightness of our acquaintance, tell you how much I feel your great loss. I think I remember your husband most clearly as I saw him at some great house near you where there were some Servian delegates. He came through the undistinguished crowd, an image of mental and physical perfection, and one of the Servians turned to me in obvious excitement to ask his name. He has always seemed the only poet, whose influence has always heightened and purified the art of others, and all who write with deliberation are his debtors.
>
> My wife joins with me in sending you our sympathy.
>
> Yours, W B YEATS [1]

It's entirely characteristic that, wanting to pay a tribute to a man he had known, Yeats should dwell upon his physical presence as something arresting or commanding in itself. For Yeats this was a matter of principle; it shows him trusting the image just as fearlessly outside the world of poetry as inside that world. This way of standing by the image through thick and thin is one of the most striking things about Yeats, and it's something that has been noticed time and again. But there's something else in the letter which is just as characteristic, though this is noticed much less often – I mean, the sentence: 'He has always seemed the only poet, whose influence has always heightened and purified the art of others, and all who write with deliberation are his debtors.' I can conceive that to someone who is not a poet or not a practising artist or craftsman of some sort, it may appear that, in saying this about Robert Bridges, Yeats is not saying very much. He's saying that Bridges was never anything but a good influence on other poets. And 'influence', we may think, is something that interests critics and commentators but doesn't interest or concern the poet himself. And so we might even suppose that Yeats is 'damning with faint praise', tactfully getting round the difficulty that he doesn't think much of Bridges's poetry in itself, by

1 *The Letters of W.B. Yeats*, ed. Allan Wade (London: Rupert Hart-Davis, 1954), pp. 774–5.

saying that all the same it was always a good influence on others. But I'm sure that this isn't at all what Yeats intended; he meant this as very high praise of Bridges indeed, almost the noblest tribute that one poet can pay to another.

For if there are indeed some kinds of 'influence' that excite commentators very much and poets hardly at all, there are other sorts of influence by which a poet sets much greater store than any of the critics do. And this sort is one that Yeats points to when he appeals to 'all who write *with deliberation*'. It's the sort of influence which we describe (not very happily) as *technical* influence; a matter of quite cold-blooded 'know-how', having to do with tricks of the trade and rules of thumb – such as a note on how it's usually better to rhyme verb with noun than verb with verb. This is the sort of practical tip which a poet has in mind when he talks about 'influence', and this is what Yeats means when he talks about the influence of Bridges. 'Tricks of the trade' – that's what I said. And in fact 'trade' is the word that Yeats uses himself: 'Irish poets, learn your trade,/Sing whatever is well made…' Or if it isn't trade, it's craft:

> All things can tempt me from this craft of verse:
> One time it was a woman's face, or worse –
> The seeming needs of my fool-driven land;
> Now nothing but comes readier to the hand
> Than this accustomed toil.

'Accustomed toil' – there the point is even clearer. Yeats gave himself all sorts of airs, claimed special privileges and access to special sources of wisdom – and all in the name of poetry; but equally, whenever he speaks narrowly of the act of composition, he talks of it in terms which are quite disconcertingly matter-of-fact, as a skill or a body of skills to be learned and practised, to be learned *through* practice, except (and here we come back to 'influence') – except for such skills as can be learned through following good models, inherited as it were from accomplished masters, from masters such as Bridges.

Yeats, in a word, was very thoroughly and completely a *professional* poet. And it's because of this that we know he intended his tribute in the letter about Bridges to be a very noble tribute indeed. He must have hoped that such a tribute might be paid to him after he too was dead. And so I ask if the tribute that Yeats paid Robert Bridges thirty years ago can now be paid to Yeats himself.

At first blush, it may seem that the question has only to be asked, to be answered with a resounding affirmative. Yeats, surely, is a much greater poet than Robert Bridges; and so it must follow that poets of today have far more to learn from him, that he is a far more accomplished master for them to follow. But in fact an artistic tradition doesn't work in this way, not at all. The greatest poets are hardly ever the best models to follow, the best influences on those who come after them. The tradition – the tradition in the sense of a body of transferable skills, of heritable 'know-how' – is carried far more by poets of the second rank than by the first rank. And a very little thought will show how this must be so. For it's precisely a sign of the greatest talents, that they can take risks which would be suicidal for the less abundantly gifted. This is one of the reasons for keeping, to describe such really great talents, the now unfashionable term, 'genius'. The genius is almost by definition the man who breaks the rules, the man who can get away with murder. And so, obviously, to try to follow such a model is disastrous. Even in the unlikely case that you, as a beginning poet, are yourself as great a genius as John Milton, you will still be asking for trouble in modelling yourself on Milton; because your genius, though equal to his, will be different – you will break as many rules, but they will need to be different rules. For this is the second thing about genius – that it is (not quite always, but very nearly) above all *distinctive*. What the great genius does is to twist the language to suit what he is and what he has to say. To adopt his style is to have to adopt his personality and his standpoint; and the greater he is, the more likely it is that his personality will be idiosyncratic, his standpoint highly individual. This must be so, just because the personality and the standpoint which emerge from his style are so indelibly, so magnificently *his*, and no one else's. What one wants as a model is almost the exact opposite of this – the sort of poet (so much more precious to other poets than to anyone else) whose personality is expunged almost completely from what he writes, so that one has the peculiarly winning and rare effect of the language speaking through the poet as medium, not the other way round. This effect of anonymity, an extreme of impersonality in poetry, *can* be associated with truly great poets (Ben Jonson, I would say, is the unique example of this in English), but this is a very rare occurrence; it's much more common to find this, or something like it, in poets of the second rank such as Bridges. And it's from poets like these that one can learn to use the language poetically without at the same time having to adopt a false personality and a foreign standpoint. It's for these reasons (and many others like them) that there is nothing in the least paradoxical about saying that the worst disaster which befell English verse drama was Shakespeare, the worst disaster which befell the English epic was Milton.

And so you have anticipated, of course, the point which I must make: no, we *cannot* say of Yeats, what Yeats said of Bridges, that his influence 'has always heightened and purified the art of others'. We cannot say this of Yeats precisely because Yeats was a greater poet than Bridges; because Yeats was a genius, whereas Bridges wasn't.

I have laboured this point a little because in England at any rate (much more, I think, than in Ireland or the United States), there is a very general reluctance to face up to this fact about Yeats; there is a general assumption that with Yeats we can both have our cake and eat it, can declare him a great poet and yet a 'central' poet, a highly individual voice and yet a model to be generally followed. We have him proposed to us as exemplary because he expresses a twentieth-century sensibility as faithfully as his great contemporary, T.S. Eliot, yet without having to throw over as many of the traditional skills as Eliot did. What we are asked to believe in fact is that Yeats is like Ben Jonson, one of those very rare great poets whose influence is in no way vitiated by the very fact of their greatness. I do not believe this. And to justify my not believing it, I need only point to any one of the very numerous poems I seem to come across, in which it is all too clear that the authors have lately been reading Yeats. These are poems in which the master's voice quite drowns out the pupil's. I don't want to inflict poor poetry upon you, and so I'm not including any poem like this. Anyone who reads the current magazines, anthologies and slim collections will have come across such poems for himself; they are very common, and indeed you will find the reviewers noting them.

But in any case, it would surely be very strange if Yeats *were* a poet like Ben Jonson, in this respect. It would be very strange if an Irish poet, a poet so consciously and deliberately Irish as Yeats was, should have that sort of centrality in the English tradition which some of Yeats's English admirers claim for him. I will name only one feature of Yeats's poetry which seems to me indelibly Irish; and this is its very marked *histrionic* element. Yeats was very conscious of this, and quite deliberate about it. He wrote:

> Every now and then, when something has stirred my imagination, I begin talking to myself. I speak in my own person and dramatize myself, very much as I have seen a mad old woman do upon the Dublin quays, and sometimes detect myself speaking and moving as if I were still young, or walking perhaps like an old man with fumbling steps. Occasionally, I write out what I have said in verse, and generally for no better reason than because I remember that I have written no verse for a long time.

This catches exactly what I mean by the histrionic quality of Yeats's imagination. And it may or may not be a naturally Irish way of composing poems; I am sure it is not an English way. I am not aware of any English poet who by his own account went to work in anything like this way. Certainly I cannot conceive that Ben Jonson thus dramatized himself in order to write his poems.

All the same, it is not for nothing that I keep coming back to Ben Jonson's name. For while I believe that Yeats's poetry as a whole isn't of the sort that always or often has a good influence on the art of others, yet it is true, I think, that there is one body of poetry by Yeats which comes near to this, one phase in Yeats's career when he wrote poems which *can* profitably be taken as models by other writers. And this phase of Yeats's writing life is announced when the poet invokes, specifically, Ben Jonson's name:

> *While I, from that reed-throated whisperer*
> *Who comes at need, although not now as once*
> *A clear articulation in the air,*
> *But inwardly, surmise companions*
> *Beyond the fling of the dull ass's hoof*
> *— Ben Jonson's phrase — and find when June is come*
> *At Kyle-na-no under that ancient roof*
> *A sterner conscience and a friendlier home,*
> *I can forgive even that wrong of wrongs,*
> *Those undreamt accidents that have made me*
> *— Seeing that Fame has perished this long while,*
> *Being but a part of ancient ceremony —*
> *Notorious, till all my priceless things*
> *Are but a post the passing dogs defile.*

These verses — the lines I've just quoted — are the tailpiece to a collection which Yeats published in 1914, called *Responsibilities*. And it's generally agreed that this collection marks an important stage in Yeats's development. In fact you still find people who believe they can pinpoint the stage at which Yeats grew from a good poet into a great one, or at least (to use their own vocabulary) the 'mature' Yeats takes over from the immature; and it's in *Responsibilities* that some of these critics claim to find this turning-point, a turning away from the use of a special literary language for poetry to the use of a common, colloquial language. For my part I believe that no such turning-points are to be found in Yeats, that on the contrary it's one of his glories to have moved so far and changed so continually, *always in an unbroken and gradual process*. All the same, *Responsibilities* does announce a sort of new departure for Yeats, and I'd like to give you my sense of this.

I'd do so by pointing not after all to the explicit invocation of Ben Jonson, not to that in the first place, but to the line, 'Being but a part of ancient ceremony'. For the next few years 'ceremony' is a word that recurs constantly in Yeats's poems. I need remind you only of 'The Second Coming':

> Things fall apart; the centre cannot hold;
> Mere anarchy is loosed upon the world,
> The blood-dimmed tide is loosed, and everywhere
> The ceremony of innocence is drowned...

'The ceremony of innocence...' And then there is the last stanza of 'A

Prayer for My Daughter', the poem which follows 'The Second Coming'
in the collection of 1921:

> And may her bridegroom bring her to a house
> Where all's accustomed, ceremonious;
> For arrogance and hatred are the wares
> Peddled in the thoroughfares.
> How but in custom and in ceremony
> Are innocence and beauty born?
> Ceremony's a name for the rich horn,
> And custom for the spreading laurel tree.

As those last lines in particular make clear, 'ceremony' is the word that
Yeats uses for what he finds most valuable, at this stage of his life, in the
aristocratic way of life. He recognized that way of life in the household of
Lady Gregory at Coole; and he envisaged himself at this time as a
specifically privileged retainer of such a noble house, the poet maintained
by the family to serve them by his poetry just as their grooms and
chambermaids served them in humbler ways. This was a relationship
between poet and patron which Ben Jonson celebrated in many of his
verse-epistles, and which he preferred to being patronized by the public
at large, just as Yeats preferred it after his disappointment with the Abbey
Theatre audiences. In fact of course, as Yeats realized, this sort of poet–
patron relationship was common all over Europe at the time of the
Renaissance, as much in the Italian city-state of Urbino as in Elizabethan
England. And Yeats at this time in his life tries to impose this Renaissance
relationship, and the valuable things in that relationship, upon the quite
different and as he thinks inferior relationship between poet and reader
which rises out of twentieth-century society.

Accordingly, it's at this time, when Yeats sees himself, not as an
isolated individual dramatizing himself and his personal predicaments, but
as a professional hired to serve a patron; when he sees himself above all as
in the lineage of Ben Jonson and the poets of Renaissance Europe – it's at
this time that Yeats strives for and sometimes attains that impersonality,
that effect of anonymity, which alone can make a poet the best sort of
model for others to follow. Consider only the last two lines of 'A Prayer
for My Daughter': 'Ceremony's a name for the rich horn,/And custom
for the spreading laurel tree.'

The images here – of the cornucopia, the horn of plenty, and the
laurel tree – are the most hackneyed images imaginable. And that is only
to say, the most traditional. These lines could have been written by any
good poet writing in any western European language at any time from
the sixteenth century to the present day. That at least is the effect that
Yeats was striving for; and I think he attains it. This *had to be* the effect.
For what the poet is saying is that 'ceremony' in the sense of time-

hallowed precedent, immemorial unwritten usage, is supremely important in life; and so he's in duty bound to conform to his own prescription, and in that part of his life which is his writing to use no devices but those which are authenticated by precedent, taken out of common stock, traditional.

And this is the first lesson which a poet of today can most profitably learn from this body of Yeats's poetry: that hackneyed, conventional images are in themselves no worse, and in fact are probably better for most purposes, than unprecedented images. The young poet can learn, in fact, that all his efforts to be above all original, distinctive, himself and no one else – all these exertions are probably wasted labour.

He can learn something else. He can notice, in this last stanza of 'A Prayer for My Daughter', how many of the words are abstract words – 'arrogance', 'hatred', 'custom', 'ceremony', 'innocence', 'beauty'. To be sure, it's no accident that this cluster of abstractions comes in the last stanza out of ten: the preceding nine stanzas have given these words the meaning that the poet can now take for granted; he's earned the right to use them. All the same the 'prentice-poet can learn from this that he almost certainly has an excessive fear of abstract words; that his efforts to be always concrete, always specific, never to state a thing but always to embody it in an image – these efforts too, like his efforts to be original at all costs, are largely superfluous.

This is related, I think, to the point about how Yeats came to use common speech in his poetry, the speech of the street-corner instead of the speech of the library. By and large this is no doubt true. And by and large it is also true that the young poet has to learn this, how there is no special language for poetry, no specially poetical words as against others that are unpoetical. But Irish speech-usage differs from British and American usage; and so British and American poets, at any rate, can model themselves in this respect more easily and surely on some of Yeats's British and American contemporaries than on Yeats himself. But there *is* one sort of speech which they can learn about from Yeats better than from any other master. This isn't the language of the streetcorner; it's the language of the political hustings and the leading article in the newspaper. Padraic Colum recalled how Yeats in his younger days used to tell young poets never to use a word that a journalist might use. But John Synge said to Colum, 'Words have a cycle; when they become too worn for the journalists the poets can use them again.' And writing in 1947 Padraic Colum could see that Synge had been right, and that Yeats's own practice proved it. For by the end of Yeats's life, as Colum rightly observed, Yeats was using to superb poetic effect the words of the journalists. The instance Colum gave was the line, 'The Roman Empire stood appalled'; and there could hardly be a better example. What shows up in this, I tend to think, is the Irish tradition of oratory. At any rate it's in Yeats's use of this range of vocabulary, in what I'm inclined to call *civic* speech, that he has most to teach a young poet about poetic diction.

And I limit myself to this aspect of poetry, its *diction*, because it's here that I think Yeats's practice is most instructive for us later poets. Fifteen or twenty years ago this would not have been true. At that time it was Yeats's use of metre which was most instructive, and if this is instructive no longer it's because the lesson has been very thoroughly learned already. For nothing is more striking about poems in English over the last twenty years than the way in which poets have turned away from 'free verse', to using again the traditional metres. In fact poets today mostly adhere to these traditional forms more strictly than Yeats did; yet there seems to be no doubt that no one has been so influential as Yeats in bringing about this most marked reversion to metre. And this is a point that I should have made earlier perhaps. Yeats has already been, for good or ill, more influential than any other poet writing in English in the present century.

'For good or ill,' I say. And this brings us back where we started. Yeats's influence has not been universally beneficial. His greatest poems – 'Sailing to Byzantium', 'The Tower', 'Among School Children' – these poems, which come later than those I've been talking about, have tended to lead later poets astray. For these are poems in which Yeats takes liberties which hardly anyone else can afford to take; this is what makes these poems glorious, it is also what makes them dangerous. It's the slightly earlier collections – above all, *The Wild Swans at Coole* and *Michael Robartes and the Dancer* – which contain the poems which are models of poetic diction. And of these at least I believe we *can* say that their influence 'has always heightened and purified the art of others'. And it's for the sake of these poems by Yeats that all of us who write with deliberation are now his debtors.

The Integrity of Yeats, ed. Denis Donoghue (Cork: Mercier Press, 1964); reprinted in *The Poet in the Imaginary Museum*.

XIII Michael Robartes and the Dancer

Michael Robartes and the Dancer is less intricately interrelated, and less powerfully made to serve a concealed unity, than some of Yeats's other collections. Indeed, a casual glance over these fifteen poems might see them as quite heterogeneous, their assembly merely fortuitous. In particular the collection might seem to fall between two stools, between on the one hand the extremely private life of man and wife in love and on the other hand the public life of politics and armed insurrection.

A second reading, however, reveals that all but two or three of the poems have one concern in common – the matter of woman's role in society. It is generally accepted that Professor Jeffares is right to identify the Queen of Sheba in the second poem of the collection 'Solomon and the Witch' with Yeats's wife;[1] and it seems clear that Mrs Yeats is likewise the woman in 'Under Saturn', 'Towards Break of Day', and 'An Image from a Past Life', as also, of course, in the tailpiece to the volume, where she is named. In 'A Prayer for My Daughter' the woman is Anne Butler Yeats, born 26 February 1919, though the poem makes mordant reference also to another woman, Maud Gonne. If George Brandon Saul[2] is right about the unsatisfactory poem, 'The Leaders of the Crowd', when he reads it as directed against the Dublin Bohemian circles frequented by Constance Gore-Booth Markievicz, then this poem joins 'On a Political Prisoner' (about Constance Markievicz in Holloway Gaol) and 'Easter 1916', where Constance Markievicz is remembered along with Pearse, MacDonagh, and MacBride. And whereas the speaker in the title-poem need not be identified, as Professor Ellmann suggests, with Iseult Gonne, there is in any case no doubt that in this poem the question how a woman best fulfils herself is discussed more explicitly than in any other. Each of these poems gains greatly from being read in the context of the others; and thus *Michael Robartes and the Dancer*, no less than other collections by Yeats, illustrates Hugh Kenner's contention that 'he was an architect, not a decorator; he didn't accumulate poems, he wrote books'.[3]

---

1   A. Norman Jeffares, *W.B. Yeats: Man and Poet* (London: Routledge and Kegan Paul, 1949), p. 207.
2   *Prolegomena to the Study of Yeats's Poems* (University of Philadelphia Press, 1957), p.119.
3   'The Sacred Book of the Arts', *Irish Writing*, 31 (1955), p. 26. (Reprinted in Kenner's *Gnomon: Essays on Contemporary Literature* (New York and Toronto: McDowell, Obolensky, 1958), pp. 9–29.)

How this works can be seen best with what may seem to be the most dubious case among those I have cited, 'Easter 1916'. This poem is clearer when read in the collection than it is when read in isolation,[4] because only in the collection does one see why the woman involved in the 1916 Rising is given pride of place over the male leaders who paid for their participation with their lives. And, to take another example, those who read 'The Second Coming' in the *Nation* for 6 November 1920, or in *The Dial* for that same month, missed a dimension of the poem which appears when it immediately precedes 'A Prayer for My Daughter'; 'a rocking cradle' in the third line from the end takes on poignancy, and witnesses to personal involvement, when taken along with 'this cradle-hood and coverlid' in the second line of the poem which succeeds it – the ominous prophecy made in 'The Second Coming' is uttered, we are made to realise, by a man whose newborn child gives him a stake in the tormented future he prophetically sees.

Apart from the five lines of 'A Meditation in Time of War', only three poems in the collection refuse to fit this scheme. These are the two ballads, 'Sixteen Dead Men' and 'The Rose Tree', and the poem 'Demon and Beast'. The ballads about the Rising obviously belong as corollaries to 'Easter 1916'. But 'Demon and Beast' is a more curious case, which deserves to be considered at some length.

'Demon and Beast' is an exception among the poems *of Michael Robartes and the Dancer*. But then, it would have been an exception in any of Yeats's collections, wherever it had appeared in his work, since it records a state of mind which the poet knows to be, for him, exceptional. 'The poem... describes how the artist is momentarily seduced by the beauty and profusion of nature into relinquishing his proper task. He is suddenly abandoned by the passions that ensured his subjectivity and his power to create; he grows objective – his mind becomes a vessel, instead of a vortex of energy, the fountain's basin instead of its abundant jet.'[5] As the terms 'subjective' and 'objective' suggest, 'Demon and Beast' can be glossed out of *A Vision* or the prolegomenon to that symbolic system *Per Amica Silentia Lunae* (1918),[6] but I agree with Peter Ure that 'in the poem the struggle is more broadly and more poetically described as a war between extreme passions, the demon of hatred and the beast of desire', both images for 'a state of intense self-absorption and subjectivity'.[7] That

4   For instance in the limited edition of twenty-five copies by Clement Shorter (1916); in *The New Statesman* for 23 October 1920; or in *The Dial* for November 1920.

5   Peter Ure, 'Yeats's "Demon and Beast"', *Irish Writing*, 31 (1955), p. 50. (Reprinted in *Yeats and Anglo-Irish Literature*, ed. C.J. Rawson (Liverpool University Press, 1974), pp. 104–13.)

6   See Cleanth Brooks, in *The Permanence of Yeats*, ed. James Hall and Martin Steinmann (New York: Macmillan, 1950), pp. 80–1.

7   Ure, *loc. cit.*, p. 47.

state – of intense self-absorption in unremitting internal conflict – was not only the state which Yeats thought natural to himself, but it was also the only state out of which, so he maintained, a severe and worthwhile art could be created. In believing this Yeats aligned himself with the visionary painters of nature, Blake's disciples Palmer and Calvert, not only against Wordsworth's 'heart/ That watches and receives', but against Ruskin and against his own friend Ezra Pound, and against any theory of poetry which holds that the poet's attention to nature may sometimes be akin to, for instance, the biologist's discipline of attentive and humble observation. The poem is thus of capital importance in defining the assumptions on which Yeats proceeded, and the challenging cost of those assumptions – more important in the perspective of Yeats's *oeuvre* as a whole than in the context of this particular collection. It is out of place in this collection, but it would have been out of place anywhere; and that, indeed, is just the point.[8]

With this exception, and the exception also of 'Sixteen Dead Men' and 'The Rose Tree', all of *Michael Robartes and the Dancer* is devoted to exhorting women above all to hate and avoid abstraction. The emphasis is by no means new in Yeats, nor, of course, peculiar to him. What is new is that Yeats, freed at last from his passion for Maud Gonne with her distracting devotion to abstractions, is now able to see woman as peculiarly responsible for escaping from 'what Blake calls mathematic form, from every abstract thing, from all that is of the brain only, from all that is not a fountain jetting from the entire hopes, memories, and sensations of the body'.[9] It is worth recalling this from *The Cutting of an Agate* (dated '1903–1915'), because the stress there laid upon 'the body' explains why the female figure is called 'the dancer'. Frank Kermode has shown that this symbolic significance investing the figure of the dancer was something that was with Yeats from the 1890s, when he shared it with Mallarmé.[10] And to the extent that the dancer of the 1890s was a female figure, with Salome as prototype, the casting of woman in this crucial role was not unprecedented in Yeats's writing. On the other hand, it is only at this point that the body of the dancer is presented in all its corporeal vigour, as much in the shamelessness which ends 'Solomon and the Witch' ('O! Solomon! let us try again'), as in:

> While Michael Angelo's Sistine roof,
> His 'Morning' and his 'Night' disclose
> How sinew that has been pulled tight,
> Or it may be loosened in repose,

8 For a brilliant exegesis of this poem (the last lines are particularly difficult because so compact), see Ure, *loc. cit.*
9 Yeats, *Essays and Introductions* (London: Macmillan, 1961), pp. 292–3.
10 *Romantic Image* (London: Routledge and Kegan Paul, 1957).

Can rule by supernatural right
Yet be but sinew.

Though Yeats had yet to visit the Sistine Chapel, he had seen
Michelangelo's 'Night' and 'Morning' in the Medici Chapel in Florence
as long ago as 1907; and yet it is only now that 'body', still opposed in the
abstract to 'mind' or 'thought' or 'spirit', takes substance in Yeats's poetry
through images taken from the great sculptor of the nude.

If at this point, however, we consult the first edition of *Michael Robartes
and the Dancer*, from the Cuala Press, we find that Yeats apparently
expected us to make much heavier weather of it.[11] At least, his Preface to
that edition suggests as much:

> A few of these poems may be difficult to understand, perhaps more
> difficult than I know. Goethe has said that the poet needs all philos-
> ophy, but that he must keep it out of his work. After the first few
> poems I came into possession of Michael Robartes' exposition of the
> *Speculum Angelorum et Hominum* of Geraldus, and in the excitement of
> arranging and editing could no more keep out philosophy than could
> Goethe himself at certain periods of his life. I have tried to make
> understanding easy by a couple of notes, which are at any rate much
> shorter than those Dante wrote on certain of his odes in the *Convito*,
> but I may not have succeeded.

This seems to refer to a different book of poems from the one we have
been reading. Philosophical? Difficult to understand? Certainly 'Demon
and Beast' is both, and so, necessarily, are the gnomic verses celled 'A
Meditation in Time of War'. But the poems to which Yeats supplies
notes are neither of these, but 'An Image from a Past Life' and 'The
Second Coming'. And as we learn to expect of Yeats's notes, these do not
'make understanding clear', but only confound it. The notes to 'The
Second Coming', for instance, speak of life as 'a double cone, the narrow
end of each cone being in the centre of the broad end of the other'; they
supply a neat diagram to illustrate this; and they explain that within the
double cone there are 'two gyres... which circle about a centre'.
Moreover,

> the circling is always narrowing or spreading, because one movement
> or the other is always the stronger. In other words, the human soul is
> always moving outward into the objective world or inward into itself;
> this movement is double because the human soul would not be
> conscious were it not suspended between contraries, the greater the
> contrast the more intense the consciousness...

11 Churchtown, Dundrum: Cuala Press, 1920.

This is familiar to any reader of A *Vision*. What is not clear is what it has to do with the poem. We draw close to the poem only later:

> This figure is true also of history, for the end of an age, which always receives the revelation of the character of the next age, is, represented by the coming of one gyre to its place of greatest expansion and of the other to that of its greatest contraction. At the present moment the life gyre is sweeping outward, unlike that before the birth of Christ which was narrowing, and has almost reached its greatest expansion. The revelation which approaches will however take its character from the contrary movement of the interior gyre. All our scientific, democratic, fact-accumulating, heterogeneous civilisation belongs to the outward gyre and prepares not the continuance of itself but the revelation as in a lightning flash, though in a flash that will not strike only in one place, and will for a time be constantly repeated, of the civilization that must slowly take its place.

This does not help us to understand 'The Second Coming'; so far from clarifying the poem before us on the page of *Michael Robartes and the Dancer*, it replaces that poem by another which is narrower, more hectoring and more idiosyncratic. There are lines from the poem –

> The best lack all conviction, while the worst
> Are full of passionate intensity...

or

> Things fall apart; the centre cannot hold;
> Mere anarchy is loosed upon the world...

which have seemed to speak memorably to the condition of men who have not consulted Yeats's note, for whom 'scientific' and 'democratic' might be hallowed words, as for the author of the note they are not. The poem swings wide enough to embrace such readers; the different poem envisaged in the note excludes them. And the writer of the poem invites such readers. For his title, 'The Second Coming', invites into the poem all those who have had access to the Christian scheme of things as it is known far outside the circle of professing Christians. On the other hand, if we follow the implications of the note even a little way, into the theory of the Dionysian great year, we realise that 'The Second Coming' is a misnomer, even a deliberate trap, since for Yeats when he wrote the poem Christ's advent was not, as it is for Christians, the first coming of the divine into the human dimension. Behind it in time lay, for instance, that advent which he was to celebrate in 'Leda and the Swan'. Thus by his title the author of the poem invites many readers whom the writer of the note is to exclude.

And unfortunately the note to the Cuala edition was not the last gloss that Yeats was to write on his own poem. In his Introduction to *The Resurrection* (*Wheels and Butterflies*, 1934), after Yeats has told how as a boy he 'took satisfaction in certain public disasters, felt a sort of ecstasy at the contemplation of ruin', he asks himself: 'Had I begun *On Baile's Strand* or not when I began to imagine, as always at my left side just out of the range of the sight, a brazen winged beast that I associated with laughing, ecstatic destruction?'[12] And he adds in a footnote: 'Afterwards described in my poem "The Second Coming".' But, of course, it is not described in 'The Second Coming', where the beast is neither winged nor brazen:

> The Second Coming! Hardly are those words out
> When a vast image out of *Spiritus Mundi*
> Troubles my sight: somewhere in sands of the desert
> A shape with lion body and the head of a man,
> A gaze blank and pitiless as the sun,
> Is moving its slow thighs, while all about it
> Reel shadows of the indignant desert birds.

It may be that we are refusing to read the poem which Yeats intended to write; but we can do no less, for the intention was never fulfilled. And if we follow the introduction to *The Resurrection* any farther, we find ourselves blurring this memorable and masterly poem into unsatisfactory Nietzschean plays of Yeats's youth, where a brazen beast is also seen in vision.[13]

The two 'technical' terms in 'The Second Coming' – 'gyre' and '*Spiritus Mundi*' – ought not to obscure the fact that the poem, as it stands in *Michael Robartes and the Dancer*, is self-explanatory. Poetically, all the meaning of the poem is in the calculated collision in the last line of the words 'slouches' and 'Bethlehem': 'Slouches towards Bethlehem to be born.' What the poem says is that when the superhuman invades the human realm all that the human can say of it is that it is non-human: there can be no discriminating at such a time between subhuman and superhuman, between bestial and divine. Whatever further gloss the poem may need can best be supplied by the poem which immediately follows it, 'A Prayer for My Daughter', which takes up from 'The Second Coming' not just 'cradle' but also 'ceremony', also 'innocence'. From a human point of view a time-scale of solar years can never be so affecting as a scale of decades, and those readers were surely not wrong who found the poem piercingly relevant between 1939 and 1945.

Yeats was not only the man who wrote the poems; he was also, unfortunately, the first and by no means the most intelligent of those who have

12 *Explorations* (London; Macmillan, 1962), p. 393.
13 See Giorgio Melchiori, *The Whole Mystery of Art* (London: Routledge and Kegan Paul, 1960), pp. 35–43.

attempted to explain them. This appears again with 'An Image from a Past Life', for Yeats's note to this poem does even more damage than his note to 'The Second Coming', and we resent it less only because there is less in the poem to be damaged:

> When I wrote 'An Image from a Past Life', I had merely begun my study of the various papers upon the subject, but I do not think I misstated Robartes' thought in permitting the woman and not the man to see the Over Shadower or Ideal Form, whichever it was.

One would like to believe that the whole business about the fictitious Michael Robartes, and his fictitious researches, is nothing more than an elaborate spoof. But although at times Yeats's tongue is undoubtedly in his cheek ('notes, which are at any rate much shorter than those Dante wrote'), at other times he writes in a grave tone which asks to be taken seriously. And if the long note is taken seriously, the poem cannot but collapse under the weight of it. In particular, one cannot help remembering how in a few years a poet was to express virtually the same perception as in Yeats's poem, without any fuss at all:

> O wha's the bride that cairries the bunch
> O' thistles blinterin' white?
> Her cuckold bridegroom little dreids
> What he sall ken this nicht.
>
> For closer than gudeman can come
> And closer to'r than hersel',
> Wha didna need her maidenheid
> Has wrocht his purpose fell.
>
> O wha's been here afore me, lass,
> And hoo did he get in?
>   – *A man that deed or I was born*
>   *This evil thing has din.*

MacDiarmid's poem suggests that 'An Image from a Past Life' might have gone better into a folk-song or ballad-form like 'The Rose Tree',[14] which is as fine an achievement as MacDiarmid's poem, and fine in the same way, in having all personal manner purged away so as to seem an anonymous product of the folk or the city street. However, although in *The Wild Swans at Coole* Yeats had already begun casting some of his best love poems into the form of songs (see 'Solomon to Sheba' from that collection), his love poems in *Michael Robartes and the Dancer* are cast in a more stilted, less satisfactory idiom.

14 'The Rose Tree' was written, according to Richard Ellmann, on 7 April 1917. It was published in the *Nation* for 6 November 1920, and in *The Dial* in the same month.

In the Preface to the Cuala edition Yeats described himself, justly enough, as one 'who has spent much labour upon his style'. Yet in 'The Leaders of the Crowd', in 'Towards Break of Day', even in the title-poem, it is possible to see an unsatisfactory strain between the sinewy rapidity of the syntax and the vagueness of the diction. Writing to H.J.C. Grierson in 1926, Yeats was to declare:

> The over childish or over pretty or feminine element in some good Wordsworth and in much poetry up to our date comes from the lack of natural momentum in the syntax. This movement underlies almost every Elizabethan and Jacobean lyric and is far more important than simplicity of vocabulary. If Wordsworth had found it he could have carried any amount of elaborate English.[15]

Addressed as the letter is to Grierson, editor of Donne, the expression 'every Elizabethan and Jacobean lyric' must comprehend the poems of Donne. And indeed the fruit of Yeats's study of Donne can be seen many years before the letter was written, certainly as early as *Michael Robartes and the Dancer*:

> Was it the double of my dream
> The woman that by me lay
> Dreamed, or did we halve a dream
> Under the first cold gleam of day?

'Towards Break of Day' does not live up to the promise of these, its opening lines. But the suppression of the relative pronoun, 'which' or 'that', is surely learned from Donne (though Pope could have taught it no less) and, together with the artful stringing of the words across line-breaks, it reveals what Yeats calls 'natural momentum in the syntax'. There is a similar energetic rapidity at the start of 'Michael Robartes and the Dancer':

> Opinion is not worth a rush;
> In this altar-piece the knight,
> Who grips his long spear so to push
> That dragon through the fading light,
> Loved the lady; and it's plain
> The half-dead dragon was her thought,
> That every morning rose again
> And dug its claws and shrieked and fought.[16]

---

15 *The Letters of W.B. Yeats*, ed. Allan Wade (London: Hart Davis, 1954), p. 710.
16 Jeffares thought the picture described was Paris Bordone's *St George and the Dragon* in the National Gallery, Dublin; but T.R. Henn suggests also Cosimo Tura's *St George and the Dragon*, seen by Yeats in the Duomo at Ferrara in 1907.

But here the expression 'her thought' is not weighty nor sharp enough to make its impact as the syntax whirls us past it. The rural-archaic or 'Shakespearian' flavour of 'not worth a rush' prepares us to take 'was her thought' as 'was in her thought'. We read the sixth line to mean 'It was the dragon she was thinking about', and only on a second reading do we grasp the intended meaning, 'It was her thought (or rather, her thinking) that was the dragon'. Yeats declares that with natural momentum in his syntax Wordsworth could have carried any amount of elaborate English; but here 'thought' is not so much elaborate English as slack English.

However, the rapid syntax finds appropriate diction in the splendid poem, too often overlooked, 'Under Saturn':

> Do not because this day I have grown saturnine
> Imagine that lost love, inseparable from my thought
> Because I have no other youth, can make me pine;
> For how should I forget the wisdom that you brought,
> The comfort that you made? Although my wits have gone
> On a fantastic ride, my horse's flanks are spurred
> By childish memories of an old cross Pollexfen,
> And of a Middleton, whose name you never heard,
> And of a red-haired Yeats whose looks, although he died
> Before my time, seem like a vivid memory.
> You heard that labouring man who had served my people. He said
> Upon the open road, near to the Sligo quay –
> No, no, not said, but cried it out – 'You have come again,
> And surely after twenty years it was time to come.'
> I am thinking of a child's vow sworn in vain
> Never to leave that valley his fathers called their home.

The reported speech, even the characteristically Irish intonation of that speech, are accommodated so effortlessly in these lines that the reader's ear supposes it to be *vers libre*. But, in fact, there is only one line, the penultimate one, which cannot be scanned as an alexandrine;[17] and I conceive that it is the ordering energy of syntax which sustains the rhythm through a measure which is notoriously too long for English breath to manage, normally.

It is not John Donne, however, who presides over 'Prayer for My Daughter', but another writer of 'Elizabethan and Jacobean lyric', Ben Jonson. In management of syntax and indeed in diction, too, Jonson, in many of his poems, is not readily distinguishable from his great contemporary. But in one genre which they both practised, the verse-epistle,

---

17 The elisions and/or substitutions – 'mem'ries', 'lab'ring', 'you've' for 'you have', and so on – which by too scrupulous metrists are condemned as licentious in Yeats, are, in fact, decorous and proper in verse such as this which, like Donne's, is histrionic, miming impassioned speech.

Jonson can be distinguished from Donne because he is so obviously superior; and in these poems he is superior (so it has been argued) because Jonson was so much more at ease than Donne was in his relationship towards the patrons to whom verse-epistles are addressed. The poet-patron relationship had interested Yeats at least since *Responsibilities* (1914), and Ben Jonson is named in the tailpiece to that volume:

> *While I, from that reed-throated whisperer*
> *Who comes at need, although not now as once*
> *A clear articulation in the air,*
> *But inwardly, surmise companions*
> *Beyond the fling of the dull ass's hoof*
> *— Ben Jonson's phrase — and find when June is come*
> *At Kyle-na-no under that ancient roof*
> *A sterner conscience and a friendlier home,*
> *I can forgive even that wrong of wrongs,*
> *Those undreamt accidents that have made me*
> *— Seeing that Fame has perished this long while,*
> *Being but a part of ancient ceremony —*
> *Notorious, till all my priceless things*
> *Are but a post the passing dogs defile.*

In this passage it is not so much the line which names and quotes Jonson as it is the line about 'but a part of ancient ceremony', which looks forward by way of 'the ceremony of innocence' from 'The Second Coming', to 'A Prayer for My Daughter':

> And may her bridegroom bring her to a house
> Where all's accustomed, ceremonious;
> For arrogance and hatred are the wares
> Peddled in the thoroughfares.
> How but in custom and in ceremony
> Are innocence and beauty born?
> Ceremony's a name for the rich horn,
> And custom for the spreading laurel tree.

'Ceremony' is Yeats's word for what he values most in an aristocratic organisation of society, as he envisaged it on the model of his own relationship with Lady Gregory. It is part of what is implied in the elegy for Major Robert Gregory, the son of that noble house, when Gregory is called 'our Sidney', just as it is implied also in the many references to Urbino, and to Castiglione's record of the Renaissance court in such a city state. This was the relationship between poet and patron which Jonson celebrated in many of his verse-epistles, a relationship which he preferred to being patronised by the public at large, just as Yeats preferred it after his disappointments with the Abbey Theatre audiences, and with the Dublin city fathers who had tried to haggle about Hugh Lane's bequest of pictures.

In 'A Prayer for My Daughter' what stands out first as very like Jonson, and quite unlike Donne, is the treatment of classical myth:

> Helen being chosen found life flat and dull
> And later had much trouble from a fool,
> While that great Queen, that rose out of the spray,
> Being fatherless could have her way
> Yet chose a bandy-leggèd smith for man.
> It's certain that fine women eat
> A crazy salad with their meat
> Whereby the Horn of Plenty is undone.

Classical mythology has been so much naturalised, has penetrated so far from the instructed *élite* among the folk, that classical references can be homely while still exalted. 'Being fatherless', for instance, has more to do with family life in rural Ireland than on Mount Olympus. And Jonson's classical erudition worked in just this way – towards a habituation, a *complete* translation of ancient Greece and Rome. The same neo-classicism at its Jonsonian best uses 'radical' – 'radical innocence' – to link through its Latin etymology with the sustained imagery from vegetation.

But equally Jonsonian, and equally unlike Donne, is Yeats's unembarrassed use of a literary property so hackneyed as the horn of plenty. The cornucopia, the laurel tree – no images are more hackneyed. But that is only to say that none are more traditional. What Yeats achieves by them is just the effect that he attained in more modest compass and less surprisingly in 'The Rose Tree'. It is the effect of anonymity. And, in fact, no other effect would do, in a poem which celebrates above all the time-hallowed unwritten laws of social usage; the style, in other things besides imagery, is itself hallowed by usage – as it has to be, if style and content are not to pull apart. In thus demonstrating how on some occasions and for some purposes a hackneyed image is better than an 'original' image, in showing, too, how to move towards and rest among abstract words ('custom', 'ceremony', 'innocence' and 'beauty', all in the same two lines), this poem by Yeats is a standing challenge and reproach to some of the most cherished prejudices of modern poetic theory, long incorporated into pedagogy. Just for this reason, no doubt, it is often overlooked.

In *The Death of Synge* ('Extracts from a Diary Kept in 1909'), Yeats wrote:[18]

> F– is learning Gaelic. I would sooner see her in the Gaelic movement than in any Irish movement I can think of. I fear some new absorption

18 *Autobiographies* (London: Macmillan, 1955), p. 504.

in political opinion. Women, because the main event of their lives has been a giving themselves and giving birth, give all to an opinion as if it were some terrible stone doll. Men take up an opinion lightly and are easily false to it, and when faithful keep the habit of many interests. We still see the world, if we are of strong mind and body, with considerate eyes, but to women opinions become as their children or their sweethearts, and the greater their emotional capacity the more do they forget all other things. They grow cruel, as if in defence of lover or child, and all this is done for 'something other than human life'. At last the opinion is so much identified with their nature that it seems a part of their flesh becomes stone and passes out of life.

This obviously is saying what 'A Prayer for My Daughter' was to say about Maud Gonne:

> An intellectual hatred is the worst,
> So let her think opinions are accursed.
> Have I not seen the loveliest woman born
> Out of the mouth of Plenty's horn,
> Because of her opinionated mind
> Barter that horn and every good
> By quiet natures understood
> For an old bellows full of angry wind?

But it chimes also, because of the imagery of stone, with lines from 'Easter 1916':

> Too long a sacrifice
> Can make a stone of the heart.

However, it is only in *Michael Robartes and the Dancer*, where Con Markievicz takes her station among so many other women, that this chime can be heard. Moreover, the assertion is made in 'Easter 1916' altogether more hesitantly and self-doubtingly than in either 'A Prayer for My Daughter' or *The Death of Synge*. For it comes only after the stone has been much discussed and much imaged in earlier lines:

> Hearts with one purpose alone
> Through summer and winter seem
> Enchanted to a stone
> To trouble the living stream.
> The horse that comes from the road,
> The rider, the birds that range
> From cloud to tumbling cloud,
> Minute by minute they change;
> A shadow of cloud on the stream
> Changes minute by minute;

A horse-hoof slides on the brim,
And a horse plashes within it;
The long-legged moor-hens dive,
And hens to moor-cocks call;
Minute by minute they live:
The stone's in the midst of all.

And here, although it is certainly the stream that is called 'living', and is associated with the lively and life-giving activities of sexual pairing ('hens to moor-cocks call'), yet the stone troubles the stream in a way which goes beyond the literal fact that it makes the running water eddy and popple. Moreover, the stream, with its unseizable mutability, the sliding and plashing which it induces, is clearly a much less stable and certain image to set against petrifaction than is the rooted and hidden tree which is set against it in 'A Prayer for My Daughter'. And the waterfowl which haunt the stream are no more like the linnet which haunts the tree than they are like the ducks of 'Demon and Beast' which are called 'absurd' and 'portly' and 'stupid'. They are called 'happy' also; but 'Demon and Beast' makes it plain that their happiness was bought on terms that were too easy, by a lax and passive abandonment to the course of nature. At this point, in fact, 'Easter 1916' goes past the point where exegesis can track its meaning. The imagery of stone and birds, rider and horse and stream, has a multi-valency which discursive language cannot compass – and this accrues to these images simply because of the beams which fall upon this poem out of the other poems in the same collection. Because Yeats holds and keeps faith in the discursive language, for instance by the sinewiness of his syntax, as his contemporaries Eliot and Pound do not, a moment like this when perceptions pass beyond the discursive reason is poignant in his poetry as it cannot be in theirs, and we do not dream of grudging him the right to acknowledge his defeat and to retire baffled before it, as he does in the last section of the poem.

On the other hand, up to 'Hearts with one purpose alone', the poem has been, though profound, straightforward. In a letter written to Lady Gregory on 11 May 1916, which shows Yeats already at work on the poem ('I am trying to write a poem on the men executed – "terrible beauty has been born again"'), Yeats reports what Maud Gonne thought of the Easter Rising: 'Her main thought seems to be "tragic dignity has returned to Ireland".'[19] And through the first two sections of the poem this is the meaning which Yeats, too, is reading out of the event. In the refrain 'A terrible beauty is born', 'terrible' must surely point to Aristotle's definition of the tragic emotion as compounded of terror and pity; and so it strikes off against 'the casual comedy' and 'lived where motley is worn'.

19 *The Letters of W.B. Yeats*, p. 613.

It is doubtless true that in the months before the Rising the Republican army was, in fact, a joke to the Dublin clubmen. But more than accurate reportage was involved for Yeats. It is a fact of literary history that the Anglo-Irish literary tradition since the seventeenth century, up to and including Synge, had scored all its most brilliant successes in comedy, even in stage-comedy; whereas Yeats, from the days of his youthful campaigning for the National Literary Society, had hoped and worked for an Irish literature that should be, on the contrary, heroic. That hope he had abandoned in 1912. The events of 1916, which proved that Irishmen were capable of a tragic gesture, seemed to show Yeats that he had abandoned hope too soon, and in the poem he seems to reproach himself for this. Yet does he, in fact, reproach himself? Certainly there is no evidence from elsewhere that the Rising made Yeats embrace with renewed enthusiasm the hopes he had entertained for Irish national culture in his youth. The truth is that the poem is an expression of self-reproach only so far as 'Hearts with one purpose alone'. At that point Yeats's reflections on the Rising move beyond Maud Gonne's, and only at that point does Yeats ask himself if the Rising makes him revise all his scheme of values. He decides that it does not; or rather, since the pity of the subject rules out any decisions being taken, he does not decide that it does. And this is perhaps the most impressive thing about the whole poem, with the impressiveness of a human utterance rather than a fashioned artifact – that the 1916 leaders are mourned most poignantly, and the sublimity of their gesture is celebrated most memorably, not when the poet is abasing himself before them, but when he implies that, all things considered, they were, not just in politic but in human terms, probably wrong.

An Honoured Guest, ed. Denis Donoghue (London: Edward Arnold, 1965).

XIV Cypress versus Rock-Slide: An Appreciation of Canto 110

Students of *Thrones* – students, I'm afraid, rather than simple readers – have had to realise that, when they might recognize a landscape familiar from early Cantos, super-imposed upon it were features of a quite different topography, one that Pound had learned to inhabit only from more recent reading. I think of the opening lines of Canto 101, where the topography of 'the roads of France' – that landscape of Ussel and Ventadour, Chalais and Aubeterre, which has been hallowed in the poet's memory since his earliest youth – is 'spliced', as it were, with the mountainous Asian landscape described in J.F. Rock's *The Na-khi Kingdom of South-West China*.[1] In Canto 110 as a whole the same thing happens with another of the two or three sacred landscapes, that of Lake Garda; and the talismanic word which announces the Na-khi landscapes is 'juniper', just as in Canto 101.

This over-all strategy is prefigured in the very first lines of the Canto, where the practised reader can just make out the roads of France behind another relatively new topographical image, that of Torcello with its Byzantine basilica in the lagoon of Venice:

> Thy quiet house
> The crozier's curve runs in the wall,
> The harl, feather-white, as a dolphin on sea-brink

For the crozier's curve, as succeeding lines bring out, is the toppling crumble of a wave-crest; and 'the wave-pattern cut in the stone' is a phrase that more than once in earlier cantos has accompanied one of the French place-names, Excideuil.

This superposition of places is obviously of a piece with what has attracted much more attention from critics – the layering and overlayering of *times*, that structural principle in the Cantos, 'the rhyme in history'. The rhyme in geography is as frequent, and may be no less structural.

In any case it lends itself very happily and immediately to *phanopoeia*. The imagination, when it moves over geographical spaces, discovers in

---

1 Joseph F. Rock, *The Ancient Na-khi Kingdom of Southwest China*, 2 vols (Cambridge, Mass.: Harvard University Press, 1947).

memory, and then formulates and casts upon the reader's mind, *images*:

>   – wake exultant
>   in caracole
> Hast'ou seen boat's wake on sea-wall,
>   how crests it?
> What panache?
>   paw-flap, wave-tap,
>   that is gaiety…

The swing of the ridge of water, as the boat that made it veers alongside and away from the sea-wall, is no less an image, for being experienced by us kinetically (thanks to the lineation, especially) more than as a vivid 'picture'. And, sure enough, Canto 110 is one of those where phanopoeia is unusually prominent, sustained and delightful.

We need to remember, however, that the three famous categories – *phanopoeia, logopoeia, melopoeia*[2] – are not mutually exclusive; that, if the three terms stand for different ways of writing, no piece of writing that is more than a few lines long can afford not to draw upon resources of all three kinds, though doubtless in no given case will all be drawn upon equally. This opening passage of Canto 110 is a case in point. For its *structure*, in the sense of what strings it together from first to last and on to what will follow, is not in its images but in logopoeia, that 'dance among words' of which the extreme and defining manifestation is the pun. It is a pun on 'crest' which takes us to 'panache', and that catches up not just 'caracole' by way of common origin in the idiom of French chivalry, but also by etymology (*penna*, a feather) the 'harl, feather-white'.[3] 'Caracole' hangs over, to take up fifty lines later a passage about cavalry-charges, though that, when it comes, has been prepared for in another way, by allusions to *Hugh Selwyn Mauberley*. Indeed, logopoeia cedes to phanopoeia as the binding principle of this Canto, only after the most raucous and 'mechanical' of all the puns, at lines 39 to 41:

> The purifications
>   are snow, rain, artemisia,
>   also dew, oak and the juniper
>
> And in thy mind beauty, o Artemis,
>   as of mountain lakes in the dawn…[4]

---

2   The categories are Pound's. *Phanopoeia* refers to a pictorial poetry, based on images. *Melopoeia* is musical. *Logopoeia* is 'the dance of the intellect among words' – i.e. word-play. See *Literary Essays of Ezra Pound*, ed. T.S. Eliot (London: Faber, 1954), p. 25. [Ed.]

3   Or 'herl': barb or fibre of the shaft of a feather, *esp.* peacock or ostrich.

4   John of Trevisa, 1398: 'Artemisia is callyd moder of herbes and was somtyme halowed… to the goddesse that hyght Arthemis.'

As for melopoeia, the way or aspect of writing which has to do with the ordering of sounds, this is what presides over the lineation and indentation which imitate a swinging wave. But in this passage the function of melopoeia is less than structural; as we cannot fail to recognize if we remember earlier Cantos which have similarly used the 'Hast thou' or 'Hast 'ou' formula from Jonson's 'A Celebration of Charis' – for instead, Canto 47 ('Hast thou found a nest softer than cunnus'), or Canto 74 ('Hast 'ou seen the rose in the steel dust'), or pre-eminently Canto 81, where the memory of Jonson's cadence not only informs, but is the substance of, the verses of lute-music which incorporate it. Canto 110 is logopoeia leading to phanopoeia; its melopoeia, though crucial to it, is structurally subordinate.

All the same, the Jonsonian formula draws our attention, and repays it. From 'Hast 'ou seen' in line 7, to 'can you see' in line 24, is a big jump:

> can you see with eyes of coral or turquoise
>   or walk with the oak's root?

Line 21 has declared: 'The water is blue, and not turquoise.' And so, from being asked ('Hast 'ou seen boat's wake...'?) whether we have seen the natural with the delighted keenness that nature's bounty demands and deserves, we have come to be asked whether we are capable of a seeing that is not natural at all but the reverse, a way of seeing proper to the anti-nature that is Art. It is elsewhere in the *Drafts and Fragments*, in Canto 116 (p. 26 of the Faber edition)[5] that Pound acknowledges:

> And I have learned more from Jules
>   (Jules Laforgue) since then
> deeps in him

And I have no dout that Eva Hesse is right, in her *New Approaches to Ezra Pound*, to remark how 'Laforgue discovered in the Berlin aquarium those "deeps" that were to become for him "the symbol of promised Nirvana"...: the motif of nature in reverse, an immutable anti-world that he once described as the "immobile unique bliss of inorganic aggregates".'[6] Nature in reverse... If Art holds up a mirror to Nature, then of course what we see in Art's mirror is Nature reversed, her left hand mirrored as our right, her right as our left; and this is repeatedly the burden of these *Drafts and Fragments*, where for instance Mussolini's 'record' (p. 25) and Pound's own (p. 27) are both described as 'palimpsest', and where (p. 13) the presence which rises through water, associated with 'pity/*compassione*, /*Amor*'. is no longer seen, as in the *Rock-Drill* Cantos, as crystal through

---

5   Davie's bracketed references are to the first edition of Pound's *Drafts and Fragments of Cantos CX–CXVII* (London: Faber, 1970). [Ed.]

6   Eva Hesse (ed.), *New Approaches to Ezra Pound* (London: Faber, 1969), p. 29.

crystal, but as 'Gold mermaid up from black water'. The Paradiso now celebrated is no longer crystalline and radiant, but is described, with more than a touch of wryness, as 'A nice quiet paradise'. And yet the perception had been with Pound many years before, though only now does he get it into focus: his essay on 'The Hard and Soft in French Poetry' had decisively opted for Gautier against Verlaine, for a poetry that chiselled hard surfaces, drawn to images of gems and metals, and he had found himself in the same territory (though indecisively) in that very Gautieresque poem, *Hugh Selwyn Mauberley* (wherein the gemmology was explicated years ago by John Espey).[7]

Moreover Pound acknowledges the connection. For after moving from 'artemisia' to 'Artemis', and so from word-play to phanopoeia, he writes a very beautiful and beautifully controlled passage, with explicit references to *Mauberley* embedded in it:

And in thy mind beauty, O Artemis,
        as of mountain lakes in the dawn,
Foam and silk are thy fingers,
                Kuanon,
and the long suavity of her moving,
        willow and olive reflected,
Brook-water idles,
        topaz against pallor of under-leaf
The lake waves Canaletto'd
        under blue paler than heaven,
the rock-layers arc'd as with a compass,
        this rock is magnesia,
Cozzaglio, Dino Martinazzi made the road here (Gardesana)

'Brook-water' and 'topaz' are the Mauberley references, and unless one takes the force of their allusions to the English Pre-Raphaelites ('the Burne-Jones cartons') the word 'Canaletto'd' will seem a gratuitous vulgarity, instead of what it is — a crucial admission that Art distorts Nature in the course of (and by the very force of) mirroring her; merely because to mirror is to reverse.

Why else indeed does the presiding deity have to be Artemis? Daniel Pearlman's momentously helpful chapter on *The Pisan Cantos*[8] has prepared us for this in a way, by showing how and why the female goddesses, Kore, Delia (i.e. Artemis), and Maia, are throughout that sequence invoked as intercessors for the poet with the male deity of day, Helios; and how it is not until Canto 83 that their intercession works so

7   John J. Espey, *Ezra Pound's Mauberley: A Study in Composition* (London: Faber, 1955).
8   Daniel Pearlman, *The Barb of Time: On the Unity of Ezra Pound's 'Cantos'* (New York: Oxford University Press, 1969), pp. 237–92.

that the poet can reconcile himself to Helios, and can see that solar principle as other than the feared and hateful killjoy of clock and calendar.
Particularly to the point of the present argument is the moment in the
Pisan sequence, which Pearlman glosses, at which Artemis, in her manifestation as Diana of Ephesus, is invoked as the patron of metal-workers.
As Pearlman explains, however, the tension is relieved in the Pisan
sequence when Artemis is seen as another face of Aphrodite; and so one
may still wonder why in Canto 110 it is Artemis who is invoked, not
Aphrodite nor any beneficent goddess compounded of both. Yet the
answer should be plain: Canto 110, so concerned as it is with art as nature
reversed, has to have lunar landscapes, lit with a reflected light, a world of
day in reverse. The ethical implications of Artemis – for instance her
having stood ever since Canto 30 for strict justice as against Christianized
pity, her strictness redeemed into compassion only when she is merged
with Aphrodite – are for the purposes of Canto 110 largely irrelevant.
The world of the sun is forward-looking ('new with the day', we are
reminded; and then, 'Mr Rock still hopes to climb at Mount Kinabalu');
in the moon world, where all is reversed, we look backward – in memory
and in elegy, though it be the elegy only of anecdote, as when Victor
Plarr talks of Gallifet's cavalry-charge, and though the memories be of
nothing more remarkable than restaurants – 'Dieudonné, Voisin'. To an
old man what stands against the rock-slide ('Bunting and Upward
neglected') is, paradoxically, that funereal tree, the cypress; and the
entombed hero who may yet some day wake again is the moon's lover,
Endymion.

None of the irony of these reversals is lost upon the old poet, if only
because among the matters reversed is his own earlier self, its programmes
and aspirations. For after all, in Pisa and after, he had aspired to a daylight
poetry, a sunlit politics and ethics, however the Pisan ordeal may have
made him flinch and look for intercessors, *reculer pour mieux sauter*. Now,
however –

> Over water bluer than midnight
>   where the winter olive is taken
> Here are earth's breasts mirroured
>   and all Euridices,
> Laurel bark sheathing the fugitive,
>   a day's wraith unrooted?
>   Neath this altar now Endymion lies.

This is a mountain lake no longer 'in the dawn', but perhaps at night or
at night-fall. The image is distorted, as previously by Canaletto when its
blue was 'paler than heaven', so now by some other agency – its water is
'bluer than midnight'. Its mirror-images preserve and give back to us
everything we could ask for, but in reverse – its olives are winter olives,

its sunlight is moonlight, the breasts of its earth will not give suck.

And yet it has denizens of its own, Daphnes that the deathless and deathly laurels of art have preserved from the sun's ravishment, Euridices that the sunlight would wither if their poet-lovers were to draw them to the upper air. In this lunar world every Daphne is a Euridice, preserved or embalmed in art's mirror. And so 'unrooted', with its saturnine question-mark, is a magnificent stroke of wit: 'Daphne afoot in vain speed' from the sun-god (p. 20) becomes *rooted* when her prayer is heard and she changes into a laurel-tree, but of course rooting and fructification from the root belong in nature, from which the magical metamorphosis of art has rapt her; so when was she a wraith, then or now, before the transformation or after it? She is embalmed in memory's backward look, engraved there by affection, in her and her lover's 'nice quiet Paradise':

> Byzance, a tomb, an end,
>   Galla's rest, and thy quiet house at Torcello

The cost is grievous, and it is counted. And yet by the end of the Canto the bargain is struck, its terms accepted:

> Falling spiders and scorpions!
> Give light against falling poison!
> A wind of darkness hurls against forest
>   the candle flickers
>   is faint
> Lux enim –
>   versus this tempest.
> The marble form in the pine wood,
>   The shrine seen and not seen
> From the roots of sequoias

In this night-piece the saving light that is prayed for can only be moonlight. *Fiat lux.* The lunar light is not all, nor only, reflected light. Roots *can* hold and thrive under this lake-water – the roots of the sequoia, most tenacious and longest-lived of trees. And so the Canto ends on an affirmation:

>   There is power
> Awoi or Komachi,
>   the oval moon.

The names of the heroines of Noh plays ('Kakitsubata', one of the plays, contributed early in the Canto to 'Yellow iris in that river bed') ensure that what is affirmed is not just Art's tenacity, its triumph over oblivion and time, but also Art's humaneness, its compassion – as when, in 'Kayoi Komachi', the ghost of Komachi's lover says to Komachi's ghost, 'The devil in your rain was my invisible terror'; or when in 'Awoi no Uye',

Awoi, racked by jealousy, says, 'I would not be seen by the moon'. (Jealousy, with its tangle of thwarted feelings, determines Awoi's earlier appearance in the Canto, at line 90:

> That love be the cause of hate,
> > something is twisted,
> Awoi…)

Because of its confessional directness, Canto 116 will understandably attract more immediate admiration than Canto 110. But the phanopoeia of Canto 110, if it is necessarily more oblique, comprehends more of the complexities of the veteran poet's chastened attitude – self-accusing certainly, discouraged even, yet mustering still enough confidence in the necessary obliquities of art to employ them in the very discourse which questions them, counts their cost, and in the end all over again decides to trust them.

Agenda, 8.3–4 (Autumn–Winter, 1970).

XV The Adventures of a Cultural Orphan

When Ezra Pound's daughter alludes by her very title to her father's *Indiscretions*,[1] the ironies are manifold: and none of them are lost on Mary de Rachewiltz. She herself, born out of wedlock, was a scandalous indiscretion on her parents' part; and the consequences were less than disastrous for the professional career of her musician mother chiefly because those who were in the know behaved with discreet and unappealing correctness for twenty years. At the end of the war in Europe, when Pound paid for his massive indiscretions over Rome radio by being arraigned as a traitor to his country, it was taken to be all the more important, so as not to further inflame American opinion against him, that Mary and her mother should retreat even further into the shadows, unacknowledged. Thus, discreet is what she has been, perforce, throughout her life, chiefly because her father has been so much the reverse. It strikes one as a story out of the nineteenth century rather than the twentieth. And yet in the end it is some of our twentieth-century suppositions that are made to look silly. For according to our apprehensive tender-mindedness towards our children and their 'rights', this child, farmed out to foster-parents and repeatedly made to feel that her existence was an encumbrance and an embarrassment, should have grown up emotionally crippled, maladjusted and thwarted, incapable of fidelity or trust or good humour. In fact, however, the Tyrolean peasant couple who were her foster-parents were kind and wise and good; she was radiantly happy in her life with them, and is still in her memories of them; and Mary de Rachewiltz herself emerges from her own pages as exceptionally serene and strong with an emotional and domestic life of firm ties and secure satisfactions. It is a happy outcome, though the happiness has been earned and paid for, time and again, at a very high price. And it looks as if the best the child-psychologists will be able to do is regard it as the exception that proves their rule!

When in 1920 Pound, prompted by A.R. Orage, called upon his memories for the weekly instalments in *The New Age* which were subsequently collected as *Indiscretions*, he found in his personal and familial past

---

1 Mary de Rachewiltz, *Discretions* (London: Faber, 1971).

nothing to hide, therefore nothing to reveal. How to be indiscreet about what, as it disconcertingly turned out, was blamelessly respectable? His daughter, by contrast, has plenty to hide if she chooses; plenty to reveal if she can manage it without cheapness. In fact she hides very little, so far as we can judge. And yet her title is not wholly ironical: for it is in revelation, not in suppression, that she has most need of tact and good taste, of 'discretion'. She has to avoid, and does, any vulgar hint of 'the inside story', of 'now it can be told'. Because her story has cost her dear, she does not sell it cheaply to us, but supplies it for the most part obliquely and allusively, especially through allusions (neatly indexed for us) to her father's writings and the *Cantos* in particular. This makes her book different from classics or near-classics of a similar kind, such as Stanislaus Joyce's *My Brother's Keeper* or, more remotely, *The Life of George Crabbe by His Son*. And in this respect too Mary de Rachewiltz is following Pound's precedent: for the style of his *Indiscretions* alludes throughout, in distinctly unsubtle fashion, to Henry James. At times his daughter deliberately but more subtly strikes the same note, as when she tells of her foster-mother ('Mamme') bringing her as a little girl to visit her parents staying briefly in the nearest town:

> And from now on whenever the scrupulous biographer will report a concert in Budapest, a performance in Vienna, a trip to Frankfurt, Wörgl, Salzburg, it may be assumed that the journey was interrupted, for a few hours or for a few days, in Bruneck.
>
> On a balcony on the Hotel Post, the Herr and the Frau, enthroned on wicker chairs. I pastured a flock of thin caoutchouc flat-bellied geese precariously floating in a bowl of water at their feet. And I wanted to stroke the shoes dangling in front of my eyes, so smooth and shiny. '*Net!*' Mamme warned watching over me from the doorway. *Net*. I must not touch the Lord and the Lady's shoes and I must call them Tattile and Mamile.

Pound's subtitle to *Indiscretions* – *Une Revue de Deux Mondes* – shows the point of his allusions to James: he sees the story of his early life as a contribution to that typically Jamesian fable, 'the international theme'. It is the fact of the *deux mondes*, of the Old World in tiers of boxes along one side of the stage and the New World equally cognizant of the spectacle from the other side, which gives to the items of his family history a representative or symptomatic or even clinical interest such as they certainly do not have in themselves, for their own sake, nor for the most part by virtue of any raciness or pungency in the language that is found for them. Mary de Rachewiltz respects and endorses her father's sense of himself as the heir to the earliest expatriate generation of James and Berenson and others, as 'the last American living the tragedy of Europe'. Thus she writes of the Pisan Canto 81 ('Pull down thy vanity'):

And the cry of AOI is an outburst more personal than any other in the *Cantos* and expresses the stress of almost two years when he was pent up with two women who loved him, whom he loved, and who coldly hated each other. Whatever the civilized appearances, the polite behavior and the façade in front of the world, their hatred and tension had permeated the house.

> *Les larmes que j'ai créés m'inondent*
> *Tard, très tard je t'ai connue, la Tristesse,*
> I have been hard as youth sixty years.

Until then the attitude toward personal feelings had been somewhat Henry Jamesian: feelings are things other people have. One never spoke of them or showed them.

There are sides to Pound which are not accounted for in this image of decorous over-refinement. It may be felt that there is in the father a vulgar streak which the daughter has not noticed: she was wounded and bewildered, for instance, when she visited him in St Elizabeths in 1953, by his amused tolerance for the rabble-rousing roughnecks who visited him there. All the same, a Jamesian hauteur, or a fastidious unease about seeming to 'make a scene', does indeed seem a good reason why intense and confessional utterances like these (another example: *J'ai eu pitié des autres. Pas assez*) get themselves said in French. Pound chooses for the expression of intense feeling the decent obscurity, if not of a learned language, at least of a foreign one.

What we have in Eliot's and Pound's lives, more than in their writings, is the touching drama of the New World come back to experience (and not vicariously – not in Pound's case, nor in Eliot's, nor in James's before them) the agonies of the Old. Eliot and Pound acknowledged in effect that, since they had got sustenance from European springs, it devolved upon them as a duty to declare their allegiance when the European centre fell apart. When we think what it meant to make such declarations (what it meant for Pound, and what it cost him), the question whether they chose right is less significant than the fact that they chose at all. What Pound chose to invest in the Old World was nothing less than a child. (Eliot never risked so much.) In Mary de Rachewiltz's book we have that child's testimony: and it is, in the end, to the effect that she endorses the investment that her father made of her. From whatever place on the political spectrum we observe this gesture being made, it is in any case, on its own account, poignant in the extreme. Her devotion to her father is evident, and it is touching. For if she had resented him, and what he let her in for, this would have been entirely understandable. Because of him she found herself, time and again, on the wrong side. Between the wars the Pustertal, where she grew up, was Italian territory: but it was wholly Austrian in feeling, and accordingly the Italians were much disliked there

– the child, schooled by her distant parents to feel pro-Italian, and required by them to observe Fascist youth disciplines as none of her Tyrolean associates did, was impaled on divided loyalties long before the war came. When towards the end of the war she worked in a German military hospital, she found herself on the wrong side of another cultural and political divide, apprehensive lest her having thus worked for the Germans should be used to strengthen the American case against her father. Pound called his *Indiscretions* a *revue de deux mondes*: *Discretions* gives us the adventures of a cultural orphan in and out of three or four worlds, not just two. Because Mary de Rachewiltz is so clear-sighted about the successive plights that she found herself in, her loyalty to her father is the more remarkable, and the more moving. (For all that, on a second reading one notices her asking more than once why, in instance after instance, it is her father who gets the benefit of the doubt, her mother who has to take the rap.)

Pound, most pedagogical of poets, was as much of a demanding schoolmaster towards his child as the most securely established Victorian father could have been. And what he demanded, year after year, was a vocational allegiance not merely declared but acted upon. For this writer's child turned out to be herself a writer, hypersensitive towards language – as indeed she could hardly fail to be, having to master, on top of the Austrian patois she spoke with her foster-parents, first the Italian language, then the English (in which she is not quite infallible even today). It seems now, with hindsight, as if she could not have saved herself except by being a writer, an artist in language. At any rate, what the expatriate American father demanded of his Austro-Italian daughter was, in whatever circumstances and at whatever cost, the literary conscience – exact fidelity in language to the recognizable contours and spatial dispositions of the physical world, due allowance made for the emotional disposition or compulsions of herself as disciplined but also involved spectator. It is a requirement that few fathers of our day, brow-beaten as we have been and morally blackmailed with the guilt of having conceived any son or daughter whatever, will dare to enunciate, let alone to enforce. So much the worse for us; for our sons and our daughters! What Mary de Rachewiltz made of the cruel assignment is enough to make her father not just satisfied but proud. Not for nothing did he insist that she learn, at one and the same time (and out of the same text, Hardy's *Under the Greenwood Tree*), both the English language and the principles of imagistically scrupulous writing in that language. The pay-off is here, in this book. It is a unique witness, as beautiful as it is brave.

The Listener, 23 December 1971; reprinted in *The Poet in the Imaginary Museum*.

XVI The Universe of Ezra Pound

Hugh Kenner makes the point that discussion and explanation of *The Waste Land* and of *Ulysses* began as soon as each work was published, and has been continuous ever since, whereas this is not at all the case with the *Cantos*. As he says, 'Not until the 1950s, when controversy over *The Pisan Cantos* had made the topic urgent did serious discussion commence, and to make its points serious study had to talk as though out of access to a critical tradition that in fact had never existed.' This is exceptionally graceful and modest. For the fact is that 'serious study' began with Hugh Kenner and no one else. It was his *Poetry of Ezra Pound* that then, in the 1950s, broke the ground that all his elders had quailed before, so flinty as it was, so densely overgrown with ignorance and misapprehension and prejudice. Every book and article since then has built upon his, or rather (to stay with the first and better metaphor) we have straightened a furrow here, kicked up and thrown out some flint that Kenner had missed, scotched afresh or tried to circumvent some tough briar that he had cut back but not uprooted. Can one think of another living critic who, returning to the studies that he thus pioneered, would have resisted the temptation to be at least sardonic from time to time about those of us who have followed him? I confess I cannot. And so the first thing to applaud in *The Pound Era*[1] is its exceptional civility, its good manners.

For instance, Kenner never brags. And yet there is plenty to brag about. For in proceeding as he did in *The Poetry of Ezra Pound* – talking 'as though out of access to a critical tradition that in fact had never existed' – he took appalling risks. He was chancing his arm, and his professional future, time and again. And he was in any case making enemies. For by assuming that a tradition of criticism existed, assuming the existence of a consensus of information and opinion, Kenner was goading, almost taunting, the rest of us into finding out whether such a consensus was possible. To speak for myself, I was sure it was not; and it was with rancorous confidence that I applied myself to boning up on the subject, probing Kenner's hypotheses and his readings. It was many years later that I had to recognize that the daring young man, for all his aggressive aplomb and unabashed brilliance, was to all intents and purposes in the right. It was not that he had 'done his homework', for at that time he

1   Hugh Kenner, *The Pound Era* (Berkeley: University of California Press, 1971).

hadn't. He has done it now, and this big handsome book is the record of that. The triumph is that the homework, now it is done, vindicates nearly all along the line what the young Kenner gambled on, trusting his unsupported intelligence, enthusiasm and taste. It is a triumph, and he could have been excused for exulting a little. He does not.

On the contrary, *The Pound Era* is a melancholy book, full of pathos. Its theme is 'the vortex' as a concept of cultural history, its validity tested against the historical record of one point in the cultural history of the present century when the concept was actualized, when the vortex became a fact – a spinning funnel of artistic and intellectual energy which, in London about 1913, sucked in the diverse and mutually enhancing talents of Pound himself, of Eliot, of Percy Wyndham Lewis and Joyce, of Gaudier-Brzeska, even – on the outermost rim, as it were – of William Carlos Williams. The pathos – the tragedy even (it is not too strong a word) – is in how the spin had barely begun before it was aborted, and the energies so concentrated were dispersed. And it was no one's fault; it was the fault of the First World War, or of whatever the forces are (Pound came to be sure what they were) that make world wars. Yet, if it had not been that war, it would have been something else, or so I read the story: the vision is Pope's in *The Dunciad*, of how a Vortex when it appears, for instance in the Scriblerus Club, is always doomed – how a fruitful concentration of several talents can never be more than momentary, one more luminous island briefly appearing in, and at once overwhelmed by, the seas of stupidity, meanness and disorder which, washing to and fro, account for the immeasurably greater part of human history. *The Pound Era* charts how the vortex began, how one talent after another was sucked into it, how it briefly and beautifully spun; but mostly it is concerned with what happened to the survivors when each of them had been flung far from the others, trying to live and create through the long aftermath, with that effective radiance still in their memories. Hence the pathos. (And who will write *The Pope Era* – ranging Pope and Swift and Gay, and Arbuthnot and Bolingbroke, into an analogous pattern?)

However, Hugh Kenner also permits himself more sanguine sentiments than these. And whenever he does so, these come before us countersigned by Buckminster Fuller. No harm in that. Fuller serves Kenner very well – for instance in the exposition of what C.H. Douglas is all about (far better than anything we've had earlier), and pre-eminently in the terms, 'self-interfering pattern' and 'patterned integrity', as of a knot, to characterize the sort of forms that the artists of the 1913 Vortex were concerned to create. Elsewhere Fuller presides over a series of observations beginning with the 1860s and 'the first thoroughly American structures: houses whose toothpick frames could support a roof before the walls were closed up, in a self-sustaining lightness Buckminster Fuller's geodesics would one day geometrize... The walls were simply windbreaks, clapped on later. American craft works by structure, not accretion, and an American poetic is unembarrassed by open spaces between the members (hence Whistler's and Fenollosa's hospitality to an oriental aesthetic of intervals).'

Observations are characteristically rapid, darting and persuasive. (Kenner quotes in illustration two poems by Zukofsky, and one sees readily enough how the comments illuminate George Oppen too.) But plainly Pound's is an 'aesthetic of intervals' no less. And this brings up the question which Hugh Kenner raises but never faces squarely: how far the Vortex of 1913, though its scene of operations was London, was a peculiarly *American* achievement. I am not wagging a querulous Union Jack if I confess that in one respect *The Pound Era*, like *The Poetry of Ezra Pound*, makes painful reading for an Englishman; in both books arrogant obtuseness, complacent inertia, and a drastically rapid winding down of energies (as in *Hugh Selwyn Mauberley*) are the defining characteristics of the England in which, and the English among whom, the Vortex happened. Englishmen from all previous centuries are dutifully honoured, as Pound's and Williams's ancestors no less than Thomas Hardy's; but the Englishman of the present century is a byword for enervation on the one hand, for philistinism on the other. It's significant for instance that *The Pound Era* begins by evoking Pound's expatriate American forebear, Henry James, but nowhere does it honour the corresponding or counterbalancing English parent, Thomas Hardy, though there is evidence that Pound seldom recalled the one illustrious precedent without making a hasty obeisance to the other. And at least in intention Hardy's use of Aeschylus in *Tess*, of Sophocles in *The Woodlanders*, and of Virgil in the 'Poems of 1912–13', seems to be in parallel with Joyce's use of Homer and Pound's of Ovid – Hardy's forms are, at any rate schematically 'self-interfering patterns' as theirs are, 'patterned integrities'.

The issue becomes important when Kenner considers those two from the original Vortex who chose to survive and operate in England; that is to say, Eliot and Lewis. The tale that is told of Lewis is harrowing, not to say hideous. It could not be otherwise. For however much we may admire *Time and Western Man* or *Self-Condemned* or the portraits of Eliot and Pound and Edith Sitwell, no one can think that the genius which in 1912 produced the 'Alcibiades' design for *Timon of Athens* (Kenner has a glittering and memorable page about it, facing an illustration) was in any way fulfilled in the forty-three years that followed. What went wrong? Kenner hints at defects or at any rate idiosyncrasies of character which made 'The Enemy' a self-indulgent *persona* for Lewis to adopt. Indeed he accounts for the worst raucousness of Pound in the years of the Chinese History cantos by suggesting that Pound was trying to occupy, against the grain of his own nature, the Lewisian polemical *persona*. But on the other hand perhaps it was not Lewis's fault, but the fault of his milieu: 'By the mid-1920s a massive triviality, a failure of will on a truly forbidding scale, was allowing English culture to lapse into shapes characterized by child-ishness, self-indulgence, utter predictability.' It is not that I object, or call for documentation; I can supply the documentation myself, and am more than half-persuaded that indeed, whereas at enormous cost Pasternak and Akhmatova and Mandelstam could survive as artists in the Russia of Stalin, no artist could survive in the England of Baldwin and Churchill. After all, Lawrence and Auden and Graves all fled its shores. Perhaps I am unreasonable to wish that if indeed this is Kenner's considered belief, he should have come right out and said it.

Moreover there remains the case of Eliot, who embedded himself in that English milieu ever more firmly. Unless we believe the *Four Quartets* are slack and boring (and Kenner does not think so, nor do I), it has to be explained why the milieu supported Eliot where it could not support Lewis. Readers of Kenner's earlier book on Eliot, *The Invisible Poet*, will know the outlines of the very special case that Kenner takes Eliot to be. But the pages on Eliot in *The Pound Era* are not up to the level of *The Invisible Poet*; in particular the knowing nudges and winks with which we are led through anecdotes of Eliot in action as the London clubman fail to convince that this was his finest performance at playing possum. They suggest instead what most Englishmen believe who dislike, as most Englishmen do, the whimsical pretensions of the clubman; they believe that Eliot sold out, and there is evidence that that is what Pound believed also, though he was always too loyal to say so. But in that case the *Four Quartets* are still not accounted for. And in fact Kenner does not account for them.

In all of this we are concerned only with the buttresses, not the central edifice, of Kenner's massive design. But some of the buttresses are moulded very finely, especially the indignant and compassionate pages given to Lewis in war-time Toronto and post-war London:

> Meanwhile the New World went on providing, it supposed, access to all that man's heart can desire: mountains and fir trees, water and wheat and sunlight. Do men need men? Do they need cities? The New World inclines to think not. Her sage is Thoreau. She feels that her cities are her problem areas; that some economic process, no doubt related to the concentrations of capital, makes them exist and metabolize thought and wealth; but that they turn cancerous.
>
> But Europe is a place of cities, and the reliance of a Wyndham Lewis on his city is so complex that a city on a lower plane of organi-zation than the old London's deprived him virtually of existence. (In that respect post-war London was like Toronto.) He was not one of the millions whose gratitude has confirmed the New World in its hypotheses, who deprived in Europe took life and hope from the gift

of elements in an elemental continent. It was not for elements Lewis hungered but for community: for all that can cross neither frontiers nor oceans: the web of relationships, indescribably fragile, that made his career possible. Even his enmities were such relationships.

But if this convinces us, less than ever can we duck the question why, if post-war London failed Lewis so completely (as completely as Toronto), it seems to have suited Eliot so well. If we think that the Garrick Club gave Eliot that community which Lewis starved for the lack of, we seem to be saying that Eliot's standards of fellowship were less exacting than Lewis's. Or is it that a painter depends on a 'web of relationships' more than a writer does? Or else again was it Eliot's religious consolations which made him less dependent on those relationships? I suspect that this last explanation is the one nearest the truth. But Hugh Kenner, perhaps wisely, leaves Eliot's Christianity out of account.

As for Kenner's central argument, we come near to the heart of it when we read, 'All manner of modern preoccupations...linguistics, anthropology, biology, folklore, economics, so interrogate present phenomena as to open up tunnels in time, down which we see to an archetypal past whose shadows, under our transparent present, lend weight and nerve and import. And as with Madame Sosostris and her Tarot pack, the seer is inseparable from what is seen.' We have heard other voices saying something like this. (They have been saying it more glibly, and with more confidence, since *The Poetry of Ezra Pound*.) Kenner says it with force because he substantiates it with readings *in* nineteenth-century linguistics and biology and anthropology, arguing for 'ecological' as the word to define what all of these come to have in common, in their procedures and assumptions. But what he says uniquely and irreplaceably is something else, though intimately related: for the view down a tunnel is, though especially radiant, diminished as well as enhanced by the recessive perspective, and this was what the nineteenth-century – James, not much less than Pater or Morris – especially savoured; whereas (so Kenner compellingly argues) in 'Homage to Sextus Propertius', two times have become as one, and we are meant to be equally aware of both dictions (and yet they seem the same diction). 'The words lie flat like the forms on a Cubist surface. The archaizing sensibility of James's time and Beardsley's has simply dissolved.' In other words, once Pound has got over the archaizing Wardour Street of his first collections (and Kenner, I am glad to say, sees these for the 'prentice-work they are), he writes a poetry in which the scene at the further end of the time-tunnel is laid out on the same flat plane as the present scene at or around the tunnel's entrance. Gone is the vista through delectably receding planes of increasing remoteness; gone is what Kenner calls 'aerial perspective' or else 'the tone of time', imaged as the successive coats of varnish painted on to make a modern painting seem as brown as an Old Master. If Schliemann and others had made the remote past no longer remote but immediate, then a modern sensibility must honour that immediacy – as in Pound's poems, and consistently in *The Cantos*, it does.

The licence which this gives, for treating Sappho or Ibycus or Wei Wang as contemporaries (their monumental ancientness torn down or split open), is hair-raising. And in *The Pound Era*, as not in *The Poetry of Ezra Pound*, Kenner's scholarly hair does rise on his head when he observes for instance his poet trusting De Mailla, and Chu Hsi behind him, so as to misconstrue completely the relations between Confucianism and the Tao in Chinese culture. Yet in Pound himself – so Kenner would say, and I agree with him – such blunders, though they must be registered and their damaging consequences allowed for, can be forgiven and excused, so apparent everywhere is Pound's piety towards the past that he rifles and sometimes, unintentionally, inverts. A different situation confronts us when, as now, not only 'the tone of time has vanished' (that varnished brown), but also the *sense* of time, of its long perspectives backward, and of *pietas* towards them; when, as now, readers and writers alike confidently invoke the shade of Pound to preside over works in which 'the immediate' means 'the unremembering'. Kenner, presumably as practising pedagogue, acknowledges the existence of this new barbarism when he brings evidence to show how both Dante and the Provençal poets were common currency among Anglo-American intellectuals when *The Spirit of Romance* appeared, but twenty years later were taken to be recondite in the extreme.

The Pound Era is a work of literary scholarship, whereas *The Poetry of Ezra Pound* was an achievement of largely unsupported critical insight and intuition. But ultimately the later book, much as it profits from hard-won learning deftly and elegantly brought to bear, stands or falls – just as the first book did – on criticism, on the act of reading attentively, though generously yet with vigilance. And in *The Pound Era* the proof of that comes early, in the fifth and sixth sections, immediately after the *tour de force* of scholarship which recreates ('The Muse in Tatters') the fragmentary terms on which Pound, or any one else at that date (or at this) had access to Sappho. These sections, 'Motz el son' and 'The Invention of Language', which establish the importance of Arnaut Daniel for *The Cantos* despite the relative paucity of direct or even oblique references to him, seem to me a really great exercise of the critical intelligence, meaning by that an articulating of just how the words on the page, and coming off the page, in fact work upon us as we read. Once again, one wants to take the secondary term in a comparison and move it into primary place, so as to ask: who will write the book or the essay on Blake which is prompted by Kenner's passing comment that 'the moral virtues Blake the engraver attributed to outlines Pound the poet associated with bounded sounds, and preferably bounded terms'? ('Bounded terms' is relatively easy; what we need to recover, which Kenner's discussion leads us to, is 'bounded *sounds*'.)

Scores of half written or loosely conceived monographs and dissertations must now be stalled; Kenner has been before them, has said tersely and memorably (and yet with appropriate qualifications) what they would have said laboriously. For Kenner has circumnavigated the Pound universe; and there is no aspect of it which is not charted more completely and accurately, thanks to his exertions. As *The Poetry of Ezra Pound* inaugurated one phase of Pound study, so *The Pound Era* completes it. From now on, there ought to be fewer books about Pound; and those few, if they are to justify themselves, will have to be very good.

Paideuma, 1.2 (Winter 1972).

XVII Eliot in One Poet's Life

What I have to say will sound egotistical and self-regarding. And so I owe it to myself to say that these were the terms of the assignment I was given – I was to be personal, almost confessional. And it's no good pretending that I find this unpleasant. On the contrary I feel a happy gratitude to the University of York[1] for inviting me unequivocally as a man who has written poems, very much on holiday from my avocations as critic and journalist and teacher.

One reason for having such avocations, and for pursuing them so strenuously as I do, is to keep a man busy, so that he need not at all often stop to make sense of himself and of his life so far as he has lived it – a sort of taking stock which inevitably, in the very nature of the case, is for the most part depressing. Thinking about what I was to say today has compelled me to this sort of salutary exercise. And in fact I found it much less depressing than surprising: once I bent my mind to the question of T.S. Eliot in my life, I was extremely surprised.

The surprise was that I discovered, as soon as I thought about it, that the late Mr Eliot has been a presence in my life more insistently influential than any other writer whatever. There is no doubt of this; and yet when I recognized it, it was with astonishment. Without being conscious of doing so, I had got into the habit of regarding him as just one of the larger-than-life effigies which are disposed, as inspiring or minatory presences, in the vaguely apprehended landscape of my private universe. But it isn't so, I realise; more than Shakespeare or Pasternak or Samuel Johnson or Wordsworth (the list could be extended), it is Eliot who presides most densely over my sense of myself, and not just my sense of myself as writer.

To begin with, his effigy has stood there longer than any other. It has been there ever since I was a schoolboy. This does not mean, alas, that as a pupil of Barnsley Grammar School I discovered Eliot's poetry for myself, still less (what would be more extraordinary and interesting) that I discovered the whole of English poetry through first responding to Eliot's. No, I discovered English poetry through Walter de la Mare – a far more likely way of discovering it, and not a bad way either. And if *The Waste Land* and 'Prufrock' were already known to me by 1938, when I was 16, it was because alert and ambitious schoolmasters had pressed them

1   This article was first given as a lecture at the University of York. [Ed.]

upon me. And I was a very ambitious schoolboy, in those days when British education was more élitist and competitive than it is today. So I responded very readily to Eliot's early poems, in the terms in which my schoolmasters presented them to me – that is to say, as commando obstacle-courses which one was not expected to complete, only to fail at more or less creditably. And I have to confess that *The Waste Land* even today lives in my mind in rather this way – as a famous challenge and ordeal, a sphinx's riddle; which is to say, not (strictly speaking) as a poem at all. Now that the publication of the drafts has made it a focus of argument once again,[2] I see others confessing in print that it is a sphinx's riddle to them too, and often enough they complain of Eliot or of Eliot and Pound between them, for having made a frustrating tease out of what should have been complete and satisfying. This may well be right. On the other hand it may be that what seems unsatisfying about *The Waste Land* is not anything intrinsic to the poem but rather has to do with the reputation of the poem, with how its reputation was first made and has been sustained ever since, in large part as an excitingly advanced exercise for the Modern Sixth. (I do not need to spell out the implications of this for teachers of literature and students of literature and people who construct the syllabus for an examination or the curriculum of a course – to put modern or near-contemporary books on the syllabus is not always proof of enlightenment, and it may harm the authors that it means to help.)

Thus the Eliot who stood in effigy in the landscape of my young mind was not the author of *The Waste Land*, of 'Gerontion', of *Ash-Wednesday*. At some point (I think after I left Barnsley for Cambridge) the look in the eyes of the statue changed a little, and he became the author of 'Marina'. For that is the first poem of Eliot's that I discovered for myself, and so cherished it, as I cherish it still. But originally the effigy was not of Eliot the poet, but of Eliot the author of those seminal essays, 'The Metaphysical Poets', 'Andrew Marvell' and 'Homage to John Dryden'. I don't like to confess this, but I fear there is no doubt of it. The proof is in the poems of mine, all long ago destroyed, which I was writing in the 1940s, when I had joined the Navy after a year at Cambridge. For those poems, as I painfully recall them, had nothing to do with Eliot's practice as a poet but had everything to do with what he was taken to have recommended in theory. Had he not re-established connections for us with the seventeenth-century poets of strenuous wit – with Donne and Herbert and Marvell? And so the poems that I wrote at that time were painstakingly structured on the extended comparisons and the farfetched hyperbolical conceits of John Donne's 'The Good-morrow' or Marvell's 'To his Coy Mistress'. And in this I think I was not alone – as late as 1954, when Thom Gunn

2   T.S. Eliot, *The Waste Land: A Facsimile and Transcript of the Original Drafts, Including the Annotations of Ezra Pound*, ed. Valerie Eliot (London: Faber, 1971).

published his first collection, *Fighting Terms*, we can see a serious and ambitious poet still strenuously acting the part, brought up to date of course, of mad Jack Donne, the libertine of the Elizabethan stews and law-courts.

I want to dwell on this, even though it takes us still further from what Eliot wrote as a poet to what he wrote (or was thought to have written) as a critic. I should like to be helpful if I can, and it may be that there are still young writers who can be sidetracked for years, as I was, by Eliot and some of the commentators on Eliot, into thinking that the seventeenth century (or the eighteenth, the sixteenth, the fourteenth) is immediately accessible to us if we only exert ourselves. Accessible, I mean, *creatively*... For that delusion was what had me balked and at a standstill, in my own writing, through most of the 1940s. I thought that since John Donne had a valuably unified sensibility – I was told that, and I was persuaded, and could see it for myself – a sort of duty was laid upon me to regain it, and help others regain it. If any one had murmured that a lot of water had flowed under bridges since the deaths of John Donne and George Herbert, I should have known how to reply. For that water which had flowed by was 'romanticism', and I knew that duty required me to have no truck with *that*! 'Romantic' was for me and my friends the ugliest imputation that could be thrown at anyone or anything, a sentence of death from which there was no appeal. There is an early poem by Kingsley Amis, called 'Against Romanticism', which catches the note very accurately. And yet why should I treat such nonsense as a thing of the past? For I notice that in the mouths of my students today 'romantic' seems to mean just what it meant in our mouths thirty years ago. And if this is so, there is the more reason for me to say this: that what liberated me into writing to some purpose was the sudden realization that what we call 'the Romantic movement' was not a fad or a fashion or an aberration but something which happened to the mind of Europe and the Americas about the beginning of the last century, and that what happened was – like it or lump it – irreversible. We are not called upon to approve or disapprove; one does not approve or disapprove of a landslide, one notes that it has happened and begins to try putting life together in the new landscape which it has created. Just thus, as a drastic breach or geological fault, does Romanticism exist in the cultural past of each one of us. We are all post-romantic people; there are no exceptions or exemptions. And in particular no one can climb back into some lost garden of the seventeenth or eighteenth century except by crossing that fault-line, and arriving permanently travel-stained from the long trek. Which means, I take it, that no twentieth century poem that is worth anything will be structured like a poem of John Donne's.

And no poem by T.S. Eliot is thus structured. But as I've explained, my friends and I in the 1940s weren't looking at the poems but at the criticism. And Eliot had declared himself 'a classicist'. Not altogether foolishly we took that to mean that we not only could but *should* pretend that the nineteenth century had never happened; that it could be erased from the record by a sheer act of will; and that it could somehow be bypassed as we threaded our way back to Boileau or Pope, to Shakespeare or Donne, ultimately to Dante. This was a damaging delusion that we laboured under, and I owe Eliot a grudge for having, more than anyone else, foisted it upon us.

You will recall that at the same time as he declared himself a classicist (he wasn't of course – it was just a coat-trailing manoeuvre), Eliot announced that he was Royalist in politics and Anglo-Catholic in religion. And you may wonder that we were not offended and alienated by this provocative espousal of positions that were unblushingly conservative, if not indeed reactionary. But I would ask you to remember rather precisely the generation that I belong to. I was seventeen in the year of the Molotov-Ribbentrop pact, when Hitler's Germany and Stalin's Russia agreed to carve up Poland between them. A year later, when I went to Cambridge, there was still in Rose Crescent the Left Bookshop to remind me that this was the university from which John Cornford and Julian Bell had gone to die in Spain. But that bookshop did not survive long; current affairs, and the news of the war, as we heard them over the radio, belied its left-wing utopianism all too evidently. And this was the time too when Orwell and Koestler and others began to reveal the duplicity of Russian policies and promises in Spain and elsewhere. The break between the generations was very sharp; for men and women who had gone up to university only eighteen months before me had had the time to invest something in the ideology of the Popular Front, and to this day that investment (as I know, for I am speaking of my closest friends) makes them wryly suspicious and resentful of Eliot as a thinker about society and as a force in politics. I had no such difficulties; for me, growing up just when I did, Eliot's pessimistic conservatism seemed tough-minded and straight-talking, a bleak but welcome wind to sweep away the tergiversations, the sentimental contradictions and self-deceptions of what Auden called 'a low dishonest decade'. And just as for my Leftist friends a couple of years older, so for me this experience was definitive; so that even today I am more exasperated by the sentimentalisms of the Left than of the Right. And even if growing up as a *petit bourgeois* in an overwhelmingly proletarian community like Barnsley had already inoculated me against the rhetoric of the Left (Had I not collected signatures for the Peace Pledge Union? Yes, I had), still it meant much to have a revered figure like Eliot asserting what looked like a plausible alternative.

(I make no excuse for touching on politics thus explicitly: every estimate of Eliot that is offered today in Britain is politically tendentious – and I do not except my own estimate. I shall suggest, later on, how Eliot's stock began to fall when the climate of political opinion changed once again. Eliot would not have expected anything else; one of the strengths of his tough-minded criticism is that he never supposes aesthetic judgements are passed in a political or religious vacuum.)

And now I have reached at last the poet, rather than the brilliantly evasive critic or the opinion-maker and trend-setter. I have reached the *Four Quartets*, poems of a nation at war; and poems which I, myself at war (I remember reading them in Arctic Russia), discovered for myself and savoured for myself, without the dubious mediation of commentators, pedagogues, exegetes. I leave aside 'Burnt Norton,' the first of the *Quartets*, because it was written and published before the war began. For that matter I find I don't know just when 'East Coker' and the others were composed, if indeed that information is available. Never mind: the poems appeared in the years of the war and were surely read by others as well as me, as war-poems. I suppose it would still be a bold anthologist who would represent Eliot as a poet of the Second World War, along with Drummond Allison and John Pudney and Alun Lewis; and if Eliot were to be represented in such an anthology, it would have to be by 'Little Gidding', the last and without doubt the most consistently splendid of the *Quartets*, which includes not only the famous Dantesque passage set in London at dawn after a bombing raid, but also –

> There are other places
> Which also are the world's end, some at the sea jaws,
> Or over a dark lake, in a desert or a city –
> But this is the nearest, in place and time,
> Now and in England.

Equally, however, when I read in 'East Coker',

> And so each venture
> Is a new beginning, a raid on the inarticulate
> With shabby equipment always deteriorating
> In the general mess of imprecision of feeling,
> Undisciplined squads of emotion

I reflect that 'raid' and 'equipment' and 'squads' are words of wartime, perhaps of that particular wartime, 1939–45. And even in 'The Dry Salvages', the least satisfactory of the *Quartets* and the most American, there is the crackling vividness of the concluding section:

> To communicate with Mars, converse with spirits,
> To report the behaviour of the sea monster,
> Describe the horoscope, haruspicate or scry,
> Observe disease in signatures, evoke
> Biography from the wrinkles of the palm
> And tragedy from fingers; release omens

> By sortilege, or tea leaves, riddle the inevitable
> With playing cards, fiddle with pentagrams
> Or barbituric acids, or dissect
> The recurrent image into pre-conscious terrors –
> To explore the womb, or tomb, or dreams; all these are usual
> Pastimes and drugs, and features of the press:
> And always will be, some of them especially
> When there is distress of nations and perplexity
> Whether on the shores of Asia, or in the Edgware Road...

where that juxtaposition of Asia with the Edgware Road I identify as a sentiment of wartime.

This passage begins with a dozen lines of rapid catalogue which may remind us of Auden at his best – consider the inventiveness, at once lexical and phonetic, of the sequence, 'horoscope, haruspicate or scry'; but it modulates from this into flat asseveration which runs the risk of being flat in a more damaging sense:

> all these are usual
> Pastimes and drugs, and features of the press:
> And always will be...

This bleakness and explicitness, this daring to seem pedestrian, is a note which Auden forfeited the chance of (so I suggest) when he left England in 1939. But in the *Four Quartets* it is everywhere, this passionate explicitness:

> We are only undeceived
> Of that which, deceiving, could no longer harm.
> In the middle, not only in the middle of the way
> But all the way, in a dark wood, in a bramble,
> On the edge of a grimpen, where is no secure foothold,
> And menaced by monsters, fancy lights,
> Risking enchantment. Do not let me hear
> Of the wisdom of old men, hut rather of their folly,
> Their fear of fear and frenzy, their fear of possession,
> Of belonging to another, or to others, or to God.

Just as in the previous passage 'haruspicate or scry' and similar inventions validated the succeeding flatness of 'all these are usual', so here the daring juxtaposition of the nonce-word 'a grimpen' and the impatiently thrown away 'fancy lights' validates the blank explicitness of 'Do not let me hear'. And it is my impression, which there is no way of proving, that this explicitness was possible only to a poet who conceived himself to be speaking for his adopted nation when that nation was united in desperation and resolve.

I am aware that it is precisely this tone in the *Four Quartets* which some readers find insupportable. They call it 'pontificating', and so it is; I can only record that when the poems first came out I was ready to accept Eliot as my pontifex, and thought that he had earned the right to that office.

It is in any case astonishing that the poet of *The Waste Land*, or of *Coriolan*, so enamoured of baffling obliquities and discontinuities, should have developed to a point where some readers can complain that he isn't oblique *enough*. In this respect the contrast between early and late Eliot is so startling that critics, myself among them, have been at pains to show that the *Quartets*, embodying by their very title the symbolist endeavour to make poetry like music, are no new departure; that they are on the contrary the natural crown and consummation of a lifelong endeavour by Eliot to find analogues in English for the achievements and procedures of the French symbolists. This is certainly true; and the delay in recognizing Eliot's French affinities is woeful evidence of our stubborn and self-congratulating insularity. Nevertheless, though the structure of *Four Quartets* both severally and as a whole is in this way musical, non-discursive (so that they are not, for instance, treatises of Christian apologetics or mystical theology), what must strike us is that within each of the relatively large blocs of verse which make up the whole – within, that is, each 'movement' of each Quartet – the writing is very markedly explicit and discursive. If it were not so, we should not hear the poems objected to as 'didactic' or 'pontificating'. And when I began to think of my own writing in relation to the Quartets, it was this aspect of their style which fascinated me most – their use of abstract words and of sustained and elaborately correct syntax. Not before time, this liberated me very fruitfully from a bundle of notions I had picked up somewhere, to the effect that poetry could and should convey meaning only through overt metaphor and what in those days we called 'image-clusters'.

But it was still impossible for me to draw *directly* on Eliot as a model. At the end of the 1940s I was indeed writing poems all too plainly on the model of the *Quartets*, parasitically dependent upon them, just as a few years before I had written all too plainly on the model of Donne. I had enough sense to realise that they were no good, those poems of mine, because in them I was only a sort of ventriloquist's doll. And in fact I would suggest that Eliot has never been a fruitful *direct* influence on other poets. In the case of the *Quartets* I found them unfruitful – so it seems to me now – because their rhythms are lax, at best no more than adequate; and it still seems to me that their prosody is the weakest thing about them – the 4- or 5-beat accentual line that Eliot uses through much of them is too capacious to be interesting, or to create cadences that are sharp and distinct. And so, before I could profit by what the *Quartets* had to teach me about diction, I had to go to other masters to learn about versification.

However, rather than pursue these technicalities, we ought to dwell on how astonishing it was for Eliot to have achieved in England the unquestioned pre-eminence that he had for all of us in the 1940s. How did it come about that a reticent and elegantly evasive, over-educated American came to occupy this position, and went on to an Order of Merit and a tomb in Westminster Abbey? Hugh Kenner has answered this to some extent by pressing hard on Pound's nickname for him, 'the Possum'. Eliot got where he did, so Kenner suggests, by 'playing possum', by lying low and shamming dead. To put it another way, as a foreigner moving in English life, Eliot's great talent was for protective coloration; and Kenner, both amusingly and justly shows how Eliot, for instance, evolved a prose style precisely in keeping with that of the *Athenaeum* and the *Times Literary Supplement* in the 1920s. A similar talent for the inconspicuously acceptable tone may be what recommended him in the circles of 'Bloomsbury'. And from this point of view it is possible to think that, by the time he joined the Church of England (in a discreetly well publicized conversion), this patiently adroit interloper from St Louis Missouri had already penetrated to the very *arcanum* of the English Establishment. But of course this is to misunderstand the status of the Established Church in England. If we can speak of a literary and intellectual 'Establishment' in this country, the Church of England is not the ark of the covenant at all – quite the contrary; to the Bloomsbury of the 1920s, as to the opinion-makers of every decade since, a profession of Christianity was very 'unsmart' indeed. And if one must be Christian, let it be theatrically Papist or eccentrically Calvinist, not at all events in that Church which has been called 'the Tory party at prayer'. From the standpoint of the literary intelligentsia, Eliot's churchmanship, so far from being a penetration into the holy of holies, was a voluntary departure into the wilderness – as Eliot himself realised, in what is one of the most vivacious and vigorous of his prose polemics, 'Thoughts after Lambeth'.

Thus it will not do to think of a wily American serpent worming his way into our trusting or mistrustful bosoms. The facts won't fit this fable. But it won't do in any case. For it rests upon the unexamined assumption that London must be the metropolis towards which an ambitious American artist will naturally gravitate. Why should Eliot, however serpentine, have sought an English bosom in any case? I began to ask myself that question when, in the 1950s, my conscious concerns turned to Ezra Pound. For Pound, about 1920 when his association with Eliot was at its closest, quite consciously repudiated England as a milieu in which creative practice of the arts could be carried on. He went to Paris, and then to Italy; and of course in the 1920s it was pre-eminently Paris, not London, where the American expatriates foregathered, to be joined there by English expatriates such as Ford Madox Ford. It has been plausibly argued that American poetry, perhaps American literature in general, came brilliantly to maturity in this century only when American writers broke the last ties of ex-colonial dependence which had tied them to London, and turned instead to Paris or Vienna or Rapallo. From this point of view. Eliot's development in the 1920s and 1930s towards bedding himself ever more deeply in English life was a striking anomaly, and was seen as such by Pound. And when we consider the English-born poets who in the same decades were finding England sterile and sterilizing – one thinks of D.H. Lawrence, of Robert Graves, ultimately of Auden – we might from time to time feel a sort of sneaking gratitude to Eliot for sticking with us, as it were. Instead I'm afraid we put the meanest possible construction on his loyalty, and we call him an Anglophile snob.

Early in the 1950s I imposed a self-denying ordinance on myself and quite consciously read no verse by Eliot at all – in a drastic attempt to root out of my own style the Eliotic cadences which were making it not mine at all. In any case by this time I was in Dublin, where for obvious reasons the master ventriloquist was not Eliot but Yeats; where Tom Kinsella for instance, a gifted and admirably serious poet, was desperately exorcising the shade of Yeats just as I was fighting free of Eliot.

When I returned to England in 1958, I found a changed climate of opinion and feeling. The younger intellectuals were turning Left once more, taking up the populist attitudes which I had been glad to see discredited at the end of the 1930s. And so the tide of sentiment had turned against Eliot once more. There was a difference however. Leftist sentiment of the 1930s, as one may see it in the Auden of those years or as surviving to the present day in Geoffrey Grigson, voiced its distrust of Eliot in overtly political terms, thinking of him for instance as the English Paul Claudel. In the 1950s and 1960s, however, this political animus against him was very often disguised behind what seemed to be a guile-less preference for generosity, magnanimity, for 'being on the side of life'. Eliot's attitudes, it was said, were constricted, mean-spirited; he seemed not to like *people* very much, in particular he didn't like or celebrate joyous sexuality.

I could see what people meant when they said this. I could sympathize and agree, and even say much the same myself – though it so happened that the generously impulsive and foolhardy poet whom I would set up against Eliot was Ezra Pound, rather than D.H. Lawrence. It was, and is, a real dilemma. One would like to love where one is compelled to praise; and Eliot is the least lovable of poets. What makes the nerves tingle, and the mind assent, should warm the heart; and in Eliot's case it doesn't. We respect, we admire, we do not love. A pity. And yet there is no rule which says that a great poet has to be likeable. Wordsworth strikes most of us as an unlikeable man, yet a very great poet indeed. What's more, the one may be the condition of the other; without the stiff-necked self-complacency that repels us in Wordsworth, he could never have persisted in the face of the obloquy and ridicule which he ran into initially. And in the same way the self-possession and bleak self-control which exhale a chill from Eliot's pages are the condition of his rare, and fastidious, accomplishment.

Moreover, when we reproach Eliot or Eliot's shade with being too guarded towards experience, not generous enough, he has anticipated us – in lines I have quoted already:

> Do not let me hear
> Of the wisdom of old men, but rather of their folly,
> Their fear of fear and frenzy, their fear of possession,
> Of belonging to another, or to others, or to God.

If one of the old men that Eliot here castigates was the old man that he saw himself becoming, surely that makes the lines all the more poignant and admirable and compelling. For fear of possession, fear of belonging to another is just what we accuse Eliot of, when we compare him unfavourably with more incautious writers like Lawrence or Pound. And so this passage may well be self-accusing. But if so, people will still resist giving him credit for it, because of the sorts of 'belonging' that he specifies: 'Of belonging to another, or to others, or to God'. That 'or to God' outrages our militantly secular culture, as of course Eliot intended that it should. We want to believe, it seems we obscurely *need* to believe, that belonging to God precludes 'belonging to another, or to others'. And Eliot won't have that, any more than the Scriptures will.

I have got to a point where I am speaking no longer of Eliot's churchmanship, but of his faith, his Christian beliefs. And although it's high time I got back on the wavelength of personal testimony (which I know I've strayed away from), this is the most awkward point at which to do so. And in fact I must duck the challenge; for bearing witness to one's religious experience and apprehensions is an exercise in which it is all but impossible to get the tone right. I will say only this: that whereas through most of the years when I've been reading Eliot I wouldn't have professed myself a practising and believing Christian, yet on the other hand I've never shared or understood the animus against Christianity as a hypocritical cheat, which I find so common, so all but universal, among my friends and contemporaries.[3] As I try to understand how this can be, I think again of that one poem of early or middle Eliot which I have said that I came across and responded to as a very young man. This is the 'Ariel' poem, 'Marina'. And someone – I think it may have been the late lamented friend of my youth, Douglas Brown – provided me with the

---

3   After a Baptist childhood and a long period of agnosticism, Davie was received into the Episcopalian Church, the American branch of the Anglican Communion, in the early 1970s. See pp. 160–2 below. [Ed.]

minimal orientation that I needed, by saying that this poem presents alle-
gorically or in symbol the movement towards conversion of a man not
yet converted, who does not know what conversion will mean, who yet
knows that he is being impelled towards it:

> What seas what shores what grey rocks and what islands
> What water lapping the bow
> And scent of pine and the woodthrush singing through the fog
> What images return
> O my daughter.
>
> Those who sharpen the tooth of the dog, meaning
> Death
> Those who glitter with the glory of the hummingbird, meaning
> Death
> Those who sit in the sty of contentment, meaning
> Death
> Those who suffer the ecstasy of the animals, meaning
> Death
>
> Are become unsubstantial, reduced by a wind,
> A breath of pine, and the woodsong fog
> By this grace dissolved in place
>
> What is this face, less clear and clearer
> The pulse in the arm, less strong and stronger –
> Given or lent? More distant than stars and nearer than the eye
>
> Whispers and small laughter between leaves and hurrying feet
> Under sleep, where all the waters meet.
>
> Bowsprit cracked with ice and paint cracked with heat.
> I made this, I have forgotten
> And remember.
> The rigging weak and the canvas rotten
> Between one June and another September.
> Made this unknowing, half conscious, unknown, my own.
> The garboard strake leaks, the seams need caulking.
> This form, this face, this life
> Living to live in a world of time beyond me; let me
> Resign my life for this life, my speech for that unspoken,
> The awakened, lips parted, the hope, the new ships.
>
> What seas what shores what granite islands towards my timbers
> And woodthrush calling through the fog
> My daughter.

I shall never write like this. I don't mean I shall never write as well as this, but I shall never write *like* this, in this symbolist manner. (I know, for I have tried and disliked the outcome.) What does seem quite clear, however, is that this way of writing – in the *Quartets* as in 'Marina' – enables the poet's sensibility to meet with his reader's at a level far below whatever dogmas may be consciously espoused by either one of them. Why, the conversion spoken of here isn't even a specifically *Christian* conversion! And so I can say, out of my own experience, that Eliot's piety is not just no more of a stumbling-block than the piety of a George Herbert, but is infinitely *less* of a stumbling-block. And yet, for as long as I can remember, agnostic readers have been explaining how they can participate in the devout poetry of Herbert while still rejecting everything that Herbert believed. The latest I have come across is Geoffrey Grigson, in a book published two years ago:

> Why can I accept the Christianity of George Herbert – though 'accept' may beg the question – and not the Christianity of Eliot or Auden, or Claudel, or any television apologist?
>
> Because Herbert had no option. He had no possible, no sensible alternative. It was his inevitable mode of evaluation.[4]

Grigson's honesty is something to be grateful for. He says quite plainly that what affronts him in Eliot and Auden is not what they choose to believe, but what they choose to *dis*believe – the secular[5] alternatives to Christianity that in our enlightened age are so abundantly on offer. What outrages him is not their credulity but on the contrary their scepticism. And on the other side of the Atlantic Helen Vendler concurs,[6] speaking of 'the religiosity of the *Four Quartets*', and asking rhetorically, 'Is nervousness cured by ethics? Can "the heap of broken images" be put together again, like Humpty-Dumpty, by a heap of moral injunctions?...' Well, we may reply, Doctor Johnson thought so. And what is Mrs Vendler's alternative? Psycho-therapy? As for me I will plead guilty to being too ready to believe in the bankruptcy of the secular alternatives. I want to believe, and have always wanted to believe, that psycho-therapy mostly wouldn't work. And so I have always been ready, doubtless *too* ready, to be persuaded by Eliot that psychologists and other social engineers are 'Those who sharpen the tooth of the dog'.

So far as I can understand my motives, they have to do with believing in the right to personal privacy, and the respectability of reticence. When I was still a boy I remember reading with a spasm of delighted assent 'ah angry letter from Joseph Conrad in which he repudiated an invitation to let his hair down in print, declaring that if he could help it no one should

4   *Notes from an Odd Country* (London: Macmillan, 1970), p. 192.
5   The original text has 'sectarian'; 'secular' is a more probable reading. [Ed.]
6   *New York Times Book Review*, 7 November 1971.

see 'Conrad *en pantoufles*', Conrad in carpet-slippers. And this was quite plainly Eliot's attitude also; some of the chill that rises from his pages is the proper and bracing chill of a man who says, 'Keep your distance. I have a right to a private life, even if I *am* a writer.' The doctrine of impersonality in art, which Eliot promulgated in a famous and influential and badly muddled essay (he seems to have meant to say not that art is impersonal but that art *de-personalizes*), is plainly a product of the same justified *hauteur* as Conrad's. And consider the success with which Eliot maintained an iron-clad reticence about the first Mrs Eliot and about Jean Verdenal. Eliot's tone is never intimate; and this is where he and Lawrence are poles apart. In a time like ours when 'personalities' are fabricated and peddled daily, when in many quarters poetry is taken to be no more than letting one's hair down or undressing in public, when as we probe for sincerity in our artists we demand the right to follow them into their bedrooms and bathrooms and on to the analyst's couch, it is small wonder if Eliot affronts us.

And yet democracy, as it used to be understood in this country more perhaps than in any other, consisted precisely in the right of the householder to slam the door in the face of the Nosey Parker, to tear up the questionnaire and put it in the waste-paper basket, the right *not* to join the Union or the club if he didn't want to, and *not* to send his child to the school that a bureaucrat had selected for him. In that perhaps obsolete sense of democracy Eliot was a democrat. And I am prepared to wonder whether it wasn't this quality of English life which made this American prefer it to the American. These are homespun speculations; but they seem to be called for, now that on all sides heads are being angrily or regretfully shaken over his allegedly reactionary politics – which were incidentally, by any objective measure, a great deal less reactionary than Yeats's, though Yeats's are excused while Eliot's aren't.

Let me try once more, for my own satisfaction, to justify my sense that Eliot has meant more to me than any other writer. It has everything to do with when I grew up. If I had been eighteen in 1920, with my heart set on some day writing memorable poems, my master would have been – would have *had* to be – Thomas Hardy. If I could have overcome my diffidence I would have made the pilgrimage to his house, Max Gate, as Robert Graves did and Siegfried Sassoon and Edmund Blunden and many another. In 1940 on the other hand, or in 1945, I would not have dreamed of penetrating to see Mr Eliot in Russell Square, and would doubtless have got a frosty or at least constrained reception, if I had. *There* is the difference. For Hardy I feel much more affection than for Eliot, but infinitely less professional respect. And the proof of the pudding is in the eating; of the poets who took Hardy for their model, as the accredited master-poet when they grew up, those who achieved most were those – pre-eminently Lawrence and Graves – who departed furthest from

Hardy's procedures and precedents. Eliot in the 1940s, precisely because the only possible relationship one could have with him was austerely professional, could be a master in the strict sense, as twenty years before Hardy never could. If in the end I had to go elsewhere to learn versification and lyric structure (where I went first was to Robert Graves, and I'm glad of the chance to acknowledge it), diction was what I learned from the Eliot of the *Quartets*. They were my model then; they are my model now. And diction is not just one aspect of poetry among others; it is the very stuff that one works with, the medium itself, language under poetic conditions. Eliot's professionalism – in the end that is what I am most grateful for; though the possum shammed dead, and perfected his English camouflage, he stopped short of adopting that disastrous English habit, indulgence towards the amateur. Between master and apprentice, between the poet of one generation and the poet of the next or the next-but-one, the only proper relationship is cool and distant, professional. For both are servants of another master yet, the tradition (so Eliot called it), the medium, the language. Eliot was never so American as when he harped on 'the tradition' in this sense. I am grateful to him, and I count myself lucky that I started my writing career, or rather I groped my way towards it, at a time when he was pre-eminently and unavoidably the sea-mark that one had to sail by.

Mosaic: The Journal for the Comparative Study of Literature and Ideas, 6.1 (Fall 1972).

XVIII Anglican Eliot

A Briton, I think, must always have a special relation to those last poems by Eliot – the *Four Quartets* – which were undertaken by a British citizen and completed in a Britain at war, and which allude continually to England's historic past and to what was then London's imperilled present. (There is an exception, of course: the third of the quartets, 'The Dry Salvages'. But Eliot, when he herded all his American references into 'The Dry Salvages', rather plainly meant – thus honouring his transatlantic pieties in one delimited act of homage – to assert his right through the rest of the sequence to speak as an Englishman.)

Eliot had undoubtedly earned the right thus to speak for his adopted nation; his patriotism is moving, and I have no intention of impugning it. Yet it is certainly to the point to ask how well he knew the country and the people for whom he offered to speak. And if I read aright the mostly ungracious comments that may be culled from Englishmen of my own generation and younger, the consensus is that Eliot knew England and the English very imperfectly after forty years. Some of the evidence for that is too familiar to be worth dwelling on – to such characteristically English voices as D.H. Lawrence's, Thomas Hardy's and William Blake's, Eliot showed himself more or less deaf. But other features of Eliot's adopted Englishness may not be so obvious to a non-British reader; and in that sentence I have slipped in one of them already – English and British are not the same, and when Eliot welcomes 'regionalism' in *Notes Towards a Definition of Culture*, this is not going to satisfy people who define themselves as Scottish or Welsh, let alone Irish. Among Eliot's British contemporaries we need think only of David Jones, Robert Graves and Hugh MacDiarmid to be reminded how there are other ways of tying historic Britain in with European Christendom beside the one that Eliot impatiently or blandly took to be the one right way – through Canterbury and Lambeth. Eliot's sense of Britain is offensively metropolitan; and not only of Britain, but of England too – his England is to all intents and purposes London, or at most the Home Counties.

This takes us at once into the *Four Quartets*. For are not three out of those four poems named after English places, all of them outside the Home Counties – Burnt Norton in Gloucestershire, East Coker in Somerset, and Little Gidding in Huntingdonshire? So they are. But in the first place every one of these locations is presented in the poem as a place of pilgrimage, accordingly as seen from the outside by the visitor from London (or for that matter from St Louis, Missouri); no sense is conveyed to us of what it is like in the twentieth century to *live* in any of these places. (Little Gidding, for instance, has existed for the last thirty years under the roar of giant aeroplanes from the USAF airfield at Alconbury; what are we to make of that, and what would Eliot have made of it?) And secondly, each of these three places is well outside the industrialized Midlands and North – the areas which have been for 150 years the heart, once throbbing and now ailing, of imperial, and later post-imperial, England. I'm not sure there is any evidence that Eliot ever travelled in industrial England at all – in that England whose damaging pressures made Lawrence's voice so shrill and yet so insistent – and in fact his leaving this England out of account, his blankness before the phenomenon of an industrial proletariat, is surely what invalidates his thinking about politics. His vision of what English society should ideally be like envisages the working class as agrarian, and the worker as peasant. Ireland in Eliot's lifetime had, as it still has, a peasantry; England had not, and has not. Charles Maurras in France, like Yeats in Ireland, was prescribing for a society which comprehended, and largely rested upon, a peasantry. It might be argued that Eliot as a political thinker made an initial miscalculation which bedevilled him to the end when he applied Maurrasian categories to a country – England – where the peasantry was long extinct. And in that case one element in Eliot's remarkably sustained and virulent antipathy to Hardy might be that Thomas Hardy, though he is too often lamentably applauded as a spokesman for English peasant-culture, in fact documents with impressive sobriety and conviction how peasant and lesser yeoman alike had in his lifetime disappeared, depressed and dispersed into an agricultural proletariat.

Thus when I call this essay 'Anglican Eliot', I intend by that a mildly acrid pun. The more Anglican, the less English – or so I want to suggest. I speak on this matter as an Anglican myself, or more specifically as a member of the Episcopal Church of America. The distinction is important; for whereas the Episcopal Church of America is of course in communion with the Church of England, it is – like the Church of Ireland and the Church *in* Wales, and the Episcopal Church of Scotland – disestablished, as the Church of England is not. And there is every reason to doubt whether Eliot would have joined the Church of England if she had not been the *established* church.

This will be contested. Did not Eliot write: 'One of the most deadening influences upon the Church in the past, ever since the eighteenth century, was its acceptance, by the upper, upper-middle and aspiring classes, as a political necessity and as a requirement of respectability'? Indeed he did; and made a beautifully calculated polemical elaboration of this point, observing (what is even truer now than in 1931) that a profession of Christian faith is nowadays for the English *intelligentsia* a very eccentric action indeed, and that a profession of Anglican faith is the most eccentric and least reputable of all. But later in the same essay – 'Thoughts after Lambeth', one of the most vivacious and brilliantly vehement of all his prose performances – Eliot embarked upon a series of disclaimers such as his practiced readers long ago learned to recognize as the overture to something outrageous:

> I do not propose in this essay to enter upon the difficult question of Disestablishment. I am not here concerned with the practical difficulties and anomalies which have made the problem of Church and State more acute in the last few years; I am not concerned with prognosticating their future relations, or with offering any facile solution for so complex a problem, or with discussing the future discipline within the Church itself. I wish to say nothing about Disestablishment, first because I have not made up my own mind, and second because it does not seem to me fitting at this time that one layman, with no special erudition in that subject, should publicly express his views. I am considering only the political and social changes within the last three hundred years...

And then, after a series of knowledgeable allusions to the Laudian church of the seventeenth century and to the Erastianism of the eighteenth, and to 'Lord Rothermere's sometime nominee, Lord Brentford' (whoever *he* was), Eliot duly proceeds to the outrageous:

> Whether established or disestablished, the Church of England can never be reduced to the condition of a Sect, unless by some irrational act of suicide; even in the sense in which, with all due respect, the Roman Church is in England a sect. It is easier for the Church of England to become Catholic, than for the Church of Rome in England to become English; and if the Church of England was mutilated by separation from Rome, the Church of Rome was mutilated by separation from England. If England is ever to be in any appreciable degree converted to Christianity, it can only be through the Church of England.

It is not hard to envisage the apoplexy with which Evelyn Waugh's Guy Crouchback might have read these bland words from the Missourian convert; nor, to move from literature into life, how they might even now be received by any scion of the Huddleston family, who as untitled gentry have held Sawston manor in the Old Faith since the thirteenth century. I do not know what the passage can mean, if not that it mattered a great deal to Eliot that the archbishops and bishops of the Church of England sit, as 'lords spiritual', in the Higher Chamber of Parliament; or that (to put it the other way around) he would have been quite unperturbed by the hackneyed gibe at the Church of England, that it is 'the Conservative party at prayer'.

This is not in the least to impugn the sincerity of Eliot's conversion to Christian faith; it is merely to point out that, when it came to deciding what Christian sect he should join, it was of the utmost importance to him that he choose what should seem to be not a sect at all but a national norm, its normality shown in that it was backed by the secular and institutional forces of the nation-state. What else should we expect of the author of *The Idea of a Christian Society*?

It is important to realize just what is involved, and to do so one needs a firm sense of the very peculiar place of the Church of England in twentieth-century English life. Eliot wrote: 'Anyone who has been moving among intellectual circles and comes to the Church, may experience an odd and rather exhilarating feeling of isolation.' The feeling was natural, and it corresponded to the reality. For just because so many of the English respect the Church of England as a matter of form, to respect it and embrace it in all seriousness is to be thought a very odd fish indeed. Eliot found himself thus regarded, and the experience was 'exhilarating'. In this way, even as he glorified in not being 'sectarian,' he was able to enjoy the sectarian's luxurious sense of being set apart, special, even a standing reproach to others. For the second time in his life, Eliot at the time of his conversion opted for isolation, for embattled independence. (The first time had been when, on his marriage, he threw up the academic profession for which he was trained.) It is entirely natural, and yet it is disastrously wrong, to regard Eliot's joining the Church of England as the smooth culmination of a policy of playing possum by which a demurely histrionic American won a commanding position in the English Establishment. How much more frank and brave, we may reflect, the doomed intransigence of his *confrère* Ezra Pound! And yet just as Pound, broadcasting from Rome to the advancing American armies, conceived himself to be an American patriot speaking for Jeffersonian America against the deluded America of Roosevelt, so Eliot, when he loyally wrote pieces for *Britain at War*, for *London Calling*, or for *Queen Mary's Book for India*, was speaking, against the deluded England of such as Harold Laski, for the England of Lancelot Andrewes, of John Bramhall and Nicholas Ferrar – an England just as little known or regarded by the British soldier as the America of Martin Van Buren was by any G.I. in the army of General Patton. In both cases – in Yeats's too, for that matter – we have a poet offering to speak to and for his nation, but in the service of a national tradition which each nation has, absent-mindedly, repudiated. Eliot might have remarked, and very forcefully too, that at least in his case the repudiated tradition persisted in the letter if not in the spirit, institutionalized – as the Church of England. Mr Graham Martin makes the point very well when he asks: 'in 1942 who but Eliot would be likely to have felt drawn away from the contemporary crisis by the "antique drum" of Charles the Martyr's confrontation with Oliver Cromwell?' But when he proceeds at once to declare, 'This aspect of the poem seems unlikely to wear well,' surely we may retort that it is likely to wear as well as the Church of England has.

The cultural value of such an institution as that Church – however 'ossified', however 'empty', however its persistence may be 'merely formal' – is something that we can find acknowledged by Eliot's peers, by Yeats and Pound. And indeed, their acknowledgement of it is what sticks indigestibly in the gullet of the neo-Rousseauistic generations who succeeded them, whose simplifications we have somehow to cope with at the present day. Yet it was in his generation Eliot who hammered this point home most insistently; and hence the particular venom that is reserved for him in the vocabulary of our neo-Rousseauists. For what they cannot forgive Eliot is that he proved his principles right in practice; that he, alone among Anglo-American poets of his generation, achieved what (in some sense, surely) they were all aiming at. His is the one incontestable success story; he spoke for his adopted nation, and that nation acknowledged his right to do so, for after all he *did* get the O.M., and he *is* memorialized in Westminster Abbey. How indigestible that cannot fail to be, for those who want to recruit poetry into the ranks of the perpetual (perpetually irreconcilable) opposition!

When I say that the English nation thirty years ago recognized Eliot's right to speak for them, of course I am not forgetting that the overwhelming majority in the British Army, the Royal Navy and the Royal Air Force did not know even his name. Indeed, I am speaking impressionistically, out of memories and on the basis of such evidence as the flyleaf of my copy of *Selected Essays*, which reveals that it was purchased in Colombo, Ceylon, in 1945, and was apparently filched by me from a mess-mate. Undoubtedly there were many, in 1942 or 1945, who preferred the wittily and impudently erudite young American of 1920 to the voice of the Establishment which spoke to us in the new poems of the 1940s. Let F.W. Bateson speak for them, wistfully honouring the scholarly and Laforguian impertinence of Eliot's youth: 'The scholarship, it was true, was only skin-deep, whereas the Anglo-Catholicism was devoted and sincere, but most of us – English and American – will continue to prefer "The Hippopotamus" and its progeny to *The Rock* and its successors.' Among those who would agree are, we may suppose, the survivors of that Bloomsbury whose *mores*, sexual and other, seem to have exacerbated (though admittedly the record is far from complete) the disintegration of Vivien Eliot, and hence of Eliot's first marriage. In any case, the fact remains – that the author of 'The Hippopotamus' could not have been the voice of an embattled nation, as the author of *The Rock* and the *Four Quartets* could be, and was.

Of course, to a later British generation than Mr Bateson's or mine, these are in any case 'battles long ago'. In Mr Jonathan Raban's very sprightly and entertaining *The Society of the Poem*, published last year in London, it is hard to decide what is more remarkable – that for Mr Raban, as for Ivor Richards nearly fifty years ago, modern British poetry should start with that American whom the late Lord Russell found so singularly lacking in vitality; or that the poems of that American which are found so momentous should still be 'The Love Song of J. Alfred Prufrock' and *The Waste Land*. It seems that our younger contemporaries are determined to hang on to the piecemeal world which *The Waste Land* presents to them, as it did to us; and that just for that reason they repudiate that world as put together again in *Four Quartets* – repudiate it, yet not with contumely. (For if there is one thing more out of fashion than Anglican dogma, it is fiercely reasoned objections to it, such as Kathleen Nott directed at *Four Quartets* a generation ago.) No, it is simply assumed that anything the Archbishop of Canterbury might countenance cannot be right; for the Church of England, now as in 1931, belongs for the Englishman in the world of public ritual and social decencies, not in the world of real private worries and desolations.

Thus Eliot was as isolated at the end of his life as halfway through it; and the tired and devious procedures of a late work like *Notes Towards a Definition of Culture* suggest that, understandably, he found the condition less 'exhilarating' as time went on. He had chosen – though (as I have argued) always on his own, quite special terms – to ally himself with the British Establishment. And in Eliot's lifetime that Establishment was, as it always is in England, non-intellectual. Like that other brilliant and quixotic immigrant, Edmund Burke, when faced with a choice between the more or less international community of intellectuals and the community of the nation, Eliot opted firmly for the latter; and was eager to defend his choice, as Burke was. Unavoidably, in both cases, the intellectuals raise the cry, 'A sellout!' – from their point of view, quite properly. The heat that is engendered, even now, in both parties to the quarrel about Edmund Burke is similarly to be expected – and, in all seriousness, it is to be welcomed – in Eliot's case.

All of this would be beside the point, it would be fruitless special pleading, if *Four Quartets* were – simply as writing, as configurations of and engagements with the English language – manifestly inferior to *The Waste Land* and other earlier poems. And, of course, on both sides of the Atlantic it is quite commonly said that this indeed is the case. I don't know what to do about this – in the first place, to vindicate a poet's use of language at that crucial level is something that cannot be done properly in a single essay; and secondly, modesty shall not prevent me from saying that I am among those who, in the medium of closely reasoned print, have attempted that vindication more than once. If I haven't persuaded Helen Vendler on those earlier occasions, I can hardly hope to do so now.

Accordingly it seems more profitable to attend to Hugh Kenner, who believes as I do that the *Quartets* (though uneven) are a substantial achievement, and to see if we can agree on what that achievement is. In *The Pound Era* Kenner offers a sort of definition when, speaking of the *Quartets*, he says: 'To unite... a *Symboliste* heritage with an Augustan may have been Eliot's most original act.' And so far as 'the *Symboliste* heritage' goes, we must be happy to concur: sluggishly and belatedly we have got round to recognizing that the title Eliot gave to these poems, together with the allusions that they make to Mallarmé, places them as part of the French *symboliste* endeavour to make poetry 'approach the condition of music'.[1] But the Augustan ingredient in the concoction is harder to isolate. And to my mind Kenner is on shaky ground when he decides that for the *Quartets* Eliot 'went to the most inconspicuous of English poets, the ones who flourished a generation after Pope and were accustomed to take up a stance in a particularized landscape and meditate'. To begin with, it is not clear who these poets are. Kenner goes on to cite Gray of the *Elegy*, hardly the least conspicuous of English poets, or of English poems; but in any case it is hard to see what other poets of Gray's generation, except some deservedly forgotten, could be made to stand with him on these terms. *East Coker* is the Quartet which best fits Kenner's case, as when he remarks: 'Of all the famous poems that have preceded it *East Coker* most resembles Gray's *Elegy*, with its churches, its tombstone, its hallowed voiceless dead, its rustic intelligences.' And we can readily agree that the two poems begin with strikingly similar sentiments:

> In my beginning is my end. In succession
> Houses rise and fall, crumble, are extended,
> Are removed, destroyed, restored, or in their place
> Is an open field, or a factory, or a by-pass.
> Old stone to new building, old timber to new fires,
> Old fires to ashes, and ashes to the earth
> Which is already flesh, fur and faeces,
> Bone of man and beast, cornstalk and leaf.
> Houses live and die: there is a time for building
> And a time for living and for generation
> And a time for the wind to break the loosened pane
> And to shake the wainscot where the field-mouse trots
> And to shake the tattered arras woven with a silent motto.

1   Though these words resemble several of Mallarmé's observations about poetry and music, they are more or less quoted from Walter Pater's 'Conclusion' to *The Renaissance* (1873). See my Introduction, p. x above. [Ed.]

But if the sentiments are like Thomas Gray's, the expression is surely very far indeed from the marmoreal succinctness of his elegiac quatrains. 'Succinct' is the last word one would think of applying to this passage, or to many passages in the *Quartets*; and I realize very well that this heavy stamping up and down on one spot – old this to new that four times over, and a time for this and a time for that, and to shake this and to shake that – is what exasperates many readers. Yet the effect is not one of dispersal and dilution, only of gloomy insistence. I think there is nothing comparable in Thomas Gray. But in *The Book of Common Prayer*, there is:

> Lay not up for yourselves treasure upon earth; where the rust and moth doth corrupt, and where thieves break through and steal: but lay up for yourselves treasures in heaven; where neither rust nor moth doth corrupt, and where thieves do not break through and steal.[2]

And who can miss, behind 'Old fires to ashes, and ashes to the earth', the order of service for the burial of the dead – 'we therefore commit his body to the ground; earth to earth, ashes to ashes, dust to dust…'? Or, behind 'Bone of man and beast, cornstalk and leaf', the piercing sentences from the same order of service: 'Man that is born of a woman hath but a short time to live, and is full of misery. He cometh up, and is cut down, like a flower; he fleeth as it were a shadow, and never continueth in one stay'? Archbishop Cranmer was not a succinct writer, and yet no part of *The Book of Common Prayer* is either diffuse or florid. The effect is, to my ear, that when we reach the quotation in antique spelling from Sir Thomas Elyot's *Boke Named The Governour* it is as if this too were from a homily spoken in a Tudor church:

> The association of man and woman
> In daunsinge, signifying matrimonie –
> A dignified and commodious sacrament.
> Two and two, necessarye coniunction,
> Holding eche other by the hand or the arm
> Whiche betokeneth concorde…

And why not? Sir Thomas Elyot was Cranmer's and Coverdale's contemporary, as was Mary Queen of Scots, on whose motto, 'In my end is my beginning', *East Coker* both begins and ends. It looks as it the component of the poem which is not *symboliste* is rather Tudor than Hanoverian. And in being so it is the more Anglican.

Yet of course Hugh Kenner had good reason to look in the *Quartets* for the note of English Augustanism, to look for it and even, in one sense, to find it. For there is no doubt that behind Eliot's writing in these poems there lie Johnson's 'London' and his 'Vanity of Human Wishes' – poems

---

2   This is in fact from the King James Version of the Bible (1611): Matthew 6.19–20. [Ed.]

which years before had provoked from Eliot the apparently trenchant but in fact characteristically slippery dictum, 'Great poetry must be at least as well written as good prose.' The poetry of the *Quartets* swings to and fro between the sonorous opalescence of Mallarmé and, at the opposite extreme, a prosaicism so homespun as to be, from time to time, positively 'prosy' or 'prosing'. It is at or about this prosaic role of the poem's language that, as Eliot says, 'the poetry does not matter'. And it is this pole of the language that can be charged by the insistent explicitness of the Anglican homiletic and devotional tradition. It was because Gray typically ignored this prosaic pole of poetic diction that Johnson, in his *Life* of Gray, cavilled at all Gray's poems except the *Elegy*. And of course it is Johnson, not the Erastian Gray, who represents the Hanoverian Church of England at its noblest and most humane. For already, ten years after the death of Pope, English Augustanism is no longer homogeneous but splitting into opposed camps, Johnson and Goldsmith on the one hand, Gray and the Wartons on the other; and Eliot as critic ranged himself firmly with Johnson and Goldsmith. Thus there *are* Augustan principles at work in and behind the poetry of the *Quartets*, but they are the principles of only one wing of late-Augustanism, the wing that was, both politically and poetically, conservative (whereas Gray in his time was thought of – and rightly – as a radical innovator). Because it is conservative, Johnson's Augustanism is not specifically Hanoverian but takes pride in holding true to a tradition of prosaic verse which reaches back, in the *Lives of the Poets*, through Denham and Cowley even to Donne, a tradition which we can without difficulty trace back further still, through Ben Jonson and Ralegh to Tudor times.

This is something more than captious infighting between me and Hugh Kenner – to whom, as it happens, I feel myself under a greater obligation than to any other critic of the *Quartets*. For it is only if we insist on the prosaicism of much of the *Quartets* that we can recognize the high tension set up between this element and, at the other pole, the Mallarméan *symbolisme*. On the one hand a form that is musical, non-discursive; on the other hand a content that for long stretches is painstakingly discursive, even pedestrian; on the one hand Mallarmé, byword for poetry that is all implication and suggestion, on the other hand Cranmer, bleakly and unsparingly explicit; on the one hand nonce words like 'a grimpen' and unseizable sonorities like 'The loud lament of the disconsolate chimera', on the other hand 'There are three conditions which often look alike/Yet differ completely, flourish in the same hedgerow'; on the one hand poetry at its most private, on the other hand poetry at its most public and, for the sake of being public, prepared to dispense with most of its customary ornaments and splendours.

It is small wonder if the product of such extreme tension is a poem remarkably uneven in tone if not in quality; a poem which has to make a formal virtue out of its own disparities, by inviting us to think that it switches tone only as Beethoven does when he completes a slow movement and embarks upon a *scherzo*. What interests me more is to ask how a poet can ever get himself in the situation of creating such a tension and attempting to resolve it. And I suppose that this might come about if a poet compelled by temperament as well as history to school himself in the ironic reticences of Henry James on the one hand and Jules Laforgue on the other, should find himself wanting to speak to and for a nation which conceives of itself as cornered into a situation which is wholly unironical because not in the least ambiguous. For such a poet (who may be wholly imaginary) I should feel affection as well as esteem.

Southern Review, new series, 9.1 (January 1973).

XIX *The Modernist* malgré lui

It would not be particularly spiteful to wonder if the flood of books about
Eliot, a river that has been in full spate for as long as any of us can
remember, doesn't have its source in the commonplaceness of this poet's
personality. Being commonplace, Eliot's personality is one that almost
anyone can sympathize with. If we add, 'except of course that he was very
intelligent', the exception will seem to some to qualify the assertion to the
point where it has no force. But this doesn't follow: the exceptional intelligence moved along tracks, and within categories (for the most part
binary and opposed), that were indeed commonplace, not just in the
United States but also in Britain, through the years 1884 to 1914 – when
Eliot was growing up. Indeed, more lamentably, the radical *either/or* (in
one gross formulation, impulsive yearning versus civic order) is what
young and energetic minds still, in 1984, experience as the choice before
them – which explains why Eliot's arcane and fastidious poetry has
become, as it did even in his lifetime, a talismanic sacred deposit which
hardly anyone is brave enough to question. Perhaps because Peter
Ackroyd[1] comes to Eliot after a study of Pound, he is brave enough to
raise the question; and though he does so only suavely and by implication,
it is this that makes his biography necessary and important.

Recently, other wary champions of Eliot, recognizing the vulnerable
commonplaceness of his ideas and of the antinomies which he dredged
from among them, have claimed for him, over and above his intelligence
in the ordinary sense (sharp and probing), another intelligence, more fluc-
tuant and fed from deeper sources, which they call – not without some
prompting from the poet's own later lectures and essays – 'musical'.
Ackroyd makes this claim. But the truth is surely that Eliot had at best a
scrupulous ear for *vers libéré* – itself, so some would argue, an inherently
coarse and compromised medium; in strict metre Hardy, and in true *vers
libre* Pound, went far beyond him. And after all to say of Eliot that he was
commonplace is only a rude way of saying that he was representative. It
is entertaining therefore to see one commentator after another insist on
the specialness of Eliot's tormented passage through life. In fact what they
see in that mirror is only their own torments (real ones, we need not
doubt) writ large and writ special.

1 Peter Ackroyd, *T.S. Eliot* (London: Hamish Hamilton, 1984).

To be particular: no one up to now has proved to us that growing up in St Louis from 1888 to 1906 was in any essential respects, as the young Eliot experienced it, different from growing up through the same span of years in Leeds or Newcastle or Liverpool. To be sure, there were indeed special dimensions to the St Louis experience – as the poet's neglected father Henry Ware Eliot encountered them, in brushes with the still not wholly extirpated redskins; but there is no evidence that the poet shared these experiences with his father, even vicariously. And as for the portentous matter of the Mississippi that washes by St Louis, Ronald Bush[2] (if not Peter Ackroyd) agrees that the celebration of this in 'The Dry Salvages' is at best on the level of Paul Robeson, willed and external, in no way comparable with the presence that the great river attains to in the pages of Mark Twain. The young Eliot grew up in St Louis cocooned by his mother from that rude actuality in a dream of Boston, and behind Boston of an imaginary, largely Italianate, Europe.

Undoubtedly Eliot's life-record might not seem so commonplace (read, 'respectable') if we were allowed access to documents not already fitted and filleted for public consumption. Ackroyd lets us know that the Eliot estate continues to stone-wall; he has not been permitted to quote from Eliot's unpublished work or from his correspondence – a prohibition that commits him to the very unsatisfactory procedure of telling us about poems from Eliot's juvenilia that he cannot put before us, even in part. Inevitably the suspicion grows, perhaps quite unjustly, that the material withheld from us contains outrageously explicit revelations. If the overt life and character are so commonplace, the buried life and person must be the opposite – an illogical but natural deduction. In the meantime the prohibition provides a field-day for interpretations called 'psychoanalytic', of which Tony Pinkney's slim book is, despite its misleadingly reductive title, an unusually sprightly and strenuous example.[3] The truth may well be that the psycho-cultural stresses that bore in on Yeats and Pound are, just because they are less typical, more interesting than those which conditioned Eliot. But psycho-analytic theory, remorselessly generalizing, cannot afford to think so. An Eliot who is ourselves-writ-large is a spectacle as consoling to psycho-analysis as to 'the common reader'.

Psycho-analytic criticism has lately become sophisticated and revisionist. If not by way of Jacques Lacan (to whom Pinkney devotes two respectful pages), then by way of Melanie Klein and D.W. Winnicott (to whom Pinkney is more subservient), Freud himself is nowadays treated as the patriarchal pioneer whose findings – however deserving of respect in the perspective of history – must be regarded as decisively outdistanced

2   Ronald Bush, *T.S. Eliot: A Study in Character and Style* (Oxford: OUP, 1983).
3   Tony Pinkney, *Women in the Poetry of T.S. Eliot: A Psychoanalytic Approach* (London: Macmillan, 1984).

and cancelled by later researches. 'Researches' and also 'findings' must always in these contexts be inside inverted commas; for of course what we have, as we move from Sigmund Freud to Anna Freud, thence to Melanie Klein and (with genuflections towards Lacan) to Winnicott, is not a science gradually refining itself but on the contrary one mythological schema superseding another. Mythology undoubtedly has its uses; and Pinkney's Kleinian pre-Oedipal mythology illuminates Eliot's prose-poem, 'Hysteria', as Freud's Oedipal mythology could not. ('Hysteria', significantly, gets in Bush's voluminous book no notice at all.) All the same, mythology is what we are dealing with; so long as we remember that, Pinkney's mythology does more than Bush's or Ackroyd's to make interesting – I will not say, to elucidate – the poet whom Randall Jarrell many years ago declared, of all modern poets, the one who most cried out for psychoanalytic attention.

The commonplaceness, of the sensibility, and of the lived witness; that we are forced back to. Bush at sometimes wearisome length establishes how the overtly 'modernist' Eliot gave way, step by step in the years after *The Waste Land*, to the incantatory poet whose first and perhaps last hero was Edgar Allan Poe. The seemingly modernist poet of *The Waste Land* and *Poems* (1920) appears in the perspective as an artfully provisional and temporary persona – not fabricated, as some have thought, at the behest of Ezra Pound, but rather a product of that intelligence, Eliot's, which showed itself at this as at all times predominantly an intelligence for manoeuvre, for polemical and rhetorical strategies. There is no question of betrayal, of 'selling out'; on this showing Eliot's was throughout a late-Romantic sensibility, which adroitly cornered the market for a time by pretending to be otherwise, which then (the market once cornered) threw off the wraps and re-appeared in its true colours. And after all we hardly need Bush's close arguments to prove this; for how else can we explain how the author of *The Waste Land* should have become, as a middle-aged publisher, the patron of Edwin Muir?

This view of Eliot's career, though it is a possibility opened up by all of these books, is not explicitly advanced by any of them. Ackroyd and Bush and Pinkney are all prepared to believe that Eliot's propaganda for a dry and impersonal otherness in the artifact answered to an urgent psychical need in himself, even as a no less urgent need for the incantatory was undermining it. It is Pinkney who does best with this, grounding his arguments on the one writer in whom Kleinian psychology intersected for a time with trained connoisseurship; that is to say, Adrian Stokes. Pinkney remarks, as we must all acknowledge once it is pointed out to us, that in Stokes's by now notorious distinction in the art of sculpture between carving and moulding, the second alternative – moulding, or modelling – though overtly it is offered as on a par with carving is, in the event, consistently discredited. Pinkney's point, if I read him aright, is that Stokes's therapy with Melanie Klein was designed to, and did, put him right about this, and restored a balance. In Pinkney's book there is a great deal of palaver hereabouts, having to do with projection and intro-jection of the mother's breast, and of the father's or the male infant's penis. But behind all this optional mythopoeia an important distinction is being made, and one that undoubtedly has as much bearing on the good poet Eliot as on the bad poet Stokes: a distinction between one and another way in which the artist, whether sculptor or poet, regards the rudely natural material that he has to fashion into art.

The obvious and yet misleading dilemma presents itself: he either surrenders to that material, or else he masters it. All the evidence we have suggests on the contrary that the successful artistic transaction has the paradoxical character of mastery-by-way-of-surrender. And many of our currently heated debates of theory, more importantly our different valua-tions of particular artistic achievements, turn on how much weight we give, in this compound, to surrender against mastery, mastery against surrender. If some people choose to take as the prototype of this mastery-surrender compound the feeding infant's experience of the maternal breast, that is neither here nor there; the contention can be neither proven nor disproven. The double-focus on the material to be shaped is in any case an abundantly documented constant in the life of many artists; and in the case of the artist Eliot the double-focus is, we may agree, the source and cause of painful, though not specially painful, tensions. Speaking as one who has invested perhaps immoderately in the stony, the marmoreal and lapidary character of the art-object, I concede that Pinkney has persuaded me, as earlier harpers on the same string haven't, that there may well be, behind such an emphatic prediction, anxieties that may be called 'depressive', at all events neurotic. As for the counter-stress in Eliot, if we call it 'incantatory', that must be understood only as a convenient short-hand; what it signifies is a preference for the rounded and melting contour, as against the chiseller's sharp edge. And undoubt-edly, from *The Waste Land* onwards, Eliot steadily took the first option. So Ackroyd can say, very justly,

> it was Eliot who in the end loosened the hold of the 'modernists' on English culture − not only did he assert the public role and 'social usefulness' of the writer in an almost nineteenth-century manner, but he also announced that the principles he derived from his religious belief were more enduring than literary or critical ones. He helped to create the idea of a modern movement with his own 'difficult' poetry, and then assisted at its burial.

Ackroyd, it will be observed, is a very temperate writer; it would be possible to put the matter of that last sentence more resentfully, by saying that Eliot, having seemed to liberate us from a Tennysonian understanding of poetry, ended up by plunging us into the Tennysonian universe more deeply than ever. At any event, such a drift towards the incantatory was not exceptional in Eliot's generation, since it has been (so one might argue) the undertow consensus of every generation for 200 years; it was Eliot's eminence, particularly as publisher, that made his acceding to the drift so influential.

What no one denies is the extreme and indeed plainly excessive conventionalism of Eliot in each of the successive roles of his public existence. As Harvard undergraduate, Oxford graduate, bank official, London publisher – Eliot played each role to the limit according to pre-ordained notions of what was proper. Ever since Hugh Kenner's *The Invisible Poet* we have been invited to reflect: Aha! it is precisely the excessiveness of the impersonation that gives it away as a historical mask, defensive camouflage. No one since Conrad Aiken has entertained the possibility that the appearance corresponded to the reality; that Eliot was in fact a profoundly conventional and conformist person. To put the case at its most plausible and pitiful – is it not true that of the most conventional and conformist people we know, only the most stupid can be thought to be unaware of the histrionically defensive mask that they wear? Some of them, to come right down to it, may be hiding behind that mask a marriage not much less tormentedly unsatisfying than Eliot's to Vivien Haigh-Wood. To use that sort of mask to conceal that sort of failure is after all (and it is only compassionate to say so) quite commonplace also. It's along these lines that we seem to understand Eliot's determined dalliance with Bloomsbury. Pound and Wyndham Lewis, his early friends and champions, disapproved of this; and Vivien was distressed by it. Yet Eliot persisted. To an insecure and therefore anxiously conformist person, it may have seemed enough that Bloomsbury was publicly esteemed as a privileged inner circle; conformity would require that Eliot make his bow there, not once but often. Harder to explain is the impression that Ackroyd cannot help but give, that in some personal relations Eliot seems to have been ruthless. Regarding his behaviour at crucial times towards his first wife, towards John Hayward and Emily Hale and Mary Trevelyan, we can only wonder if we ourselves, and commonplace characters generally, are not more hard-hearted than we like to suppose.

The difficult though hackneyed question is: supposing we detect, or think we detect, deficiencies in the poet as a moral agent in life, what bearing does this have on our judgement of his poetry? From the position that such information or speculation has *no* bearing on the poetry, we have advanced – if that is the word – to the position that Ackroyd seems not altogether certainly to adopt: so far from the man's failures in life reflecting adversely on his artistic work, it is precisely those failures that make possible and even underwrite his triumphs in art – for the art is the compensation for (the acknowledgment and yet overcoming of) the failures in living. This is undoubtedly compassionate in a way that the author of *After Strange Gods* rather notably wasn't. But in effect, as the moralistic author of *After Strange Gods* certainly recognized, it allows to the artist a special dispensation to behave badly. Eliot, to give him some credit at last, wouldn't buy that: sin is sin, and hell is hell, for the artist as for any other human creature. Eliot's Christianity – unappetizing as it is for many Christians, and lop-sided though it must seem to most – has at any rate this great virtue: it is not designed to get him off the hook. And indeed his embracing of Christian faith, on these particularly disadvantageous terms, is the one event in Eliot's life that lifts him far above the commonplace, just as it is the extra dimension to his experience that lifts him above Pound, in all other respects so much more decent and generous, and above Yeats. It is sadly true that after his conversion Eliot seems even more deficient in Christian charity than he was before; but at least he is no more charitable to himself than he is to others. And his Christianity was serious in other ways. When in later life he disparaged his poetry – even as he continued to practise it, and was quite avid for the rewards it brought him – he meant what he said: as between salvation and damnation, his poetry counted for nothing, unless indeed it counted towards damnation. This is a dimension of Eliot's experience that none of his commentators do justice to; and indeed there is no currently acceptable mode of critical biographical discourse that can accommodate it.

From time to time in Bush's book we recognize the author of his earlier, irreplaceably thorough study, *The Genesis of Ezra Pound's Cantos*. But writing about Eliot, Bush has let his once admirable thoroughness deteriorate into a sedate assumption that he has all the time in the world. What reader, one asks oneself, does Bush envisage, with the leisure to proceed at this ambling and yet arduous pace? And the answer can only be, I fear: a fellow-professional (for Bush is Associate Professor at Cal Tech). Eliot's anxiously conventional urbanities, for instance as London clubman, had at least the virtue of discouraging such heavy-breathing professionalism among his commentators. This strenuous expansiveness in Bush is a great pity; for he asks the probing questions about *Four Quartets* which Ackroyd, in an unusual lapse, idly skims over (Pinkney, for his part, passes by the *Quartets* with a casual reference to their 'equanimity' – which certainly reveals the limitations of *his* critical approach). Ackroyd astutely notices how American readers have tended to resist the *Quartets*, whereas the British have taken these poems to their collective heart perhaps too readily. This difference is likely to persist; for even if we agree with Bush that there is something seriously wrong with at least 'The Dry Salvages', no British reader is likely to think, as Bush wants him to, that Eliot's misjudgement about it was of a sort once diagnosed by Emerson and denounced again in Eliot's lifetime by William Carlos Williams. Eliot's sensibility may indeed have been Romantic or post-

Romantic; but this is not to say that to get the correct perspective on his achievement we need delve no further back than the nineteenth century.

Ackroyd's touch deserts him lamentably, I think, when he proceeds to his peroration:

> Both as a writer and as a man, his genius lay in his ability to resist the subversive tendencies of his personality by fashioning them into something larger than himself. His work represents the brilliant efflorescence of a dying culture: he pushed that culture together by an act of will, giving it a shape and context which sprang out of his own obsessions, and the certainties which he established were rhetorical certainties. In so doing he became a symbol of the age, and his poetry became its echoing music – with its brooding grandeur as well as its bleakness, its plangency as well as its ellipses, its rhythmical strength as well as its theatrical equivocations.

This is distinguished writing; yet surely this dying fall should be resisted. For what is this culture that is declared to be 'dying'? English? Anglo-American? European? And what does it mean in any case to say of a culture that it is dead or dying? Surely we may think that a culture dies only through a failure of nerve on the part of those who should sustain it, and purvey its values; by a willingness on their part to assist in its premature obsequies. It would be more modest and more plausible to say that Eliot's poetry witnesses, not to the death of a culture, but only to the end of an era. What happens surely, at the time of such an end, is that the ruling élite and the governing class (there is normally much overlap between them) prove themselves incapable of exercising the rule that history has delegated to them. In Eliot's lifetime the high bourgeoisie of England – so it might be argued – proved itself a class or a caste from which in this way virtue had departed. Eliot, who as an American did not have to ally himself with this caste, in fact chose to do so. (This is the meaning of his Bloomsbury connections.) The era of their dominance is decisively over, though the veneration accorded not unjustly to Eliot's handling of language has the effect of concealing the sterility and frivolity of those for whom he chose to act as spokesman. What will survive the dissolution of this hegemony, and its suppression by some other, is that part or aspect of Eliot's writing which makes it part of the by no means dying culture of Christendom.

Times Literary Supplement, 12 September 1984.

XX A Fascist Poem: Yeats's 'Blood and the Moon'

There have been so many commentaries on Yeats's poetry that no one – certainly not I – can claim to be conversant with all or even most of them. However, to the best of my knowledge, no one has yet read out of Yeats's 'Blood and the Moon' the dismaying and alarming meaning that I find it presents to me. The poem first appeared in spring 1928, in Pound's Paris magazine, *The Exile*; and this may be to the point, for I read the poem as expressing a fascism more thorough-going than Pound would have professed at that time, and in some ways more unpalatable than Pound would profess at *any* time. This is not in the least to extenuate Pound's fascism, but it *is* meant to suggest how much more indulgent we have been, and continue to be, towards Yeats's fascism than towards Pound's. When we are compelled – for instance, by Conor Cruise O'Brien – to recognize that in old age Yeats was quite consciously and voluntarily a fascist, we still try to huddle this aberration away into his very last collection, as we find it for instance in the unmistakable allusions to racism and eugenics in 'Under Ben Bulben', the poem of 1938 that stands last in the *Collected Poems*, declaring:

> Know that when all words are said
> And a man is fighting mad,
> Something drops from eyes long blind,
> He completes his partial mind...

The point of looking at 'Blood and the Moon', undoubtedly a less impressive poem than 'Under Ben Bulben', is to establish, if I am right, that Yeats was no less a fascist a good ten years earlier.

Since 'Blood and the Moon' is not a very well-known poem, I must be allowed to quote it in full:

I

> Blessed be this place,
> More blessed still this tower;
> A bloody, arrogant power
> Rose out of the race

Uttering, mastering it,
Rose like these walls from these
Storm-beaten cottages —
In mockery I have set
A powerful emblem up,
And sing it rhyme upon rhyme
In mockery of a time
Half dead at the top.

II

Alexandria's was a beacon tower, and Babylon's
An image of the moving heavens, a log-book of the sun's journey
    and the moon's;
And Shelley had his towers, thought's crowned powers he called
    them once.

I declare this tower is my symbol; I declare
This winding, gyring, spiring treadmill of a stair is my ancestral stair;
That Goldsmith and the Dean, Berkeley and Burke have travelled
                                                          there.

Swift beating on his breast in sibylline frenzy blind
Because the heart in his blood-sodden breast had dragged him down
    into mankind,
Goldsmith deliberately sipping at the honey-pot of his mind,

And haughtier-headed Burke that proved the State a tree,
That this unconquerable labyrinth of the birds, century after century,
Cast but dead leaves to mathematical equality;

And God-appointed Berkeley that proved all things a dream,
That this pragmatical, preposterous pig of a world, its farrow that so
    solid seem,
Must vanish on the instant if the mind but change its theme;

Saeva Indignatio and the labourer's hire,
The strength that gives our blood and state magnanimity of its own
    desire;
Everything that is not God consumed with intellectual fire.

III

The purity of the unclouded moon
Has flung its arrowy shaft upon the floor.
Seven centuries have passed and it is pure,
The blood of innocence has left no stain.

> There, on blood-saturated ground, have stood
> Soldier, assassin, executioner,
> Whether for daily pittance or in blind fear
> Or out of abstract hatred, and shed blood,
> But could not cast a single jet thereon.
> Odour of blood on the ancestral stair!
> And we that have shed none must gather there
> And clamour in drunken frenzy for the moon.

IV

> Upon the dusty, glittering windows cling,
> And seem to cling upon the moonlit skies,
> Tortoiseshell butterflies, peacock butterflies,
> A couple of night-moths are on the wing.
> Is every modern nation like the tower,
> Half dead at the top? No matter what I said
> For wisdom is the property of the dead,
> A something incompatible with life; and power,
> Like everything that has the stain of blood,
> A property of the living; but no stain
> Can come upon the visage of the moon
> When it has looked in glory from a cloud.

It is awkward to have to start accounting for this poem by bringing in information from outside it, but it will save time to do so. Accordingly, I start with what Joseph Hone says about it in his pioneering biography (*W.B. Yeats 1865–1939*, 1942), where we learn that this is one of two poems written under the immediate impact of the assassination of Kevin O'Higgins, Ireland's authoritarian 'strong man', whom Yeats knew well and admired, shot down on a Sunday morning in July 1927. Particularly pertinent is Hone's quoting from *On the Boiler*, the last piece of prose that Yeats wrote, where (I quote Hone) 'he was to place O'Higgins in his Irish "saga" with Berkeley, Swift, Burke, Grattan, Synge, Lady Gregory'. This is important because it suggests that the litany of names in the second section of the poem is only accidentally Anglo-Irish and Protestant; it is meant to be *Irish*, and the addition of O'Higgins makes it so. Yeats, when he added that name in *On the Boiler*, made the point explicitly: 'If the Catholic names are few on the list, history will soon fill the gap...'

History *will...* The future tense gives another clue: the litany of names in the poem is not backward-looking, elegiac, but forward-looking and menacing. And indeed the poem itself virtually says as much:

> A bloody, arrogant power
> Rose out of the race...

As an account of Ireland's recorded past this is just untrue, as Yeats's Irish readers would be the first to realize. The bloody power did not rise out of the Irish race, but was imposed upon it – time and again, from the days of the Anglo-Norman overlordship that left behind the tower Thoor Ballylee in which and about which Yeats is writing. Thus, he is writing of an Ascendancy that *will* come; the Ascendancy that has been is a sort of guide to this, but with the difference (less crucial to Yeats than to many) that the new Ascendancy will rise out of the race – naturally, so a fascist would say – whereas the Ascendancy that has been was imposed by a colonizing power on the race subjugated and colonized. It is natural, when we first encounter the roll call of Goldsmith and Swift, Berkeley and Burke, to suppose that it serves the same purpose as when a similar roll is called in other poems and in a famous Senate speech; that is to say, to stand for the minority, once ascendant but now dispossessed, for which Yeats in the Republic is making himself a spokesman. But this is a blind, a false scent deliberately laid by Yeats who, in 1928, as Cruise O'Brien explains, chose not to express his fascist sentiments openly. The charge of 'fascism' has yet to be substantiated, as I am aware; but at least we must realize that in this poem more is going on than meets the eye.

'Uttering, mastering it' – the avowed mockery with which this 'powerful emblem' is set up derives from the difference between 'uttering' and 'mastering'. To utter and articulate the race consciousness is certainly in one sense to master the race. In fact it may be the most perdurable sort of mastery. But it differs from other sorts of mastery in that it is achieved without the spilling of blood; those who achieve the sort of mastery that is utterance (and they include all the names in the second section of the poem) are shut out from the blood tie that, in the third section, binds together master and mastered, the assassin and his victim, the leader and his henchmen, the native Irish, the Norman-Irish, and the Anglo-Irish. This is the point of bringing in the figures of Percy Bysshe Shelley and the Alexandrian and Babylonian astronomers. Some commentators – for instance, Denis Donoghue in a volume called *An Honoured Guest* – can see in these allusions nothing but a muddling distraction. But they are crucial, because they show that the Anglo-Irish names which follow are introduced not just as Anglo-Irish (which we have suspected already), but also not as *Irish* – they are the names of utterers, articulators, in a word *intellectuals*. 'His towers, thought's crowned powers', in relation to Shelley, is a jawbreaking, uncouth expression, but what it says is important. The tower is Yeats's 'ancestral stair', partly because it is Irish, but far more because Yeats is an intellec-tual. Yeats is of the Ascendancy to come only in being the self-appointed laureate and apologist of that Ascendancy that will be, as Burke and the rest were apologists for the Ascendancy that once was.

Thus, in the third section ('we that have shed none'), the 'we' is not modern man as against men of the past. The 'we' is Yeats *and* Shelley *and* Burke *and* Berkeley *and* Goldsmith. And all of them are in drunken frenzy because they all want the blood bond which they are debarred from through being articulators, apologists, utterers. This means, so the poem says, that the assassins and their victims are 'innocent' in a way the artic-ulators never can be. And it is surely here – in the grotesque inversion by which 'innocence' is reserved for those who spill each other's blood – that the charge of 'fascism' can be made to stick. Yeats is a great poet, and we can respect the honesty of the logic that led him to this point; but what he says is sick and loathsome:

> Odour of blood on the ancestral stair!
> And we that have shed none must gather there
> And clamour in drunken frenzy for the moon

Moreover, the attempt to 'shoot the moon' is doomed to failure; even though the purity of a lunar monument like Berkeley's philosophy is never tarnished, yet even for Berkeley the end is in frustration, since power is humanly attainable whereas wisdom isn't – if only because the dead, who are truly wise, can never communicate their wisdom. (The commentators tell us, no doubt correctly, that the butterflies are, as in Dante, disembodied spirits too fragile to break into the lighted tower of human contemplation through the window to which they flutter. What it is beneath a commentator's dignity to say is that they are also, doubt-less, the night moths which the elderly poet saw outside the windowpane when he raised his eyes from the page he was working on.)

Thus every modern nation is – like the tower of Thoor Ballylee, with its concrete roof and unrepaired top storey – 'half dead at the top', not just because in non-fascist states the élite is not self-chosen, and thus not 'natural'; but also because, even in the fascist state to be hoped for, the clerisy, the apologists for the régime, will be excluded from the blood tie, disabled by guilt at this exclusion, and by frustration at knowing that their objective (the moon – they are lunatics) is unattainable.

Certain reflections present themselves. For it would surely be quite wrong to leave the impression that 'Blood and the Moon' has merely *diagnostic* significance, as showing the socio-political aberrations that one great poet, or even a generation of poets, could fall into. On the contrary, this poem, that seems at first sight so intensely, even parochially, Irish in its terms of reference, turns out when we look at it to be passing judge-ment on matters that are not peculiarly Irish at all. We may note in the first place that on our reading of the poem the poet is given no specially privileged status. He, and the artist generally, is downgraded, radically – Goldsmith, for instance, is presented as a mere epicure of the intellect, and the one poetic icon that is set up in the poem (the tower) is ravaged with mockery that is self-mockery; the writers in the poem are seen in their capacity as intellectuals, members of a clerisy, not as image-makers. Does this mean that fascism has no role for the image-maker to play? However that may be, it is not for nothing that I have used the Coleridgean term, 'clerisy'. Let us call it 'intelligentsia', if we find that more fashionable term more comfortable. Certainly what the poem is concerned with is the function of 'the intellectuals', considered as a distinct and in some degree corporate body in the modern state. And from that point of view the poem surely is an extreme formulation of the anguish felt by the intellectual under the repressive tolerance (as we used to call it some years ago) which is wished upon him by modern societies such as the British and the American. In Yeats's writing early and late this is a constant theme – the wish of the writer to be *held responsible*, to be *called to account for* the consequences of his own utterances:

> Did that play of mine send out
> Certain men the English shot?

Yeats wants the answer, yes! And if certain penalties attend upon the answer 'yes', he wants, quite desperately, to undergo those penalties. The supposedly enlightened toleration which permits a writer to say what he pleases, on the supposition that he will never be brought to book for the consequences, is what every writer must be glad of in his private and domestic capacity, at the same time as he indignantly deplores it, in his capacity as a member of the same international élite that includes, or once included, Boris Pasternak and Osip Mandelstam. The writer who believes in the nobility and necessity of his calling may even be pushed to the extreme and paradoxical position of yearning for those régimes, fascist or communist, in which his activity is thought important and influential enough to be worth persecuting and proscribing.

Trying to Explain (Manchester: Carcanet, 1980).

XXI Poets on Stilts: Yeats and Some Contemporaries

One of the poems of Yeats that has attracted least attention is in *Last Poems*. It is called 'High Talk'; and one reason why it is seldom noticed is, I should like to think, that it ends with Yeats at his most foolish and least plausible. However, up to the last three lines it contains much that is pleasing, and it addresses itself to one feature of Yeats's writing which I think we should, in 1982, be particularly concerned with:

> Processions that lack high stilts have nothing that catches the eye.
> What if my great-granddad had a pair that were twenty foot high,
> And mine were but fifteen foot, no modern stalks upon higher,
> Some rogue of the world stole them to patch up a fence or a fire.
> Because piebald ponies, led bears, caged lions, make but poor shows,
> Because children demand Daddy-long-legs upon his timber toes,
> Because women in the upper storeys demand a face at the pane,
> That patching old heels they may shriek, I take to chisel and plane.
>
> Malachi Stilt-Jack am I, whatever I learned has run wild,
> From collar to collar, from stilt to stilt, from father to child.
> All metaphor, Malachi, stilts and all. A barnacle goose
> Far up in the stretches of night; night splits and the dawn breaks loose;
> I, through the terrible novelty of light, stalk on, stalk on;
> Those great sea-horses bare their teeth and laugh at the dawn.

Some of the affection I feel for this obstreperous piece is without doubt eccentric. It intrigues me, for instance, that one of the more memorable phrases, 'Daddy-long-legs upon his timber toes', appears to be derived, and brilliantly adapted, from a peculiarly brutal ballad of the Royal Navy. This ballad, which is attributed to Henry Phipps, first Earl of Mulgrave and Viscount Normanby (1755–1831), commemorates, as the refrain has it, 'Howe, and the Glorious First of June!' – that is to say, Admiral Lord Howe's victory of 1 June 1794, when he took the Channel fleet to engage the French 500 miles off Ushant. It is imagined as spoken by a sailor who has lost a leg in the engagement:

My limb struck off, let soothing art
    The chance of war to Poll explain;
Proud of the loss, I feel no smart
But as it wrings my Polly's heart
    With sympathetic pain.
Yet she will think (with love so tried)
    Each scar a beauty on my face,
And as I strut with martial pride
On timber toe by Polly's side,
    Will call my limp a grace.

I cannot think this was an allusion that Yeats intended us to, as we say, 'pick up'; and yet, if it had been brought to his notice, I cannot believe that the Yeats of the *Last Poems* would have been disconcerted by it, least of all by its brutality. For Yeats at the end of his life was very deliberately a brutal poet. And one need not have a particularly weak stomach to catch one's breath at some of his brutalities. For instance. in 'Under Ben Bulben':

You that Mitchel's prayer have heard,
'Send war in our time, O Lord!'
Know that when all words are said
And a man is fighting mad,
Something drops from eyes long blind,
He completes his partial mind,
For an instant stands at ease,
Laughs aloud, his heart at peace.

Or there is, later in the same poem, the perhaps unintended but unmistakable reference to eugenics:

Scorn the sort now growing up
All out of shape from toe to top,
Their unremembering hearts and heads
Base-born products of base beds.

In so far as the mutilated Jack Tar of Mulgrave's ballad was presumably the base-born product of a base bed, Yeats's readiness to identify with him on the score of 'timber toes' seems positively humane and egalitarian compared with those later lines.

Readers who are affronted by the late Yeats's brutalities, particularly if they connect them with those flirtations with fascism that Conor Cruise O'Brien has documented, deserve in my view more of a hearing than we are usually prepared to give them. However, I'm not going to engage such objections directly, but only as they may or may not arise from those more narrowly *stylistic* objections that Yeats in 'High Talk' anticipates and retorts to. For this poem about a poet on stilts is surely a poem about *stilt-edness*, about putting on airs, talking tall. Is that the same as having a high, a lofty style? It's an important question. At any rate, Yeats shows himself very conscious that he is talking of a personal peculiarity; as for stilts, he says, though his are lower than what poets of the past have stalked upon, still, he says, 'no modern stalks upon higher'. And it is surely true that no twentieth-century poet in English, of comparable stature, has so insistently as Yeats affected the high style. It is just that about him, I suggest, that accounts for our having such a divided mind about him.

For we must surely start by recognizing, now in 1982, that Yeats's status is far from secure – his status, I mean, as one of the masters of modern poetry in English. To be sure this may mean only that Yeats is still alive, still a living presence among us; of him – as of Pound and Eliot and Stevens and others – we may say that, if ever he ceases to provoke animosity, then indeed he will be *dead*, marmoreally intact in his niche in the unquestioned (and seldom inspected) canon. But there is a difference, all the same. As I look back over thirty years, I am sure I see that the troubles and disquiets about Yeats have been growing, in a way or to a degree that is not true of the poets I have just bracketed with him. Yeats's status is uncertain, and growing more so. This has been truer on the European shore of the Atlantic than on the American shore. But isn't that what we should expect? Since 1969, to Irish Republican patriots as much as to Ulster separatists or the families of British soldiers, it has become plain that there yawns an appalling gap between on the one hand tall talk about Cathleen-na-Houlihan and her four green fields, or 'Cromwell's Curse', or 'the indomitable Irishry', and on the other hand the moral and civic squalor of present-day Belfast or Crossmaglen or Derry. Is it to be wondered at that on all these sides, from all these bodies of sentiment, there should be heard voices angry at, and contemptuous of, the poetic voice that disguised in sounding phrases the actuality of trip-wires, and the random long-distance murder and mutilation of infants? If we want poetry and the socio-political actuality to be drawn together, here we have a case of it; and the equation does not work out in favour of the poetic vision, nor of its supposedly privileged status. But in any case the groundswell against Yeats had been growing long before events in Northern Ireland gave to some of his poems an unwelcome topicality. Of many instances I might cite I will take C.H. Sisson, in his *English Poetry, 1900–1950: An Assessment* (first published in 1971, but surely written long before). Here Sisson, an English poet now in his sixties and plainly in some important respects a follower of Ezra Pound, decides that 'Yeats was a Victorian Great Man, extending himself by force of will right up to the outbreak of the Second World War, and adapting for his own use certain technical lessons of the twentieth century...' If, in that formulation, 'Victorian' doesn't speak with quite the baleful force that Sisson intends by it, consider some of his other formulations: 'One has only to put Yeats's work beside that of Hardy to be aware of the stiffness of his clothes. There is no psychology in Yeats, only magic. There are no people, only dolls – of elegant and dramatic appearance, very often.' Or consider this comment on one of the Crazy Jane poems ('I had wild Jack for a lover'): 'Those who think that realism should look up their Villon.' Almost identical is his response to 'Men Improve with the Years', where Yeats seems to ask us to see him as 'worn out with dreams;/A weather-worn, marble triton/Among the streams' – on which Sisson remarks: 'If anyone thinks that serious he should refresh himself with a course of Sir Thomas Wyatt.' When Sisson's book was reprinted late last year, it was this last comment which moved the *TLS* reviewer to protest: 'it simply will not do to attack magnificence, which is one of the poles of English poetry, in the name of authenticity, which is the other'. But of course this in its turn 'simply will not do'. For are we, admirers of Yeats, to settle for the supposition that what we admire is an *inauthentic* magnificence? Whatever 'the authentic' is (and it's a fashionable and therefore very slippery notion), we surely can't relinquish claim to it so easily. Moreover 'magnificence' (by which I understand, among other things, the high style) may indeed in the past have been 'one of the poles of English poetry'; but the question is, precisely, whether we can continue to regard it thus, in the second half of the twentieth century.

None of this would matter very much if C.H. Sisson were only another hack-reviewer, an academic picking up a few easy pounds or dollars from week-end reviewing. But Sisson on the contrary is a serious non-academic practitioner, whose poems and verse-translations have of recent years earned him wide esteem. (And he is also, to confound the ideologue, very much on the political Right, a high-flying monarchist Tory, of a sort now very rare on the British scene.) His aversion to Yeats – for that is what it amounts to – deserves to be taken seriously, especially since Sisson is (so my reading persuades me) in some degree representative.

In 'High Talk' Yeats, I suggest, foresaw Sisson's sort of aversion, though he could hardly have foreseen its vehemence or how widespread it has become; and Yeats defends himself and his stylistic procedures. To be sure the little poem is not in itself tall talk. On the contrary, in every particular down to the deliberately stumblebum metre, the piece, so long as it holds up, is in Yeats's comic vein – a very distinctive vein, exploiting Yeats's own Tony Lumpkin sort of comicality. Accordingly we must take care not to be over-solemn about it. But some of the lines enter reasonable pleas for Yeats's habitual preference for talking tall:

> Because piebald ponies, led bears, caged lions, make but poor shows,
> Because children demand Daddy-long-legs upon his timber toes,
> Because women in the upper storeys demand a face at the pane,
> That patching old heels they may shriek...

We are given three reasons, one after the other, why Yeats writes as he does. The line about the children says in effect that children have the right to demand of the father or the father-figure an emblem of virility; and the line about the women makes the same claim for them – that they rightly demand emblematic virility of the men who are, or might become, their lovers. Neither plea can easily be disregarded; it is at all events arguable that in the years since Yeats died it is not coincidental that, as man for good and pressing reasons has come under pressure to relinquish such traditionally masculine roles as the freebooter or the man-at-arms, so parental and sexual roles inside the household have fallen into confusion and disarray. What does it mean, nowadays, to be manly? What image of manliness can we cherish, now that so many of the traditional images for it prove to be more than we can afford any longer? *Machismo* is a fact, north as well as south of every border, and it may well be that simply to deplore it is not good enough, that we ought to ponder it more than we do. (In Yeats's vocabulary, incidentally, when women 'shriek' they do so from sexual excitement as often as from fear.) The other reason that Yeats gives, the one that he puts first, having indeed anticipated it in his very first line, is even more interesting. The poet, he insists, is a showman, a performer, an entertainer – as he is also in that more probing but also more confusing late poem, 'The Circus Animals' Desertion'. Indeed this emphasis is constant with Yeats, if not from the first at least from the time of his earliest involvement with the Abbey Theatre. From then on Yeats sees the poet's role as essentially histrionic. Nowhere is he more explicit about this, or more challenging, than in *The Bounty of Sweden*, his reflections on getting the Nobel Prize; but it is implicit in everything he writes. One may conjecture that the general public finds this easy to stomach, though leaders of opinion don't – which might explain how queasily opinion-making critics approach a writer like Ernest Hemingway who, as is notorious, practices a histrionic *machismo* in his art as well as his life. At any rate, one sees already one retort that could be made to C.H. Sisson: And what sort of show do *you* put on? What sort of performance? What do you do that 'catches the eye'? Admirers of Sisson's verse (I am among them) do not find it easy to meet such challenges. For Sisson's poetry, though it has many virtues, certainly isn't, in any ordinary sense, *entertaining*. And the same is true of many other writers at the present day, who are cherished by an *élite* but ignored by the public at large, which sees in their work only bears that are led by the nose, and lions that are 'caged'.

It is worth dwelling on this. Indeed it prompts reflections too many, and too far-reaching, for us to deal with them all. But in the first place, Yeats is commonly considered a very arrogant poet, and indeed was at considerable pains to give that impression; but in this readiness to be the entertainer – to be sure in a noble household, only before a *fit* audience – Yeats was perhaps the humblest poet of his time. Since C.H. Sisson compares him with Thomas Hardy, we may remember the distinctly 'huffy' tone that Hardy the poet takes towards his readers. Yeats is thought to be arrogant, and Hardy to be humble; but a very little thought can reverse the equation. Again, when Sisson finds Yeats wanting by comparison with Hardy, he says: 'There is no psychology in Yeats, only magic. There are no people, only dolls – of elegant and dramatic appearance, very often.' But may we not retort, with at our elbow the author of 'High Talk', that 'dolls' are just what an entertainer, for instance a puppet-master, is concerned with; and that if he makes his dolls elegant, and of dramatic appearance, that is part of the entertainment he offers us, for which we should be grateful? Once again we see the possibility of a reversal of roles. For Yeats is often thought of as a towering Aesthete: one who frequently asserts the superiority of 'Art' over 'Life'. And yet the author of 'High Talk' and of 'The Circus Animals' Desertion' reveals an almost cynical scepticism about the claims of Art, such as I think Thomas Hardy never entertained.

Accordingly dolls are named, and the nature of a doll is pondered, in many poems by Yeats. One such poem is the sequence 'Upon a Dying Lady', which celebrates the conduct upon her death-bed of Mabel Beardsley, Aubrey Beardsley's sister – a scene of great importance for modern poetry, since it is feelingfully recalled more than once by Pound in *The Pisan Cantos* and without Yeats's poem, the force of Pound's allusions will be missed. The second of Yeats's seven-part sequence is subtitled 'Certain Artists bring her Dolls and Drawings':

Bring where our Beauty lies
A new modelled doll, or drawing,
With a friend's or an enemy's
Features, or maybe showing
Her features when a tress
Of dull red hair was flowing
Over some silken dress
Cut in the Turkish fashion,
Or, it may be, like a boy's.
We have given the world our passion,
We have naught for death but toys.

Though 'Upon a Dying Lady' is not widely known nor much remarked upon (we shall find reasons for that before we are done), I'm sure Sisson is right to regard it as one of the triumphs of Yeats's middle period. 'Triumph', however, is hardly what he makes of it. His approval is grudging, to say the least:

For a moment Yeats's desire to make a pretty, formalized scene and his feelings of pity in the presence of the dying woman become congruent. It is not grief that the poem conveys; it is hardly concern for the chief character; it is a sense of the propriety of her having been so perfect a piece of furniture in the poet's *ambiance*.

That last phrase is hard to forgive. For Yeats had made it clear, even in this poem (not to speak of what he had been writing many years before this) that what Sisson calls his '*ambiance*', if indeed Yeats has made it his, had been deliberately acquired by him from sustained study of those who, he had decided, were most 'learned in old courtesies'. And those teachers were predominantly from the Renaissance, Italian principally but also English. Thus in this poem Giorgione is named, and one of the dolls was, we are told, 'the Venetian lady... her panniered skirt copied from Longhi'. Elsewhere the school of courtesy has been located in that Renaissance court of Urbino which Castiglione celebrated in *Il Cortegiano*, The Book of the Courtier. And what we call Yeats's middle period is characterized by the emergence of a new style in his verse which permits him, among other liberations that it brings him, to make contact over the centuries with those English poets who came nearest to being analogues of those courtly Italians – Ben Jonson, John Donne, Philip Sidney. Thus the '*ambiance*' to which Mabel Beardsley's behaviour is found proper is not a set of whimsical predilections peculiar to Yeats or shared only with some of his intimates like Pound; it is the ambience of the High Renaissance. In that ambience Sisson's word, 'propriety', carries more weight than he seems to allow for; it is the principle of *decorum*, a principle which in Renaissance thinking determined alike what behaviour is proper on a deathbed, and what style (for instance high, middle or low) is proper for celebrating such behaviour. If we see this poem, like many more by Yeats in his middle period, as aspiring to the company of great Renaissance poems, we may be moved to remark of Milton's 'Lycidas', as Sisson does of 'Upon a Dying Lady', that 'It is not grief that the poem conveys; it is hardly concern for the chief character...' Mabel Beardsley 'puts up a good show'. If she was scared to death, she was determined not to show it. And Yeats salutes her for that, as one fastidious showman salutes another. What we are saying is that not only are walkers-on-stilts and puppet-masters and ballad-makers prepared to be entertainers and performers, so also are poets as haughty about their calling as Ben Jonson and John Milton. And if Sisson and others think we live in a different world from them, Yeats doesn't.

Moreover, Mabel Beardsley didn't think so, either. Sisson admits that 'the scene and the properties introduced are closely modelled on reality'. They are indeed. Mabel Beardsley is not co-opted by the poet into a world not hers. On the contrary, time and again in the poem Yeats stays scrupulously close to the recorded facts about Mabel and her dead brother, and that dead brother's art, and the interests they shared (for

instance, transvestism). Particularly striking and admirable is the fact about
the Beardsleys which Yeats goes out of his way to acknowledge in the
fifth poem of the sequence. This he calls 'Her Race'; and the title is both
sardonic and defiant, as we soon see:

> She has not grown uncivil
> As narrow natures would
> And called the pleasures evil
> Happier days thought good;
> She knows herself a woman,
> No red and white of a face,
> Or rank, raised from a common
> Unreckonable race;
> And how should her heart fail her
> Or sickness break her will
> With her dead brother's valour
> For an example still?

Yeats's snobbery is notorious; for instance his constant endeavour to make
out that his own shabby-genteel and mercantile background was a great
deal grander than it was. And not only feminists have protested that Yeats
is interested in women only when they are high-born or beautiful, preferably both. These verses give the lie to that, or at least they show that he
could conquer these prejudices when the occasion required it. For they say
quite unequivocally that Mabel Beardsley was not beautiful, and that (as
was indeed the case) the Beardsleys' social origin was shabby and obscure.
And thus 'race' in the title means not anything one is born to, but what
some distinguished individuals can grow into. Aristocracy, breeding, can
be *acquired*. Act tall, talk tall, and you *grow* tall – it is what Yeats implies
elsewhere. Indeed, is it not implied in 'High Talk'? It is not an anti-
democratic sentiment, unless we think democracy endangered whenever
diction rises above common parlance, as it does here in the beautifully
judged slight archaisms of 'uncivil', 'narrow natures', 'unreckonable',
'valour'. But of course if you think, as Yeats seems to have thought, that
the sixteenth and seventeenth centuries had ideas about human dignity
which we have lost since and need to recover, then there is no way for
your diction not to be archaic in some degree, and thereby elevated,
'high'. 'Uncivil', for instance – if civility by the time Yeats was born had
taken the meaning it has when someone says, 'You, keep a civil tongue in
your head!' and if like Yeats you want to restore the connection between
civility (good manners) and civilization, the only way to make the point is
by so adjusting the level of your diction that 'civil' or 'uncivil', when they
occur in your discourse, will recover at least some of the precious meaning
they once had, which they have now lost or are losing.

I have just sketched a defence of stilted poetry – or of one kind of such poetry – which Yeats does not include with the three defences that he offers in 'High Talk'. And indeed the broadly comic mode of that poem could hardly have allowed him to do so. But in any case Yeats was a great deal less sure-footed in these matters by the time he wrote 'High Talk' than he had been twenty years earlier when he wrote 'Upon a Dying Lady'. A distressing number of Yeats's later poems are very slapdash performances, and people who attack Yeats unfairly, like C.H. Sisson or in the United States the late Yvor Winters, are I suspect understandably exasperated[1] by those all too many devoted Yeatsians who refuse to distinguish between Yeats's poetry and his *rant*. What but rant is that 'barnacle goose' who suddenly flies out of nowhere into the last lines of 'High Talk'? Or those allegedly 'great' sea-horses who bare their yellow teeth and 'laugh at the dawn'? What has the dawn done that it should provoke horse-laughs? One sees in a schematic way what Yeats has in mind: in these last lines he will exemplify that tall talk which through previous lines he has been contending for. But this is tall talk of a sort that has nothing to do with high style. These lines certainly raise the emotional temperature – to fever-pitch in fact, where we can expect, and duly we find, delirium. But the 'height' of the high style has nothing to do with emotional temperature, but with decorum, with *keeping*. And Yeats's last three lines are totally *out of keeping* with what has led up to them. In these lines, and for that matter in 'High Talk' as a whole, Yeats is writing an English which no longer remembers the English of Ben Jonson or John Milton, Philip Sidney or Thomas Wyatt or John Donne. And it is very much open to question whether, in a language without such memories, the notion of high, middle, and low – of *levels* of style – any longer has meaning.

And yet we still talk as if these terms have meaning. At least, some of us do; and poets, rather than critics. Here for instance is an American poet now in his fiftieth year, talking last year about himself as a poet:

> Yes, I am certainly a high-style poetic writer. I was then and I am now. Whatever the merits of the low and referential style of poetry which was dominant in the 1950s when I began writing, I have not been able to obtain those merits.

This is Allen Grossman, born a Jew in Minneapolis in 1932, author of five collections of poetry, of which the latest, just out from New Directions, is called *Of the Great House*. What a Yeatsian title! And sure enough Allen Grossman knows what he is about, and what his allegiance must be:

> I began writing in a serious way... in college. My work was to find a lineage, an ancestry or family other than my human and personal family: an affiliation in which I could find some outcome of desire

different from that promised me in the social world. In a clear way, I began as a creature of the Yeatsian kind and have continued to develop the implications of that beginning to this day.

For Grossman, you perceive, being 'a high-style poetic writer' means at the present day being 'a creature of the Yeatsian kind'. It also means, as is made clear in these comments and is clearer in others I could quote, being at the present day very isolated on the poetic scene, aware of swimming against the tide. What that flowing tide is, what Grossman means by 'the low and referential style of poetry', appears from what he says of the late Robert Lowell:

> the whole history of Lowell's writing, down to his last work... is an experiment to discover whether there is some power of writing which can situate itself at the point of intersection between the life lived and the transcendental exactions of art... Lowell's discovery, I think, was that poetry written at that zero point of coincidence between world and mind really has no meaning and no end, really confers no consolation...

I think this is inaccurate about Lowell, who in his youth indulged in plenty of tall talk, some of it plainly derived from Yeats; it applies only to the Lowell who emerged with *Life Studies* in 1955 (the same year, incidentally, as Ginsberg's *Howl*). For my part I am of Robert Lowell's generation, and when I hear the word 'transcendental' I reach, if not for my revolver, at least for my knuckleduster. And yet I recognize real truth in what Grossman bitterly and contemptuously says, of poetry that 'really has no meaning and no end, really confers no consolation...'. It is true, I think; alike in the United Kingdom and the United States, and even in Ireland, much of the poetry that is published is so much on a level with the world that it feeds off and feeds back into, is skimmed so immediately and humbly off recognizable actuality, that it does indeed seem to be just an item of that actuality, with no access to, and no claims upon, any other reality. Thus I have sympathy with Grossman, and with his conviction that the Yeatsian legacy in style is something we cannot ignore. Moreover Grossman's own poetry, so far as I know it, is interesting enough to confirm the respect I feel for him (though I don't detect Ben Jonson in it).

And yet... (This is my last point and I think an important one.) Should any poet declare himself as 'high-style', or for that matter 'low-style'? Surely on the contrary the Renaissance principle of decorum required the *complete* poet to command all three levels of style, and to show his 'invention', his tact and sensitivity, in knowing when and how to move or switch from one level to another. The greatest poets of our century – I have in mind Eliot and Pound, a little less certainly Hardy – show just this ability. And Yeats beside them does seem a good deal less flexible.

XXII   The Franglais of Criticism; the English of Translation

From a brief report in *The Times* for 17 February this year we learn that 'about a twentieth of French is now [1983] made up of *anglicismes*', and that '*Le Monde* now contains an English word in every 166.' We can hardly expect that a daily newspaper should explain how these statistics were arrived at, and the questions they beg are obvious: *whose* French is now one-twentieth anglicisms? The French of a Gascon peasant-proprietor? Of a butcher in Lyons? Of a student on the Left Bank? And so on. Still, supposing these statistics to represent what is *perceived to be* the truth (and no one seems to have challenged them), Philip Howard, who supplies them, comments comfortably: 'The common market in languages with loan-words is as natural and healthy as travel to other countries. It has always happened since the Tower of Babel, and it always will.' And he cites some entertaining and innocuous instances: for instance 'a *cul-de-sac* has no meaning for a Frenchman'; and *comité* for 'committee' was approved by the Académie Française as long ago as 1762. On the other hand, much to their credit I think, French patriots have seldom regarded this development with such equanimity. For them there has been something new about Franco-English linguistic trading through the last several decades, as Howard acknowledges by quoting from Theodore Zeldin's authoritative *The French*: 'The real cause of dissatisfaction with foreigners in France comes not from the French feeling humiliated by borrowing from America or from other countries; but from an annoyance that foreigners are not borrowing much in return.' That annoyance should nowadays be muted; for in one field at least, academic literary criticism (particularly in the US, but latterly in the UK also), gallicisms have become so much the order of the day that the currently acceptable idiom of discourse, in literary criticism and literary theory, is a franglais tipped much more towards the French than the English component. The trade with the French in this area is so self-conscious, and carries so much *cachet* (you see!), that it is surely of a quite different character from that 'common market in languages' that has 'happened since the Tower of Babel, and... always will'. The phenomenon is so widespread that it could be studied in relation to any number of modern authors in English – Joyce certainly, Stevens, many others.

And so, if it is one thing that crops up in relation to recent writings on Pound, this is not because Pound is a special case, though it is true that Pound's fascism attracts attention from those (rather numerous) who have imported from Paris, along with a post-structuralist vocabulary, an allegiance to the political Left. (The union is sometimes declared to be not accidental but necessary; but that need not concern us.)

It is convenient, and almost unavoidable, to begin looking at recent criticism of Pound with Massimo Bacigalupo's massive and very distinguished book of 1980, *The Forrmèd Trace.*[1] And what distinguishes Bacigalupo's book is in the first place that it is blessedly free of the franglais I have been describing, of which since his book came out there have been really abominable instances, particularly in criticism of Pound under the auspices of Jacques Lacan. It is not that Bacigalupo hasn't read the French theorists, though he has kept such a distance from their idiom that he has deceived some reviewers into thinking he hasn't. His command of elegant but seldom self-regarding literary English is really remarkable in one who is not a native speaker. A second mark of distinction about the book is precisely its massiveness; and that is to say quite simply its usefulness for anyone wanting to understand what is going on, for good or ill, on page after page of *The Cantos*. It has other claims on us: notably, a thin but distinguished line of writing about Pound in Italian, something which international Pound scholarship has tended to ignore, in Bacigalupo's pages asserts itself as something that can be ignored no longer. For obvious reasons Italians have the right to a special say about the author of *The Cantos*, and they say their say from a special and specially valuable standpoint. As a post-fascist Italian, Bacigalupo for instance is keenly aware, and documents unforgivingly, how Pound to the very end defiantly celebrated the defeated fascist state of Mussolini. On the other hand, and much less happily, Bacigalupo takes over from older, self-consciously European observers such as Montale or Milosz a haughty attitude to American literary culture in general, to the extent of hinting repeatedly that what went wrong with Pound's poetry can be laid at the door of culpable naïveté and ignorance endemic in the American tradition that he was heir to. (Bacigalupo's grasp of that tradition seems to me, I must say, too uncertain for this thesis, as he argues it, to be taken seriously.) However, his special though by no means exclusive concern is, as his subtitle makes clear, 'the later poetry', meaning in effect the cantos after *The Pisan Cantos*, published as *Rock-Drill*, as *Thrones* (Cantos 96 to 109, published 1959), and as *Drafts and Fragments*. And it is in relation to these writings, which have — *Thrones* especially — stuck in the craw of many of us, that Bacigalupo breaks new ground.

1   Massimo Bacigalupo, *The Formèd Trace: The Later Poetry of Ezra Pound* (New York: Columbia University Press, 1980).

194 *Modernist Essays*

This happens when he isolates very convincingly, as the determining principle of this later writing, something he calls 'transcription'. Transcription is the kind of word-play that occurs when the poet in the act of composition has before him a polyglot text, for instance a Chinese text presented with interlinear glosses in Latin and French, or else a monoglot text (Dante in Italian, Homer in Greek) which he can make polyglot by, as it were, supplying as he goes along discontinuous glosses in other languages. Transcription as thus understood needs to be distinguished very firmly from translation; since it has for its object not the rendering however loosely of a foreign text but rather, as Bacigalupo demonstrates, the generation of mythology or metaphysics out of lexicography by way of interlingual puns. This distinction, however, will be resisted rather strenuously. For 'intertextuality', a principle much cherished by modern criticism, not necessarily but habitually lumps together all forms of trafficking by a modern writer with an anterior text. One hears for instance of 'hidden translation', of which indeed there is a great deal in *The Cantos*; and although Bacigalupo provides us with the term 'transcription' as distinct from translation, still he is not much interested in insisting on the distinction. I think on the contrary that he should have insisted. There is translation in *The Cantos*; there is also 'transcription'. And far more than Bacigalupo, I think we need to be clear in our minds when we are dealing with the one, when with the other. However, in practice Bacigalupo's more lenient understanding must be respected, when we see how this enables him to make sense of passages that had seemed irredeemably wayward and opaque. To say this, however, is quite different from deciding that after this demonstration the *Thrones* cantos are better than we thought they were. For in order to think that, we have to give to waywardness a value that older and sterner theories of poetry, Anglo-American rather than French, would deny. It is crucial to note for instance that transcription in this sense is like any other sort of punning in that it depends on misconstruing; and Bacigalupo shows how Pound in old age was bold and adroit enough positively to invite misconstruction, derailing the reader into false etymologies, confounding words (and proper names) that belong apart. The oddity of this is, as Bacigalupo recognizes very well, that Pound's professed principles, early and late, stressing the importance of 'calling things by their right names', had always aligned him with the sterner moralists, opposed to those post-Mallarméan theories which have put a premium on waywardness in the writer.

Mallarmé of course had his own sternness: the waywardness was to be itself a discipline, founded on the conviction that only a willed waywardness in the writer could cede the initiative to his language; and that the language, thus freed, would produce, through bizarre leapings and interlacements of sound and sense, meanings that the author could not have foreseen. Bacigalupo, who seldom misses a trick, recognizes that for his reading of *The Cantos* to stick, he has to make Pound a Mallarméan poet *à son insu*, creating in *The Cantos* a Mallarméan 'sacred book' even though he, Pound, imagined he was doing something quite different. Bacigalupo maintains this bold case by making ingenious and tricky use of 'decadent' as a concept of literary history, and by insisting on what of course is quite true – the fact that Pound in the early phases of his career was happy with many *fin-de-siècle* mannerisms and assumptions. It is just here, in fact, that Bacigalupo speaks to us with a French accent. Though he has read Derrida, and is surely in some degree a deconstructionist critic, he has been shrewd enough to cover his tracks. But he adheres to a French tradition insofar as he will have no truck with older authorities, including for instance Montale whom he otherwise venerates, when they shake their dubious heads over what, in Pound or anyone else, can be thought of as 'mere word-play'. 'Word-play', Bacigalupo would have us think, is just what poetry is, neither more nor less; and the best poetry, other things being equal, is that which allows to language – to the many languages of mankind – the maximum *play*, in the several senses of that word. Because, for such writing to succeed, the writer has to surrender all responsibility for what his words get up to in the playground he has cleared for them, he can hardly be brought to account. Hence arises a crucial tenet of deconstructionist criticism: the author *can't lose* – to just the extent that he can't win either. He has been declared unfit to plead. He is shown to behave irresponsibly, because there is no way for him to behave otherwise. In this way Bacigalupo can be repeatedly contemptuous of Pound's aberrations (not just the political ones) at the same time as he is endlessly indulgent to him. As in all deconstructionist criticism, applauding an author and condescending to him amount to much the same thing.

Michael André Bernstein's *The Tale of the Tribe*[2] appeared the same year as *The Forméd Trace*, and there is no need to ask which of the two scholars arrived first at the perception they agree on: not only that *The Cantos* are as one whole poem imperfect, but that the imperfections of this poem are the necessary conditions of what we should most applaud in it. Bernstein, a Canadian who teaches at Berkeley, is the more eager to applaud; and so his tone is throughout more mournfully charitable than Bacigalupo's, as he explains how *The Cantos* not only did, but had to, fail. 'Fail', though, has to be put inside quotation marks, because it is consistently an implication of Bernstein's discussion that failure on such a scale, in such a heroic endeavour, is worth more than any conceivable triumph or perfection achieved on easier terms. Accordingly, and as we might expect, nowhere in Bernstein is there any equivalent to Bacigalupo's implication that it was Pound's American-ness that betrayed him, and ensured his failure.

2   Michael André Bernstein, *The Tale of the Tribe: Ezra Pound and the Modern Verse Epic* (Princeton University Press, 1980).

All the same Bernstein is awkwardly aware of how often, in the discourse of American critics, 'a poem's intention is equated with its actual achievement or, when this becomes manifestly impossible, the grandeur of the struggle is regarded as sufficient proof of the work's merit'. The American whom he pillories on this count, among commentators on Pound, is L.S. Dembo. And, searching for Old World commentators who shall offer an alternative to this New World indulgence, he cites Philip Larkin, John Press and… myself. He quotes from the end of my *Ezra Pound: Poet as Sculptor* (1964):

> Whatever more long-term effect Pound's disastrous career may have on American and British poetry, it seems inevitable that it will rule out (has ruled out already, for serious writers) any idea that poetry can or should operate in the dimension of history, trying to make sense of the recorded past by redressing our historical perspectives… History, from now on, may be transcended in poetry, or it may be evaded there; but poetry is not the place where it may be understood.

To this he responds: 'I think that the last twenty years of American verse indicate that Pound's ambition has by no means been discarded, that even writers with different literary and intellectual perspectives have wanted… to maintain the authority of poetry as a crucial site in which "history… may be understood".' But why should I deny this? That some later American poets have tried to take up the Poundian enterprise cannot be denied. But this cannot disprove my contention that in doing so the later poets (Bernstein discusses two of them, Williams and Olson) failed to read the right moral out of Pound's career. When they launched themselves again on the same foredoomed enterprise, Olson and Williams ruled themselves out of the company of those who are, as I say, 'serious writers'. Their persistence is the proof of their obtuseness. But I did not enjoy reaching this conclusion in 1964, nor do I take any pleasure in reiterating it now.

In any case this is a way of thinking and talking about poetry that seems to belong in a different universe from those much less buoyant and sanguine contexts, from decadence to deconstruction, that Bacigalupo would persuade us are more appropriate to the case of Pound. And sure enough Bernstein begins by locating the enterprise of *The Cantos* at the furthest extreme from Mallarmé's confessedly unattainable 'Grand Oeuvre', his 'sacred book'; ranging it instead under the rubric 'Tale of the Tribe', a rubric that Pound discovered and endorsed in Kipling. In terms of Pound's conscious and professed intentions, there is no doubt that Bernstein is right and Bacigalupo wrong; but as we have seen it is a postulate of Bacigalupo's thought that Pound knew himself and his own intentions hardly at all (though he makes an exception of *Hugh Selwyn Mauberley*, as we shall see). In any case Bernstein too is indebted to the

French. This debt, which can be tracked through his endnotes, is in his text most evident in the gallicisms that turn to wondrously novel uses the verbs 'inscribe' and 'recuperate', together with their cognates 'inscription', 'recuperation', and so on. These are, it must be said, no more than grace notes to what is in substance a thoroughly conservative and enlightening consideration of what is involved in bringing to bear on twentieth-century experience the demands traditionally associated with the *genre* of the verse epic. It is a remarkable achievement, thus to show how much virtue there still is in old-fashioned *genre* criticism. All the same, the gallicisms are obfuscating. When Bernstein remarks, 'It is precisely in those sections deprived of an easy recuperation through a definable narrator or point of view that the poem most fully asserts itself as an epic', the English speaker, for whom 'recuperate' means (*Pocket Oxford Dictionary*) 'Restore, be restored or recover, from exhaustion, illness, loss, &c.', can only infer, not only that the poem is *sick* (exhausted, suffering loss), but that according to Bernstein there are circumstances in which a poem will be better (will, for instance, 'most fully assert itself as an epic') when its sickness is least alleviated or cured or curable. And this is rather plainly a version of Bacigalupo's theorem by which the poet can't lose because he can't win. In one extreme form the theorem seems to rest on the assumption that writing as such, the very act of *écriture*, *is* a sickness, a socio-psychological malformation or maladjustment; from which position it is easy to contend that writing is most inviolably and triumphantly itself when the maladjustment inherent in it most stubbornly resists curative treatment. However, the French verb *récupérer* has a range of meanings quite unknown to the English 'recuperate'. These include (*Collins–Robert French–English English–French Dictionary*, 1978): 'salvage', 'reprocess', 'make up' (e.g. work-days lost), 'take over', 'harness', 'bring into line'. And it is accordingly plain that a French speaker, reading of *récupération* in relation to a literary text, is not compelled into a medical metaphor as the English speaker is when he reads of a text's 'recuperation'. Obviously when we hear of how a text resists being taken over, or harnessed, or brought into line, we shall by no means think that the text thereby 'fails', as we cannot help but think it fails when we hear that it resists being restored to health. On the same page there is a related instance of how gallicisms obfuscate, when Bernstein quotes Roland Barthes saying that 'Flaubert... opère un malaise salutaire de l'écriture'. This he obligingly translates in a note as 'Flaubert... works a salutary discomfort of writing' – an expression so bizarrely alien to English usage that only in a legalistic sense can it be thought to be English at all. Some critics build their entire discourse out of gallicisms like these, and one can only conclude that portentous obfuscation is their one purpose in writing.

It is not for nothing that I single out 'recuperate' and 'recuperation' as instances of how the franglais idiom of currently fashionable criticism consistently perpetrates and invites misconstruction. This is not peculiar to criticism of literature. On the contrary, in *Comparative Criticism*, 4 (1982) Marcelin Pleynet is translated by Paul Rodgers so as to ask about André Breton's hostility to Cézanne's painting: 'Is it not really much more a question of the painter's social situation and his recuperation by the market than the painting itself?' (p. 39). We may guess, with surely every confidence, that Pleynet's *récupération* (in the sense of harnessing, taking over, bringing into line) is here being represented by the English word 'recuperation'. Since, however, English 'recuperation' is innocent of these meanings, what can we find here except, at the risk of offending Paul Rodgers, simply lax and lazy mistranslation? But if we turn back a few pages to Stephen Bann's Introduction to Rodgers' translation, we read (p. 33) of how Breton's hostility to Cézanne 'may be explained up to a point by a legitimate distaste for Cézanne's recuperation by the art market'. And here we have the same irresponsible gallicism (irresponsible because obfuscatory, inviting misconstruction) perpetrated without even the sorry excuse of a French text that has to be Englished. The matter is really of some importance. In all our talk of 'deconstruction' (and 'deconstructionist'), what of the word's first cousin, 'misconstruction'? My own strong suspicion is that many of those English speakers who toss around 'deconstruction' most blithely conceive that they are playing games with the English verb 'construct', not with the verb 'construe'. Each of course has its sinister shadow in the Dictionaries: as one may 'misconstruct', so one may 'misconstrue'. For those more sophisticated, more aware of what they are doing, it appears that the prefix 'mis-', as in '*mis*translate', '*mis*construe', even '*mis*take', no longer has any meaning and may as well be dispensed with – as indeed it largely has been, in common parlance and common written usage. In order to 'de-construe' (for that of course is the proper and in its measure elegant usage, rather than the barbarous 'deconstruct'), one may as well misconstrue. Indeed, misconstruing is the most economical, obvious and effective way of *de*construing; just as, we might say regarding these instances lately before us, mistranslating is the best way to *detranslating*. 'Detranslating' is, unless I am mistaken (whoops!), a barbarous coinage all my own, which signifies, rather than the putting of French into English or English into French, the transferring of French and English texts alike into an intermediate neologized tongue, at once barbarous and mandarin, called franglais. Again, we *mis*take, we deliberately *take* an expression in a sense possible indeed but in the highest degree implausible, so as to discredit the possibility of any taking that is not also a mistaking. In this way we begin to see that mistaking, mistranslating, and misconstruing are at the heart of deconstructionist criticism, procedures so essential to it that the pejorative implications of the 'mis-' prefix must be systematically eliminated from its (and our) discourse. Again, if one may read, one may also *mis*read. But the concept of intertextuality, valuable in itself, has been misconstrued so as to yield the proposition that the misreading of an anterior text by a modern writer is at least – at least! – as legitimate and as fruitful as the reading of it. And in this way Pound, notoriously a misreader (he couldn't even copy accurately), can be elevated as the presiding genius of ways of writing which he, the historical Ezra Pound trained as a pre-1914 philologist, would have disdained and condemned. The admittedly extreme fallibility of a modern master is taken – is *mis*taken – to validate deliberate and perverse falsifying in the practice of his successors.

Michael Bernstein does not so mistake. No more than Bacigalupo, however, can he agree with me in thinking the *Thrones* cantos sterile and tedious. His defence of *Thrones* rests on what is undoubtedly the most beguiling and ingenious apologia yet offered. This is Hugh Kenner's formulation: 'the governing science of *Rock-Drill* is natural growth... The governing science of the next sequence, *Thrones*, is philology: luminous words and their meanings, seeds of mental growth.' But after Bacigalupo's elucidation of just what sort of attention to words the *Thrones* cantos incite and depend on, we must surely think that 'philology', compendious category though it is, cannot be stretched far enough to comprehend what is going on in these pages. Philology, we may agree, comprehends lexicography, but hardly a sort of lexicography that puts a higher premium on false derivations, false and fanciful etymologies, than on right ones. Nor can it be part of either lexicography or philology, considered as (even in the loosest sense) 'sciences', that lexicons should be used to generate mythologies. For that, we remember, is what Bacigalupo demonstrates: that the mental growth 'seeded' by the lexical extravagances of *Thrones* is mythopoeia. Bacigalupo supplies a description so just and elegant as to be positively poetic: 'In the ample web of *Thrones* are secret rents, through which we go beyond language, into a metalinguistic space where the panic passion for the word celebrates its final, luxuriant, and microscopic feasts.' This 'panic passion' is surely more than a love of words; rather it is a sort of lusting after them. And though Bacigalupo is more inclined to indulge with vicarious excitement in the orgies than to reprehend them, still the orgiastic, immoderate, even depraved implications of his metaphor seem to fit rather exactly what we see being done with words, and done *to* them, on many pages of *Thrones*. On some pages of our most gallicized criticism very similar microscopic feasts are served to us – though, needless to say, with much less refinement and invention. The *Thrones* cantos, and deconstructionist criticism, seem made for each other. And yet, as Bernstein recognizes no less clearly than Bacigalupo, the poet's theory of language and his professed poetics remained as far as ever from the post-Mallarméan theories that usually, or most obviously, underwrite such practices whether in poetry or criticism. As Bernstein puts it, with rather ponderous care: 'one of the major difficulties with *The*

Cantos is that they rely upon specific modernist techniques for which an adequate aesthetic analysis exists, but do so on behalf of intentions that require an entirely opposed critical framework, one which was elaborated to deal with very different works.'

As regards verse translation, and the principles that ideally should inform the practice of it, it is difficult to put down these books except with a despairing sense that in the present century no ground, no ground at all, has been gained. On the one hand in departments of Classics and of Modern Languages, as in the surprisingly many non-academic circles where the *dicta* of such departments are attentively listened to, there still survives, hectoringly assured as ever, the grotesque misconception which already in the seventeenth century Denham and Richard Fanshawe and John Dryden were challenging: the notion that fidelity and literality are the same thing. On the other hand we now have, in the deconstructionist misunderstanding of what Eliot and Pound professed and practised, the mirror image of that pedantry – a set of ideas according to which mistranslation and misconstruction, misreading and misconception and mistaking, are words void of meaning, naming operations upon texts as legitimate as, and more creative than, their opposites. Between servile literalism on the one hand and on the other free-wheeling variations *ad lib.*, the business of verse translation none the less goes on – scandalously unrewarded and unhonoured, for the most part disreputable and yet, against all the probabilities, still stubbornly and unaccountably in many instances honourable. To endorse in reverse a judgement by Charles Tomlinson in his splendidly eloquent Clark Lectures, *Poetry and Metamorphosis*, Pound was the John Dryden of our times. This is to say, he is the second greatest verse translator known to us in the history of our tongue. And yet he can be, and is, recruited into the second, the 'free-wheeling' camp of translators. But this is to misunderstand him, and to fail to take the force of what, as a verse translator, Pound did. The Pound who fiddled obsessively with 'transcription' in the *Thrones* cantos was a lesser, a crucially disoriented, character.

Bacigalupo, however, does not think so. In his annotations to the elegant though physically frail Mondadori edition of *Hugh Selwyn Mauberley* (with verse translations into Italian by Giovanni Giudici),[3] Bacigalupo reiterates with more assurance and heavier emphasis what he had already contended for in *The Formèd Trace*: the view that *Hugh Selwyn Mauberley* represents an accurate self-diagnosis by Pound which half a century later the author of *Thrones* and of *Drafts and Fragments* was still trying, in vain, to belie or to work around. Those who know even hazily the history of Pound's reputation in English will feel that they have been

---

3   Massimo Bacigalupo and Giovanni Giudici, *Ezra Pound: Hugh Selwyn Mauberley* (Milan: Il Saggiatore Mondadori, 1982).

here before. And so they have; for when no more than thirty cantos were extant, this was the verdict passed on them by F.R. Leavis, who similarly read *Hugh Selwyn Mauberley* as an all too accurate diagnosis and prognosis; arguing therefore that a long poem of epic pretensions written by Pound/Mauberley could not be anything but sterile, its seeming energies the galvanic and factitious exertions of a decadent aesthete trying to persuade himself he was something else. The wheel comes full circle; and after Hugh Kenner and John Espey and I and two dozen others have called on evidence not available to Leavis in order to prove Leavis wrong, here comes Bacigalupo, with more evidence than any of us (in particular, the original typescripts), to reinstate the Leavis reading of *Hugh Selwyn Mauberley* in all its massive and damning simplicity.

If I declare myself unpersuaded, it is not, I hope, because I have some professional investment in an alternative view of Pound's career. I contend that there are, in *The Cantos*, things of great, even momentous value, for which neither *Hugh Selwyn Mauberley* nor any other work of Pound's youth has prepared us. I will specify just one such, to which perhaps no one will attach such importance as I do. It is what I will call 'stonescape', meaning by that the man-made environments and ambiences of worked stone (stone, not concrete, not cement, not asphalt) which are to be found in the ancient and even quite modern quarters of small Italian cities otherwise so undistinguished as Palestrina or Anagni. There is a vision of human and civic dignity projected and preserved by such totally architected, totally sculpted, environments. Time and again in *The Cantos*, most often in relation to Venice but sometimes with reference to less accredited sites like Sulmona or (to go out of Italy) Poitiers, the emblematic moral significance of such an ambience is caught into words and cadences. And for this the earlier poems, up to and including *Hugh Selwyn Mauberley*, do not in the least prepare us. For such effects (to call them that, though they are *affects*, rather), the franglais of modish critical discourse has no vocabulary at all. Nor will it soon, if ever, generate such vocabulary. For Pleynet and Derrida and Lacan have all lunged out into appreciation (on their own terms) of painting; but, true to its origins in Saussure and Jakobson and Freud, their criticism is insistently verbal, as well as verbose. Architecture and sculpture, conceived of not as the providers of museum monuments for photographers but as elements and agencies in the shaping of habitable environments, escape all the nets of metonymy and metaphor. Accordingly franglais criticism has not, and perhaps will never have, a vocabulary to encompass them. Not much poetry possesses such a vocabulary; but the poetry of *The Cantos*, not steadily indeed but intermittently, does. Pound in *The Cantos* puts over into English words and cadences not just from Greek and Chinese, but out of languages more foreign still: the paved space on a tilt in morning sunlight, the three-times-over nubile swell of the romanesque apses at the east end of the *duomo*, so easily translated into Freudian terms and so manifestly degraded, emptied of significance and presence, by such a translation, which thereupon and by that token declares itself a mis-translation. The great translators, a Dryden or a Pound, will not stoop to that. Massimo Bacigalupo won't thus stoop either; but I suspect he stands beside Pound's best biographer to date, Noel Stock – that is to say, among Pound scholars who reach the point where they rather bitterly resent the man who has given them so much trouble. If one has worked on the Poundian scriptures, it is impossible not to sympathize: Pound *is* maddening, Pound is (a lot of the time) inexcusable. He is also, however, not always but often enough, a great and scrupulous poet; one who knows for instance when he is translating and when he is doing something else.

Comparative Criticism 6, edited by E.S. Shaffer (Cambridge University Press, 1984).

XXIII The Mysterious Allen Upward

Allen Upward (born 1863) remains a mystery man. I have no hope here of dispelling the mystery, not even of casting anything but very tentative light on it. My intention is only to emphasize that the mystery persists; that it is unaccountable; and that, so long as it persists, our pretensions to chart the intellectual history of our times, or the times of our grandfathers, are hollow. It is not after all as if we were dealing with a figure from the sixteenth century or earlier; Upward died by his own hand no longer ago than 1926. How can it be that a figure so historically recent, by no means a recluse but on the contrary gregarious and a prolific self-promoter, should have been consigned to oblivion so conclusively that, so far as I can make out, there exists not a single sketchy impression of him from those who knew him in life, and of his many books even the best libraries can muster only a few? This inquiry, therefore, if it can be dignified by that name, is an inquiry into the processes of cultural transmission or non-transmission. And if I may anticipate my conclusion, the case seems to prove that the period of Edward VII and George V, of Presidents Theodore Roosevelt and Woodrow Wilson, and since them the age of computerized information retrieval, no more ensures the continuity of historical memory than did the times of Henry VIII or Edward VI. In fact, rather less so.

The mystery of Upward is encapsulated in an issue ten years old of that eccentric and unreliable but invaluable London magazine, *Agenda*, which in 1978–9 carried two essays about Upward, one by Kenneth Cox, the other by Michael Sheldon.[1] How could the figure that emerges from Michael Sheldon's biographical researches – a flitting opportunist, scare-monger, and demagogue of municipal politics in England, Wales, and Ireland – have written a book, *The Divine Mystery*, which (Kenneth Cox decides) 'stands in breadth of view, in novelty of ideas, in clarity of exposition and in brilliance of *obiter dicta* at least on a par with Montesquieu'? And if Cox is right, as I'm sure he is (for the name of Montesquieu is not chosen at random), how can it be that such a book should never have been reprinted since its first publication in 1913 until 1976, and then in Santa Barbara, California?[2] Somewhere here there is a scandal; and we

---

1   *Agenda*, 16.3–4 (Autumn–Winter 1978–9), pp. 87–121.
2   Allen Upward, *The Divine Mystery: A Reading of the History of Christianity down to the Time of Christ*, with an introduction by Robert Duncan (Santa Barbara: Ross-Erikson, 1976).

cannot as intellectual historians look ourselves in the face until we have probed it.

With every month that passes, the chance of rescuing Upward from oblivion gets slimmer – not just because there can now be hardly anyone left among eyewitnesses who might testify, and not just because under imposed budgetary constraints British libraries at all levels are now shredding seldom-asked-for books from eighty or sixty years ago, but because we get further and further away from sympathizing with or understanding the world of speculation that Upward took for granted. Kenneth Cox is very good about this:

> Opportunities for self-instruction in his time were not bad: many books were cheap and some serious attempts were made to popularise science. Those were the days when educated men still thought it possible to discuss the latest theories, when you could still drop into the British Museum to do some reading and, if you wanted to know about the reformation of the zodiac in 700 BC, write to the Astronomer Royal...
>
> The mental world Upward inhabited was one where matter not divided into disciplines or bedevilled by politicians is subjected to independent and wide-ranging enquiry. He called himself a scientist and his subject 'ontology, commonly called truth'.

Nothing could be further from the assumptions and guidelines that govern nowadays the deliberations of bodies like the Royal Society and the British Academy and the Social Science Research Institute, where research proposals are, no doubt scrupulously, vetted by specialist committees and sub-committees. In such a context Upward would not have stood a chance – not of financial support (that would be out of the question), but of recognition in the sense of being taken seriously. The same goes of course for such a contemporary of his as H.G. Wells. The matter is aggravated by the fields (so we think of them, though Upward didn't) that Upward ranged over and ranged across. Cox cites them as: 'mythology, comparative religion, anthropology, etymology, theoretical physics and the paranormal'. And he pungently and prudently anticipates the objection:

> In these notorious areas amateurs soon lose their footing and proclaim as truth, or at least as plausible speculation, ideas others dismiss as moonshine. The literature of these studies is cluttered with the lucubrations of bookish old geezers not quite right in the head: not every Casaubon failed to write his *Key to all mythologies*. What makes Upward any different?

Kenneth Cox has his answer to that question, in two parts; and it is a very good answer. What is interesting is to ask why in Upward's lifetime no one asked the question, let alone answered it, except Ezra Pound and more dubiously A.R. Orage; and since Upward died the question has been asked (obliquely) and answered (partially) only by certain recent commentators on *The Cantos* of Ezra Pound.

These last, of whom I am one, deserve no great credit. Pound from first to last thrust Upward's name on our attention; and beyond a certain stage of sophistication in studies of Pound's poem, the instigation could not be ignored. But all that we Poundians made of Upward was as much of him as could be brought to bear on Pound's poetry. And this is not good enough. To begin with, among those, still a minority of the reading public, who are sure that Pound was a very great though manifestly imperfect poet, there is certainly no agreement that he was a coherent and consistent thinker; accordingly it is abundantly possible to admire Pound for making admirable poetry out of 'the lucubrations of bookish old geezers not quite right in the head', Upward among them. In the second place, those of us who are professionally or semi-professionally students of poetry are ourselves infected by the domination of 'specialisms'. How can we fail to be, since most of us are required at some point to go cap in hand to an institution like the British Academy or its American equivalents like the Guggenheim Foundation? Accordingly there is insistent pressure, which most of us at some point accede to, to regard our concern with poetry as a specialized discipline on a par with other specialized concerns in, say, organic chemistry. It is certainly significant that only poetry has imposed on its students the necessity to take *some* notice of an otherwise obliterated thinker whose cast of mind wasn't fundamentally poetic or literary at all (for Upward's poems and stories are the least valuable of his writings). That attests to the stubborn determination of serious poetry to regard the exertions of the human mind as somewhere, at some level, all one. But because we who have specialized in the study of poetry have just for that reason neglected to consider how that study locks in with others, our consideration of Upward stops short of the point where he is most challenging: that is to say, the point where, as Cox shows, he requires us to rethink the whole map of intellectual endeavour, challenging the accepted demarcations that split that endeavour into bureaucratically manageable fiefdoms.

Either that, or else when our studies force us to a frontier between poetic and other modes of thinking, we lunge across that frontier incon-siderately and foolishly. Thus thirteen years ago, carried beyond myself by excitement at Upward's *The New Word* (London, 1908, but possibly written as early as 1896), I quoted from it as follows:[3]

> The story of the waterspout, as it is told in books, shows it to be a brief-lived tree. A cloud is whirling downwards, and thrusting out its

3   Donald Davie, *Pound* (London: Fontana, 1975), p. 66.

whirlpoint towards the sea, like a sucking mouth. The sea below whirls upward, thrusting out its whirlpoint towards the cloud. The two ends meet, and the water swept up in the sea-whirl passes on into the cloud-whirl, and swirls up through it, as it were gain-saying it...

In the ideal waterspout, not only does the water swirl upward through the cloud-whirl, but the cloud swirls downward through the sea-whirl...

The ideal waterspout is not yet complete. The upper halt must unfold like a fan, only it unfolds all around like a flower-cup; and it does not leave the cup empty, so that this flower is like a chrysanthemum. At the same time the lower half has unfolded in the same way, till there are two chrysanthemums back to back...

It is strength turning inside out. Such is the true beat of strength, the first beat, the one from which all others part, the beat which we feel in all things that come within our measure, in ourselves, and in our starry world.

Rashly (with a rashness that I must say I was half conscious of) I commented, 'Upward of course did not live to see this inspired guess at "the first beat" astonishingly confirmed experimentally, when the biophysicists Crick and Watson broke the genetic code to reveal "the double helix" (that's to say, double-vortex).' I accept Cox's reprimand when he writes entertainingly that to see Upward's 'inspired guess' thus 'confirmed experimentally' is 'a pleasant fancy differing only in degree from seeing the invention of the submarine predicted in the Rigveda'. It is a true bill: a literary sensibility (mine) got itself carried away into an intellectual world I was not at home in, where for instance *proof* and *experiment* had meanings different from those I was used to.

And yet 'a pleasant fancy' seems more dismissive than is called for. It doesn't measure up to the excitement, the heightened awareness, that Upward's sentences provoked in me (and do again, now that I re-read them), nor for the unforeseen analogy that that excitement provoked me to. The formula that Cox offers me is unexceptionable: 'It is more sensible to admit that the verbal faculty, while capable at its heights of marvellous insights and syntheses, which may precede and even suggest discoveries (Heisenberg got ideas from Anaximander), produces formulations that as such cannot be proved or applied.' And yet I am not clear in what sense the faculty in Upward that produced these sentences can be called precisely verbal; nor, while accepting that such formulations cannot as such be proved, am I sure that they cannot be applied. The important point to my mind is that in these sentences by Upward we experience a powerful mind thinking powerfully about the physical and the non-physical world; and it seems wrong and self-defeating for us to scout and ignore his apprehensions merely because we cannot securely label them under hydraulics or oceanography or botany or metaphysics. At this point the preservation of what I have called the historical memory seems involved with the current articulation of the world of learning, an articulation ever more minutely intricate according as, in Cox's sardonic words, more and more of our sciences 'are both more exact and more uncertain'. Each of us may be remembered *in our discipline*; woe, and in the worst cases oblivion, attend those who have no one discipline, or have one that they stray outside of; who detect what Upward was to call, and after him Pound, 'rhymes' between disciplines – something more than analogies, yet less than equivalences.

And yet if we ask why Upward was ignored in his lifetime and has been largely ignored since, it will hardly do to suppose this was because his synthesizing intelligence flew in the face of a strong professional determination to compartmentalize. For there were other synthesizing popular educators – H.G. Wells has been mentioned – who in Upward's day received sufficient acclaim. G.K. Chesterton might be another instance. Yet if it isn't the intellectual climate that must bear the blame, on the other hand, as Michael Sheldon says, 'it seems clear that the practical factors alone are not sufficient to explain the obscurity surrounding his life and works'. By the time of *The Divine Mystery*, Upward was arguing that in all human cultures, including quite notably Christendom, the genius is doomed to the role of changeling and sacrificial scapegoat. And 'genius' was surely, and rightly, how he characterized himself. Accordingly some have suggested that his suicide eleven years later was the logical outcome. But a man does not shoot himself to prove the rightness of a theory. Years before, Upward had advanced a much more mundane but more plausible explanation of why he was, as increasingly we must think he was, vindictively overlooked:

> The reputation, and even the livelihood, of a private man of letters is largely at the mercy of great organs of opinion like *The Daily News*; their grudges are often lasting, and they have the means of keeping up a vendetta long after the public has forgotten its origin; and the law of England does not afford that protection to assailed individuals which is afforded by the law of other countries, by requiring the signature of newspaper articles and the insertion of replies. In these circumstances I can only place myself in the hands of the public, and trust to its sense of fair play to protect me in the discharge of my duty to itself and to those who have appealed to it through me.

This is from *The East End of Europe* (1908), one of Upward's books that is nowadays little read and indeed seldom to be found. I have seen it described as 'a travel-book' and also as 'a war-correspondent's dispatches'. Neither description is accurate. Better is the subtitle: 'The Report of an Unofficial Mission to the European Provinces of Turkey on the Eve of the Revolution.' The Revolution meant is the bloodless one of the Young Turks in 1908 against Abdul Hamid II. At once we see why *The East End of Europe* can never attract even such few readers as have lately been brought to *The Divine Mystery* (not to speak of *The New Word*, shamefully never reprinted to this day): where those books sail at a high and intoxicating level of abstraction, *The East End of Europe* is unremittingly concerned with the quotidian and the contingent – in a setting, moreover, the Balkan peninsula in the first decade of this century, than which few can seem more remote from the modern common reader's interests or frame of reference. And yet, whatever Upward may have distorted or suppressed (for instance, his mission was unofficial – who then financed it, and in whose interests?), *The East End of Europe* gives to his thought an extra dimension that we should not have dreamed of, after reading only *The Divine Mystery* and *The New Word*.

Here is Upward the historian; and in fact the first fifty pages of *The East End of Europe* are masterly in their concise clarity, making manageable sense of a conflict of languages and races so traditionally intractable that it has generated the baleful word *Balkanization*. As a traveller Upward is humorous and relaxed, urbane, and towards the schoolchildren whom he meets in their classrooms – Turkish, Greek, Bulgarian, and of mixed races – he is tender. Hardly ever does he fall back on that staple of travellers' tales – the lousiness or other disadvantages of his accommodation. And he eschews altogether, drawing attention to it himself, impressions of landscape; his concern is entirely with the inhabitants of those landscapes, and from that, their human and civic condition day by day, nothing is allowed to distract him. We get another surprising shaft of light on to him when he concludes his castigation of an English journalist who had preceded him: 'I confess myself unable to understand how any writer could have imagined that he could help his argument by including such passages as those in a book intended to be read by English gentlemen.' Was 'English gentlemen' written straight-faced or with tongue in cheek? Kenneth Cox seems to be right when he says that 'irony was not one of Upward's weapons'; and so I infer that, disconcerting as it may be for modern readers, Upward's appeal to English gentlemen was made in all naïve sincerity.

Again, we may feel, Upward was extraordinarily ill-advised, or else unlucky, or else perverse. For who in seventy or eighty years has cared what 'Rumelia' is, or was? It was what Upward chose to travel over, and to report on: that large Balkan territory which, as the Ottoman Empire found ever less energy to administer it, was becoming a power vacuum. Into that vacuum were rushing Bulgar, Serb and Greek, Rumanian and Albanian, each of them more or less manipulated by one of the Great Powers: Russia and Austria, Britain and France and Italy, covertly but effectively Germany – the powers which had created the vacuum in the first place, by harassing and humiliating the retreating Turk, under the seldom enunciated but always understood pretext of defending Christendom against Islam.

Upward presents the principal power struggle in the region as between Bulgar and Greek. He declares himself, firmly and indeed fervently, Hellenophile. Armed bands both Bulgarian and Greek were roaming the territory; and Upward claims to have found that the Greek bands were defensive and protective vigilantes, whereas the Bulgarian bands (*comitadji*), directly organized from Sofia, were 'Bulgarizing' by terror. More surprisingly, he is strongly pro-Turk; at least, in one anecdote after another, he presents the Ottoman administration as thoroughly mild and humane, the Pashas' rule over their Christian subjects as by and large enlightened. Indeed, a strong undertow in the book, which we become more aware of the further we read, is that, whereas the Christian communities are murderous towards each other, the Mohammedan is even-handedly compliant and considerate towards all of them. The cumulative effect is almost Swiftian. It challenges at every point the originally Gladstonian consensus that had for many years governed British policy on 'the Eastern question':

In our nurseries, if a child shows a boisterous and ungovernable disposition, we call him a 'young Turk'. A favourite figure in our nursery tales is that of the terrible Turk, with his big turban, and big beard, and baggy trousers, his curly moustache, curly slippers, and curly scimitar. The redoubtable Bluebeard, according to historians, was actually a French or Breton noble; but he is always pictured as a Turk. Such ideas, so early implanted, are never really effaced.

For a hundred years past those Powers which hope to aggrandize themselves at the expense of Turkey, and those aspiring peoples which have desired foreign aid in overthrowing their old conquerors, have deluged Europe with denunciations of the Turk. The cause of Christianity, the cause of liberty, and the cause of territorial greed have found a common enemy in the Turk. In the year 1876 two of these causes found a champion in the most powerful popular orator since Demosthenes.

Gladstone, a name which I have never heard mentioned by any Turk except in terms of sincere respect, had two supreme interests at heart – what he believed to be Christianity, and what he believed to be freedom. On many occasions in his life one of these interests pleaded against the other. Over the question of Bulgaria the two were united, and the result was tremendous.

The great statesman then at the helm of the British empire trimmed his sails to the wind, and brought the ship into port. What was genuinely Bulgarian territory was rendered independent; but the ambitions of Russia were repressed, Turkey was safeguarded, and the future was left open for Greece.

This result could not satisfy Gladstone. The General Election of 1880 was one of the few ever fought in England on a question of foreign politics, and it resulted in an overwhelming condemnation of the Turk for the 'Bulgarian atrocities' – a strangely prophetic phrase!

That decision of the electorate was loyally accepted by the followers of Beaconsfield, and their new leader afterwards emulated Gladstone in his language about Turkey and her sovereign.

'Bulgarian atrocities' is said to be 'a strangely prophetic phrase' because, whereas Gladstone meant by it atrocities allegedly committed by Turks in Bulgaria, Upward means by it atrocities that he alleges the Bulgarians have committed in Macedonia.

What is remarkable here is that, in his several fruitless attempts to enter parliamentary politics (Michael Sheldon gives us such details as we have), Upward himself seems to have campaigned on what we might now call the left wing of Gladstonian liberalism. Accordingly it may seem that in *The East End of Europe* we encounter, in the field of politics, what Kenneth Cox laboriously but valuably defines as a characteristic habit of Upward's mind:

> Upward had the kind of mind which, proceeding from a central sense of an ungraspable whole, what he called the 'All-thing', advances to an outpost of opinion only to find itself associated with persons who have arrived there by some process of ratiocination, or who have stationed themselves there for motives of self-interest, and which thereupon retires to its centre, refreshes itself at its source and advances again in a different direction, sometimes to a position diametrically opposite to the first. His writing continually takes up new starting points, working round his main preoccupations, but breaking off before a definite conclusion that can be identified and fixed.

It is rather important to see what Cox is here claiming for Upward. He is not saying that Upward 'couldn't make up his mind' – which is an incapacity that, where we have encountered it, none of us is called on to condone. He isn't saying, either, that Upward rather often changed his mind and consistently claimed his right to do so – though that's a right that we ought to recognize, as much in intellectual endeavour as in politics, though we seldom do. Nor is Kenneth Cox, as I understand him advancing a claim for 'the free play of mind', where 'free' means 'irresponsible'. Rather, if I read him right, he is making a plea for the provisional: that is to say, for assertions which, however trenchantly made (and why assert at all, it not trenchantly?), are corrigible in the light of further evidence, even of further reflection and extraneous opinion. What Cox is standing up for in fact, with Upward as prime instance, is the rights of the *speculative* intelligence.

That intelligence cannot be, in political or any other terms, partisan. And so politics, because it is of its nature partisan, cannot make use of, because it cannot trust, an intelligence like Upward's. The English electors were right therefore to deny Upward a parliamentary seat, whenever he asked for it. However there are intelligences (many more of them, indeed) that are at once keen and partisan. Such was Henry Noel Brailsford (1873–1958), the English journalist whose *Macedonia* had appeared in 1906, whom Upward girds at on page after page, and in footnote after footnote, of *The East End of Europe*; of whose retaliation in the *Daily News* Upward admits himself afraid. It would be worth someone's while to scan the columns of the *Daily News* through the relevant years to see if Upward's fears of retaliation were or were not well-founded. What is certain is that Brailsford went on to have a career, as opinion-maker, that is abundantly and even deferentially recorded; his books are still remembered, and (some of them) reprinted. Brailsford's principal publications are: *The Broom of the War-God* (a novel, 1898); *Shelley, Godwin and their Circle* (1913); *The War of Steel and Gold* (1914); *Belgium and the Scrap of Paper* (1915); *A League of Nations* (1917); *The Russian Workers' Republic* (1921); *Socialism for Today* (1925); *How the Soviets Work* (1928); *Property or Peace?* (1934); *Voltaire* (1935); *Rebel India* (1931); and *Subject India* (1943). He earned a long and respectful entry in *The Twentieth Century Dictionary of National Biography*, from which Upward's name is, alas not conspicuously, absent.

And yet, for as long as Upward was alive, his career and Brailsford's seemed to run in parallel – with this difference: that Brailsford was consistent. Brailsford was, from first to last, a left-wing thinker; and though, like all such in his lifetime, he had to make tactical adjustments from time to time (now ardent about communist Russia, now keeping his distance from it), his bent is, whatever the subject he takes up, predictable. That surely is what we mean when we characterize such consistency as 'admirable': we mean that on any given question we can be certain, within manageable limits, which way Brailsford will jump. There never was any such certainty about Upward. And to be radically unpredictable scares everybody – in the world of learning, as in other worlds.

A good case in point is Upward's attitude toward the Irish. Born in Worcester to a family attached to the Plymouth Brethren, Upward attended and graduated from the Royal University of Ireland, an institution particularly intended – largely on J.H. Newman's initiative – for Irish Roman Catholics. Why his *alma mater* should have been thus unlikely, not to say outlandish, is what no one offers to explain, unless he explains it himself in his pseudonymous autobiography, *Some Personalities* (1921), which I have not seen. (Robert Duncan, who has, did not trust it very far.) This is in itself an instance of how Upward, in his life as in his thinking, not so much eludes all categories as confounds them. We cannot even, in our ignorance of circumstances now probably irrecoverable, label the choice 'quixotic'. However that may be, it seems that Upward in his Irish years aligned himself, quite actively too, with certain Irish nationalists. Yet in *The East End of Europe* when Upward alludes to the Irish, as he does several times, his sympathies seem to lie quite elsewhere. Brailsford had argued, in support of the *comitadji*, that 'a revolutionary organisation has as much right as a recognised Government to punish traitors, and to levy taxes by force'. In one who was or would shortly be in touch with Lenin, the sentiment is not surprising. But Upward is appalled:

> The Bulgarian apologist can only excuse the atrocities of his clients by arguments which would be rejected with horror by the ordinary anarchist. According to him, if in any country a body of men, however contemptible in point of numbers, band themselves together to seize the government, they are thereby justified, not merely in employing assassination against the agents and supporters of the government in existence; they are justified in usurping authority over the ordinary peaceable inhabitants; they may rob and plunder them, they may murder those who complain, or torture those who hang back.
>
> If the anarchists of Europe should ever be tempted to act upon these principles, the world will become one great carnival of horror. And if anything could add to their wickedness it would be their extension to what is, in substance, a war of annexation waged, not against the Turkish Government, but against the Hellenist people. In order to understand the full bearing of this frightful reasoning, we must imagine Ireland an independent republic, and emissaries from Dublin landing in Liverpool to conquer that city. They will be received and sheltered in the Irish quarter; they will shirk encounters with the English police; but they will set about bringing over the Welsh citizens to their side by a campaign of savage terror.

There is no denying that this reads very quaintly in 1989. Has the IRA in fact missed a trick by not terrorizing Welsh citizens of Liverpool? It is surely a comical notion. Yet Upward's only mistake was to pick on the wrong city; read 'Belfast' for 'Liverpool', and 'Unionist' for 'Welsh citizens', and his analogy not only holds up, it is an accurate prediction. Moreover, in the areas which it controls, the IRA, like other terrorist organizations, assumes just those 'rights' that Brailsford asserts on behalf of his Bulgarians, acting in this on thoroughly Leninist principles. Should we react to Upward's 'one great carnival of horror' by exclaiming, *o sancta simplicitas*? Or should we not give him credit for foreseeing, however incredulously, what has in fact come to pass since he died?

We may wonder, it seems we *ought* to wonder, whether Upward was not 'blacked out' quite deliberately, for political reasons, by thinkers in the Leninist tradition of the Fabian Society, powerful in British public and intellectual life from Wells and Shaw and the youthful Brailsford through to Kingsley Martin, who wrote the hagiography of Brailsford for *The Twentieth Century DNB*. For of course even today to be, like Brailsford, an apologist for political terror is not held in Britain to disqualify anyone from esteem among the intellectual *élite*, nor even from public office. And yet to speculate along these lines is unthinkable. For to entertain such speculations is to subscribe in some measure to 'the conspiracy theory of history'. And that is unthinkable, because Ezra Pound is unavoidably part of the story, and once Pound is named we are in sight of such a monstrous product of conspiracy theory as *The Protocols of the Elders of Zion*. Yet most of us have seen in our own spheres of interest, including the world of learning, that plots *are* hatched, exclusions and blackballings *are* engineered, vendettas *are* maintained; that some persons who think themselves discriminated against are right to think so. The initiators of pogroms, up to and including the Nazi genocide, are still triumphing in our midst if, by their cynical manipulation of conspiracy theory, they blackmail us into refusing to acknowledge that in some circles and at some stages of recorded history conspiracies against certain individuals were hatched, were maintained, and were successful – to the point where, in the worst cases, the targeted individual was virtually written out of the historical record altogether.

Moreover, the world of professional scholarship cannot escape its share of the blame. For there is professional pride on the part of historians. Intellectual historians, like other kinds, have come to think it ignominious for them, even part of their time, to go about stooping to keyholes and listening at half-open doors or to backstairs gossip – which is what they are condemned to, if they accept that conspiracies sometimes happen. Where in such furtive researches are to be found the wide vistas, the uncoverings of dynamisms and laws operating through many eras, such as historians have felt themselves called to since Hegel if not before? For a not unreasonably ambitious historian, the trouble with a case like Upward's is that it is stubbornly particular. There is no law of history that he exemplifies, no generalization however modest or tentative that can be drawn from his life, so far as we know it. There is no way in which to make him representative. The late poet Robert Duncan, introducing the Californian reprint of *The Divine Mystery*, thought he could see one way in which Upward in his generation was a representative case:

Allen Upward has to contend with... the gap that was beginning to appear between popularizing journalism and the high styles of personal expression, as he has to contend with his lower class Plymouth origins and his Grammar School Education, with his Grub Street ambitions and his job writing, with his careers in civil service, in an England where class consciousness and a literary élitism growing out of Oxford and Cambridge associations made for his cultural isolation.

Thus Duncan (though it's way off his main concern) finds a category that Upward can be slotted into: he was 'born the wrong side of the tracks'. But it won't do. Upward lived in fact through a period when crossing from the wrong side of the tracks to the right side was, for persons of talent, comparatively easy and could be very profitable. Again, though many cases could be cited (Wells, Chesterton, Shaw), the best counter-example is Brailsford who, born ten years after Upward to a provincially non-conformist background like his, survived to write books still acclaimed as 'minor classic' or 'socialist classic'. Even Brailsford's university, Glasgow, was neither more nor less provincial than the Royal University of Ireland, neither more nor less remote from 'Oxford and Cambridge associations'. Why then is Brailsford remembered and Upward not? It seems that the socialist historian's safety net is as little as any other able to catch Upward; he falls through it, plummet-like, as certainly as through any other of the nets that scholars have woven, of ever finer mesh, to ensure that the memorable is remembered. It doesn't happen; a maverick like Allen Upward is only very partially, and by accident, rescued from oblivion.

Kenneth Cox decided that Upward is best described as 'a visionary'. But that is the merest device, even (one might say) a cop-out. 'Visionary' is a catch-all category devised to accommodate those – Swedenborg, Nietzsche, Upward (other names will come to mind) – whom none of the properly constituted committees and sub-committees will take on. It is good that such a category exists, to stop the committees and sub-committees from thinking that between them they have taken account of the entire range of intellectual endeavour. All the same, a cop-out is what it is. The sort of thinking that we agree to call 'visionary' is, where it is not self-deluding and charlatan, a sort of thinking that the currently accepted map of human thought cannot, any more than earlier now discredited maps, find room for. But just suppose that this were a primal kind of thinking which secondary kinds, theology as much as philology or physics, can batten on. In that case its exclusion from the array or hierarchy of accredited disciplines would still be justified. And the sacrificial victimization of its exponents would be understandable, indeed almost a matter of course. But that would bear out Upward's thesis that the truly original thinker is at once scapegrace and scapegoat. It is a thesis that his own life and subsequent reputation may be thought to bear out, in a quite spectacular or exemplary fashion. Brailsford of course posed no such problems.

Upward died unmarried and childless. He fathered no spiritual children either, unless we count a maverick and half-crazy American poet. Whom therefore does it help, to have his teasing obscurity worried over? The history of the modern mind is complete enough without him. Those of us who feel a little worry and a little shame on this score must be, whether we know it or not, appealing to a principle metaphysical if not religious: the *lacuna* impugns our dignity and the dignity of the intellectual pursuit we conceive ourselves to be engaged in. That is an irrational conviction: metaphysical, at best speculative. Keeping the historical record full, or as full as possible, the keeping of faith with past generations – these tasks, which we tend to think of as obvious and practical necessities, are nothing of the sort. They rest, whether we know it or not, on somewhere an act of faith.

The American Scholar, 59.1 (Winter 1990).

XXIV 'The Dry Salvages': A Reconsideration

In 1956 I published an essay, 'T.S. Eliot: The End of an Era', which focused on 'The Dry Salvages'.[1] If only because this piece has attracted some attention over the years, it seems high time that I had second thoughts about it, particularly in the light of new information that has come to light in the last thirty years or more. To do this, I must first reproduce my 1956 essay, or as much of it as is immediately relevant.

My announced object, then, was to establish that 'The Dry Salvages' 'is quite simply *rather a bad poem*'. My objections began with the very first lines:

> I do not know much about gods, but I think that the river
> Is a strong brown god – sullen, untamed and intractable,
> Patient to some degree, at first recognized as a frontier

Helen Gardner, who in her *Art of T.S. Eliot* (1949), had cited these and subsequent lines precisely to show Eliot's masterly manipulation of language, had declared that the 'strong brown god' is 'a personification which the poet's tone makes no more than a suggestion, a piece of half-serious myth-making'. But, I objected, 'the first line has not sufficiently defined the tone (a single line hardly could) for this to be true'. I might have asked, but did not: How serious is half-serious? This would have saved me from having to navigate in the tricky waters of 'tone'. However, 'tone' was what Helen Gardner had appealed to; and so it was what I stayed with when I objected to the next lines:

> Useful, untrustworthy, as a conveyor of commerce;
> Then only a problem confronting the builder of bridges.
> The problem once solved, the brown god is almost forgotten
> By the dwellers in cities – ever, however, implacable,
> Keeping his seasons and rages, destroyer, reminder
> Of what men choose to forget. Unhonoured, unpropitiated
> By worshippers of the machine, but waiting, watching and waiting.

I asked: Has the tone been settled even now, ten lines into the poem, enough to carry off the journalistic cliché 'worshippers of the machine',

---

1 See pp. 13–21. [Ed.]

and the limpness of 'watching and waiting'? Gardner herself had allowed that 'worshippers of the machine', such an inert and faded locution, called for invisible quote-marks. But where, I asked, had the poet signalled that such quote-marks were called for? I would make the point now by asking: Do we have here, in Wordsworth's phrase, a man speaking to men? Or do we not have, rather, a journalist addressing his 'concerned' readership; or a perhaps Unitarian minister addressing his 'concerned' congregation? Such are the uncertainties that one points to by complaining of instability of tone.

I back-tracked at this point to the first line, and asked of 'I do not know much about gods': 'Who could conceivably start a conversation like that without condemning himself from the start as an uncomfortable *poseur*?' I'm not sure I was well-advised to try in this way to bring the issue of 'tone' down to earth; for I leave myself open to the objection that not all poems have to be conversational, not all of them need be seen as opening a dialogue with the reader. On the other hand it is surely true that, if the poet proposes something other than this, the terms of that alternative proposal should be made clear – as, in this poem by Eliot, they aren't.

I turned next to the second section of the poem, which B. Rajan had declared to be 'as intricately organized as anything Eliot has written'. This section is, it will be recalled, a *sestina*: an Italianate form which calls for a richness of rhyming such as English of its nature is hard pushed to provide. In the first *sestine*, I said, came a very beautiful perception:

The silent withering of autumn flowers
Dropping their petals and remaining motionless

And the rhymes found for 'motionless' are, in order (with my jeering comments): 'emotionless' (how so?); 'Oceanless' (grotesque!); 'erosion-less' (he seems to mean 'uneroded'); and 'motionless', rounding out the line 'To the movement of pain that is painless and motionless', which I rudely characterized as 'incantatory gibberish'. Frequent and regularly recurrent rhyme had never been part of Eliot's repertoire; and it is unaccountable – so I thought and still think – that after so many years' experience he should have embarked on a form making so many demands on a skill he had never practised. It is poignant and unsurprising that Helen Gardner years later found, in the Magdalene College MSS, a sheet on which Eliot had jotted down rhymes for his sestina, including two that he had struck out but in desperation found himself compelled to use. These are straits that writers of English sestinas are familiar with.

My next, and last, objection was to the lines:

It seems, as one becomes older
That the past has another pattern, and ceases to be a mere sequence –

Or even development; the latter a partial fallacy
Encouraged by superficial notions of evolution,
Which becomes, in the popular mind, a means of disowning the past.
The moments of happiness – not the sense of well-being
Fruition, fulfilment, security or affection
Or even a very good dinner, but the sudden illumination –

Of these verses, I asked rhetorically:

> Is this the poet who wove to and fro the close and lively syntax at the beginning of 'East Coker', or the passage from 'Burnt Norton' beginning 'The inner freedom from the practical desire'? How can we explain that the same poet should now offer, in such stumbling trundling rhythms, these inarticulate ejaculations of reach-me-down phrases, the debased currency of the study circle? And worse is to come – Possum's little joke: 'Or even a very good dinner...'. At the dismal jocularity of that 'very good dinner', we throw in our hands. The tone that Miss Gardner thought established in the very first line can now, we realize, never be established at all.

We now know, from Gardner's *The Composition of Four Quartets* (1978), that while the poem was still in MS, Geoffrey Faber had objected in this passage to what he called 'lecture-stigmata'. All I add to his objection is to observe that the lectures of which 'stigmata' appear must have been impoverished, idle and condescending lectures. And if it should seem, as doubtless it does, that my comments were gleefully unforgiving, it should be considered, first, that in between the passages I took exception to were others that I applauded (notably the lines beginning, 'To communicate with Mars, converse with spirits'); and also, more pertinently, that in 1956 I was still a 'prentice-poet anxious to learn from my elders about matters like diction, accordingly baffled when the most esteemed of my elders, Eliot, presented me with passages so little worthy of emulation as those I protested at.

Ronald Bush, in his *T.S. Eliot: A Study in Character and Style* (1983), was so good as to call my 1956 essay a 'devastating critique'. Of course I was, and am, gratified; to not many of us is it given to be devastating. But when I look more closely at the relevant pages, I see that Bush endorses my strictures on only one of the three passages I take exception to: the one beginning 'It seems, as one becomes older'. The opening passage, and Section 2, the sestina, he passes over without comment. The reason for this is not hard to seek, and it exposes an embarrassing fact: that on 'The Dry Salvages' the Anglo-American consensus tends to split apart, nationalistically. This was, I see now, inevitable. Of the *Four Quartets*, three are plainly written by Eliot the naturalized Briton; only the third, 'The Dry Salvages', is imagined and composed by Eliot still the unalienated American. How could objections to it by me, an Englishman, not seem to be invidious? (Not, I'm glad to say, that this was ever conveyed to me except politely.) Not only does 'The Dry Salvages' most emphatically turn around American locations – the Mississippi seen from St Louis, and the Atlantic seen from Cape Ann – but the sensibility brought to bear on these locations is distinctly American, not European. In order to enter in imagination these American scenes of his boyhood and youth Eliot had to recapture the American self which he had given up (legalistically) when he became a British citizen. Nothing shameful in that, and nothing surprising. But it means, disconcertingly, that whereas the other Quartets ask to be seen down the perspectives of Old World culture, 'The Dry Salvages' is placed in the cultural perspective of the New. To come at once to the knottiest problem, in that perspective Walt Whitman is a towering figure, whereas in the Old World perspective he isn't. Indeed it's not to this day clear what the Old World has decided to make of Whitman. And it must be said that Eliot and Pound, Americans in Europe, did nothing to help the Europeans on this score. (The tragically doomed Englishman Ivor Gurney tried harder, but went unnoticed.) Because both Pound and Eliot so largely concealed their debts to Whitman, his presence in their work, and specifically in 'The Dry Salvages', can be overlooked by British readers, as it was in Gardner's *The Composition of Four Quartets*; or else can be noticed by them only disparagingly, as when Bernard Bergonzi (*T.S. Eliot*, 1972) remarked: 'The opening lines are poor, in a weakly sub-Whitmanesque fashion.' (The weakening presence that I detected in those lines was not Whitman, but Bliss Carman.) Understandably Bush, as an American reader, is far more conscious of Whitman's presence, though he sometimes associates him with William Carlos Williams, as when he advises (p. 179): 'if we seek a contemporary guide to the premises of Eliot's late work, we could do worse than turn to Williams's *Spring and All*.'

I find this implausible. But of the relevance of Whitman there can be no doubt. In 1956 I was able to use S. Musgrove's *T.S. Eliot and Walt Whitman*, from (perhaps significantly) New Zealand; but if I were to re-write the essay now, I should want to take account of the more far-reaching role for Whitman adumbrated in Cleo McNelly Kearns's *T.S. Eliot and Indic Traditions* (1987), especially since this sees Whitman behind Krishna and Arjuna, whose Indic presences I certainly dismissed or discounted too rashly thirty years ago.

On the other hand Ronald Bush's Americanism is very sweeping, very *driving*. Taking note of Helen Gardner's indeed remarkable discovery that Eliot's original *schema* called for much about the ocean but nothing about the river, he observes: 'But by the time Eliot had finished his first draft, the sea and the river were related in one venerable figure: the river of an individual life flowing into the sea of eternity.' Not in the first draft nor

in any subsequent one up to the last, can I see that in the poem river and
ocean are allegorized in this fashion. Bush goes on to say, of the lines
about the 'strong brown god': 'Steeped in the Emersonian notion that the
American self is a process, the lines remind us that Whitman envisioned
the river of life as an open road, and that after him Mark Twain put the
river road at the center of *Huckleberry Finn*. That openness of self was part
of Eliot's birthright...'. If indeed Eliot's verses are 'steeped' in a certain
Emersonian notion, Bush has to prove it, not just say so. In no time at all,
he is saying that the river 'suggests a peculiarly American self', and indeed
that 'the river is a self'. How does one politely protest that on the contrary
the river is a river, and a quite specific river, the Mississippi? Moreover, if
it were true that 'Whitman envisioned the river of life as an open road',
he would surely be a bad poet, for rivers and roads are very different.
Indeed, where the Mississippi is concerned, Eliot is at pains to insist on
the difference – both here, in the verse ('untrustworthy, as a conveyor of
commerce'), and more memorably in prose that he wrote in 1950, pref-
acing an edition of *Huckleberry Finn*:

> A river, a very big and powerful river, is the only natural force that can
> wholly determine the course of human peregrination. At sea, the
> wanderer may sail or be carried by winds and currents in one direction
> or another; a change of wind or tide may determine fortune. In the
> prairie, the direction of movement is more or less at the choice of the
> caravan; among mountains there will often be an alternative, a guess at
> the most likely pass. But the river with its strong, swift current is the
> dictator to the raft or to the steamboat. It is a treacherous and capricious
> dictator. At one season, it may move sluggishly in a channel so narrow
> that, encountering it for the first time at that point, one can hardly
> believe that it has travelled already for hundreds of miles, and has yet
> many hundreds of miles to go; at another season it may obliterate the
> low Illinois shore to a horizon of water, while in its bed it runs with a
> speed such that no man or beast can survive in it. At such times, it
> carries down human bodies, cattle and houses. At least twice, at St
> Louis, the western and the eastern shores have been separated by the fall
> of bridges, until the designer of the great Eads Bridge devised a struc-
> ture which could resist the floods. In my own childhood, it was not
> unusual for the spring freshet to interrupt railway travel; and then the
> traveller to the East had to take steamboat from the levee up to Alton,
> at a higher level on the Illinois shore, before he could begin his rail
> journey. The river is never wholly chartable; it may suddenly efface a
> sandbar, and throw up another bar where before was navigable water.

The Mississippi river is not an open road, and it never was.

This passage was brought to my attention only in 1978 by Helen
Gardner in *The Composition of Four Quartets*. In the same place she

unearthed, even more strikingly, a passage which stands behind the treatment of the ocean in 'The Dry Salvages' as the preface to *Huckleberry Finn*
stands behind the poem's treatment of the river. This prose comes (inter-
estingly) from earlier in Eliot's life, 1928, when he wrote a preface to
Edgar Ansel Mowrer's *This American World*:

> My family did not move so often as his, because we tended to cling to
> places and associations as long as possible; but with a family tendency
> to traditions and loyalties, I have a background which Mr Mowrer
> would recognize, and which is different from that of the native
> European and from that of many Americans. My family were New
> Englanders, who had been settled – my branch of it – for two genera-
> tions in the South West – which was, in my own time, rapidly
> becoming merely the Middle West. The family guarded jealously its
> connexions with New England; but it was not until years of maturity
> that I perceived that I myself had always been a New Englander in the
> South West, and a South Westerner in New England; when I was sent
> to school in New England I lost my southern accent without ever
> acquiring the accent of the native Bostonian. In New England I missed
> the long dark river, the ailanthus trees, the flaming cardinal birds, the
> high limestone bluffs where we searched for fossil shell-fish; in
> Missouri I missed the fir trees, the bay and goldenrod, the song-
> sparrows, the red granite and the blue sea of Massachusetts. I
> remember a friend of my schooldays, whose family had lived in the
> same house in the same New England seaport for two hundred and
> fifty years. In some ways his background was as different from mine as
> that of any European. My grandmother – one of my grandmothers –
> had shot her own wild turkeys for dinner; his had collected Chinese
> pottery brought home by the Salem clippers. It was perhaps easier for
> the grandson of pioneers to migrate eastward than it would have been
> for my friend to migrate in any direction.

I would not claim that this account of the New England coast is superior
to that in the poem. But it is, while more explicit, at least as interesting.
And it prompts the reflection that to any American born of the automo-
bile generations Eliot's America, where New England and 'the South
West' are worlds apart, must be at least as strange as it is to any European.
   It's particularly to the point to compare 'the ailanthus trees', here casu-
ally named as among the Missourian things that the poet missed when in
New England, with what the poem makes of them:

> His rhythm was present in the nursery bedroom,
> In the rank ailanthus of the April dooryard,
> In the smell of grapes on the autumn table,
> And the evening circle in the winter gaslight.

In 1956 I was particularly scathing about how his (the river's) 'rhythm was present in' bedroom and ailanthus and so much else. With an irritation that I confess to feeling still, I protested: 'After this statement has been issued, we know not a tittle more about the relation between river and bedroom than we did before.' Having in the interim read Ronald Bush, I suspect that the offending phrase represents a gesture by Eliot to readers like Bush who cannot be interested in non-human entities like oceans and rivers, except insofar as they can be made to 'symbolize' movements in the human psyche. Such down-grading of the non-human in favour of the human Creation may at times be invited by Emerson; it is, unless I am wrong, quite foreign to Whitman. And so 'His rhythm was present in' still seems to me a wretched locution.

Ralph Waldo Emerson continues to shoulder, or to be forcibly inserted, into discourses about Eliot. Thus Lyndall Gordon, in her *Eliot's New Life* (1988), could assure us that 'for Eliot, the historical event of the Blitz was, in Emersonian terms, a token of his being and becoming'. This went along with similarly blithe and impassive observations about how 'To Eliot, war, as a historical event, was peripheral to its private moral meaning'; and how 'Eliot was animated, not harrowed, by the horrific scene'. Add that Eliot refused to remove his estranged and long insane wife from the London blitz, even as he arranged such removal for himself, and 'Emersonian' seems an inadequate and misleading term for blank unfeeling and moral obtuseness. That possibility could not fail to reflect back on one's reading of 'The Dry Salvages', as of other poems. And that reflection or re-reading was particularly painful for those anxious to join Eliot in Christian orthodoxy.

Thus, 1988 was a very bad year for every one of us who had invested trust and respect in Eliot the poet. It was his centenary year; and it was marked not only by Lyndall Gordon's virtually authorized biography, but also by the first volume of the poet's correspondence, *The Letters of T.S. Eliot: Volume 1, 1898–1922.* If these two publications were meant to be sedately honorific, the project appallingly misfired. So far from settling doubts about Eliot, these books re-inflamed old doubts and provoked new ones. The volume of letters, it turned out, was by no means complete but comprised only 'the significant extant letters Eliot wrote up to age 34'; and since it seemed that the only judge of 'significance' had been the editor, the poet's widow, of course the selection was immediately challenged. Peter Ackroyd, who seems to have had less than full co-operation from the Eliot estate when writing his own biography, was one of several reviewers who complained at not finding a letter of 7 April 1921, from Eliot to Richard Aldington. Replying to Ackroyd's strictures in a letter to *The Times* on 5 October 1988, Mrs Eliot explained that she did not know until then of this letter, promised to print it in full in an appendix to her Volume Two (which at this time of writing has yet to appear),[2] and for good measure provided, then and there, the whole of the missing letter's final paragraph. The seemingly admirable candour of this was unfortunately somewhat smirched, since *The Times* published, immediately below Valerie Eliot's letter, one from Michael Hastings who, as author of the 1984 play *Tom and Viv,* seems understandably to have had only frosty relations with Mrs Eliot and with Eliot's publishers. Hastings revealed that the missing letter had survived in a place where Valerie Eliot might well have looked for it, among the papers of Eliot's brother-in-law, Maurice Haigh-Wood, who had showed it to Hastings in 1979. Moreover, Hastings wrote of a series of letters from Eliot to Sacheverell Sitwell in the 1920s, still in existence in 1980 though not drawn on by Mrs Eliot. Add to this Ackroyd's confident assertion that there were letters to Percy Wyndham Lewis that the editor had 'passed over', and inevitably the suspicion grew that this book of letters was a whitewash job.

Such in-fighting about testamentary dispositions and the like is not to my taste. But, sadly, allegations and prevarications about Eliot the man and his life-record cannot now be disentangled from the record of Eliot the poet. Undoubtedly Valerie Eliot, as relict of a famous writer, has had a hard furrow to hoe. Yet she seems to have got the worst of all worlds. For even as she has given the impression of covering up, what she has uncovered is sufficiently damning in any case. Consider only the controversial sentences to Aldington which, under pressure from Ackroyd, she belatedly revealed:

> Having only contempt for every existing political party, and profound hatred for democracy, I feel the blackest gloom. Whatever happens will be another step toward the destruction of Europe. The whole of contemporary politics etc. oppresses me with a continuous physical horror like the feeling of a growing madness in one's brain. It is rather a horror to be sane in the midst of this, it is too dreadful, too huge for one to have the comfortable feeling of superiority. It goes too far for rage.

To speak for myself, these sentiments do not in themselves appal. But the question inevitably arises: Who asked the young Mr Eliot, lately arrived from St Louis, to make himself thus responsible for the whole of Europe? And yet that too is not the root of the matter: the truth is surely that we hear not the voice of the young Eliot, but a voice that he thought would be more acceptable to his correspondent – surely the voice, unlikely as it seems, of D.H. Lawrence.

Such anti-democratic sentiments cannot surprise any one who has

---

2   As the present book goes to press (2004) Mrs Eliot's second volume has still not appeared. [Ed.]

studied Eliot even a little. What shocks is the tone of lofty petulance in which they are uttered. And yet this is not significantly different from a letter six years before, which Mrs Eliot prints, to Isabella Stewart Gardner:

> On the 14 Juillet I was in Brussels, having come from Ostende, Bruges, Ghent, and Antwerp. Two days later I was in Germany, and in a fortnight I wished myself well out of Germany. Not that the people were not very kind to me – the Germans have that hospitality and cordiality which characterizes the less civilized peoples. And not that I wish the Germans to be crushed – but France is so important, and defeat would do the French so much harm! This alone outweighs any consideration of right and wrong in my mind.

That letter was dated: 4 April 1915. And whereas, once again, the anti-democratic and indeed racist sentiments may or may not be thought shocking, the tone in which they are uttered undoubtedly is. We may contrast W.B. Yeats in 1924: 'The stream has turned backwards, and generations to come will have for their task, not the widening of liberty, but recovery from its errors – the building up of authority, the restoration of discipline, the discovery of a life sufficiently heroic to live without the opium dream.' The sentiments are just as anti-democratic, and in the light of subsequent history just as baleful. But Yeats's tone is measured and solemn, where Eliot's is supercilious and glib. Tone (we recognize again) makes all, or nearly all, the difference; and tone was what Eliot, left to himself, habitually got wrong. The boy who, on moving to New England from Missouri, 'lost my southern accent without ever acquiring the accent of the native Bostonian', was thereafter condemned to seeking, without ever finding, an accent that should be authentically *his*.

To think so is the only way to turn aside the implications of *Eliot's New Life*, an extraordinary work in that it presents an extremely damaging image of Eliot the man at the same time as it proposes, or pretends, to do just the opposite. A lot turns on Eliot's treatment of the women in his life; and this can be passed over rather quickly, since it isn't directly relevant to anything in 'The Dry Salvages'. On the other hand it certainly has some relevance, insofar as it necessarily questions Eliot's right to speak as a moralist, or as a moral individual. To be blunt about it, the worldly biographer must see in Emily Hale a New England spinster cruelly kept on a string through forty years, only to be brutally rejected in the end – this on evidence assembled by Lyndall Gordon herself. Yet Gordon can see her as the Beatrice to Eliot's Dante, 'a convenient focus for Eliot's evolving idea of love': a role that, Gordon has the grace to acknowledge, Emily neither understood nor agreed to, never having been asked. In the 1940s and 1950s, true to his Atlantic Alliance evenhandedness, Eliot seems to have handed out the same treatment to the English 'good sport', Mary Trevelyan. In the drama that Eliot made of his life – a more lurid melodrama than Christianity, except in its New England version, gives warrant for, though Lyndall Gordon finds it absorbing and apparently justifiable – Vivien Haigh-Wood and Emily Hale and Mary Trevelyan have only walk-on parts. The ravenousness of such egotism, suppose we agree in discerning it, we cannot help but see reflected in *Four Quartets*, among them 'The Dry Salvages'.

However, the uncertainty of tone that we have seen as characteristic of Eliot may cast doubt on the documents that Lyndall Gordon cites, for instance his communications to his woman friends. More certainly it disqualifies her reading of Eliot's response to the London blitz. Whether or not Vivien and Emily and Mary have only walk-on parts in Eliot's drama, it seems clear that the blitz supplied more than 'noises off'. Eliot thought that the latter three of his *Quartets* were patriotic poems; and they were so regarded by their first readers – for instance by me, who read them first while serving with the Royal Navy in North Russia. However Lyndall Gordon may have been seduced by 'Emersonian terms', the London blitz was experienced, by the first readers of *Four Quartets*, as something other than 'a token of his being and becoming'. Eliot, a poet who found it exceptionally difficult to express fellow-feeling, in this emergency found it possible to do so. And accordingly the lines, 'When there is distress of nations and perplexity / Whether on the shores of Asia, or in the Edgware Road', point, I believe, to far more than the unregarded 'wisdom of the East'. When Ronald Bush says of these lines, 'Better than any poet of the century, Eliot knows the dishonesty of making poetry out of this kind of language', I experience poignantly what is meant by the generation-gap. It was wartime conditions that made Asia and the Edgware Road contiguous; and if the diction is carefully stilted, the stiltedness confers dignity, as it was meant to do.

In 1959 Hugh Kenner called Eliot *The Invisible Poet*. But it was in *The Pound Era* (1971) that Kenner made fascinated much of how Eliot in his later years zealously played the part of the London clubman. Kenner would persuade us that this was just another of the masks that the poet hid behind, intimating in his solicitousness about what cheese to take from the cheeseboard his profoundly ironical perception of how trivial such preoccupations were. But I'm not sure this is the right moral to draw. For if this is a mask, it is one that all London clubmen wear, and if some are more aware of mask-wearing than others, 'mask' in their cases means something more commonplace than what it meant for W.B. Yeats, or what Pound meant by *persona*. In donning their mask the clubmen obey a social, not an aesthetic, imperative. Eliot's dexterity in doffing and donning such masks surely had a lot to do with the worldly success that he, more than any other modernist poet, achieved. But, disconcertingly, 'commonplace' is indeed the word that comes to mind. At every stage of his life, as a Harvard student, as an Oxford student, as a bank-employee, as a publisher, as an Anglican convert, as a clubman, Eliot assiduously fell in with the habits and pretensions of his peers, seeking to be not so much invisible as anonymous. This is the behaviour not of an ironical dandy but of one anxious not to offend; conscious of how hard he found it to strike upon and maintain an appropriate tone, he took over the tone and the manner that obtained in each milieu he moved in. This was surely what Pound meant by dubbing him 'the possum', after the creature that survives by shamming dead. Accordingly I like the conclusion reached by another biographer, Peter Ackroyd in 1984: 'He was a strange, private and often bewildered man who was raised into a cultural guru, a representative of authority and stability.' 'Often bewildered' – that was one possibility that never presented itself to me in 1956, precisely because Eliot's *guru* status had been so drilled into me, through school and college. Whatever else one might think about him (for of course the guru was as often resented as revered), it was axiomatic that he *always knew what he was doing*. It was on that unchallenged assumption that, after establishing what was wrong with 'The Dry Salvages', I launched into a devious and schematic argument to show that what was wrong was after all quite right; that wherever the tone seemed 'off', this had been engineered and calculated by the poet. We were meant to notice (so my argument went) that the tone had gone wrong, and to ask ourselves why the poet had engineered such wrongness. All this part of my essay now seems to me quite implausible. The material that the poet dredged up when he remembered his boyhood was too intimate for him to maintain decorum in speaking about it. This is the most straightforward explanation, and also the most compassionate.

How much does it matter? Obviously it has some bearing on the question whether *Four Quartets* is one thing or several things. If there are such fissures as I detected, and continue to detect, in the third member of that quadripartite structure, then *Four Quartets* cannot be the monumental edifice that some of Eliot's adulators pretend. (Some of his detractors too; for one may recognize a monument even as one finds it repellent.) It is hardly good enough to concede that the writing is 'uneven'; for the monumental intention, and the wish to set a seal on an artistic career, raise the stakes beyond the point where such a concession would suffice.

There is also, rather more momentously, the historical perspective. When I subtitled my 1956 essay 'The End of an Era', that rested on a too sophisticated argument which I now disown. But there is still a sense in which *Four Quartets* does indeed mark the end of the era that had produced *The Waste Land* and *Ash-Wednesday* and *Coriolan*. These were works to which one could not address the question. 'Is this a man speaking to men (and women)?' Those multi-vocal poems by the younger Eliot had been constructed – whether by design or luck is perhaps undecidable – in such a way that the question did not arise. With

Four Quartets it does arise; and in 'The Dry Salvages', because the tone so notably wobbles, the difference becomes starkly apparent. The multi-vocal poem had been disowned by its heretofore most applauded exponent; and we were back with the univocal poem in which every-thing ultimately turned on how far one could trust the voice that spoke.

   To my mind that is a grievous loss. On the other hand I do not subscribe to the theatrical understanding of literary history, by which the curtain comes down on one act (as it may be, modernism) to rise on another (post-modernism, whatever that means). Great multi-vocal poems were yet to be written – by Bunting in England, by Ed Dorn in America. Moreover, Ezra Pound would continue to publish batches of *Cantos*. Yet Eliot's secession – for that is how it must appear – undoubt-edly legitimated afresh the self-confident egotists in verse whom his and Pound's polemics had earlier driven from the scene, or at least discredited. Moreover, when 'The Dry Salvages' showed how Eliot couldn't harmo-nize his American with his British voice, this anticipated the situation we have now, when the British can't hear the American voice, nor the American the British. That is a seed-bed for cultural chauvinism. With the multi-vocal poem such questions did not arise.

XXV A Son of Ezra

Like anyone else who has been in literary life for as long as I have, I have in recent years found myself teased or trapped by interviewers into admissions that I hadn't intended, which at times revealed to me aspects of myself that I hadn't been aware of. One such self-recognition came lately when a clever and deferential interviewer, probing delicately what he saw as an authoritarian streak in my aesthetic as well as political preferences, elicited from me the protest that I wasn't born to any of the ranks of British society that expect to wield authority. My father, I said, was a non-commissioned officer, a sergeant. But after the interviewer had gone I thought to myself: the NCO *does* exert authority, though an authority delegated to him by his superiors. Might it not follow that authority is most treasured and upheld, not by 'the officer class', but by the NCO class which depends for its authority on the officers, and is bitterly resentful when the officers throw that authority away? My own brief period in possession of a King's commission didn't dislodge this notion; for in 1945, as a Sub-lieutenant in the Royal Navy, I was wholly dependent on my NCO, a Yeoman of Signals — as he and I both understood very well, though neither of us would ever say so. In practice then, I reflected, authority is a very tricky and intricate matter: so far from being a naked exercise of power — that spurious equation I had rejected on my own account long before — authority is what the subordinated yearn for, and if necessary will fight to preserve.

There are those who will denounce such a train of reasoning as fascist or proto-fascist; and they won't be deterred by noticing that it corresponds to observable facts. In the end, persons of this persuasion will settle for nothing short of eliminating the NCO as a class, or (more precisely) as a rank. No more Yeomen of Signals! Luckily this won't happen — not just because no military or para-military formation can function without such personnel, but because there is a socio-psychological type which corresponds to that rank. My father was of that type, and happy with it; and so, I reckon, am I. Accordingly I responded very warmly and immediately to my contemporary Denis Donoghue's memoir, *Warrenpoint*, much of which centres on his father who, though Roman Catholic, was a sergeant first in the Royal Irish Constabulary, then in the Royal Ulster Constabulary. Setting aside the special exacerbations inflicted by the Irish context, I eagerly share Donoghue's gratitude to his father for embodying authority in a form that must be respected and could be emulated.[1]

What has to be recognized is that the NCO who is most fiercely loyal to his superior officer is the same man who is most fiercely critical of him. The most withering criticism of the officer class comes from those sergeants and petty-officers who have had to cover up for the ineptitude of their officers, to 'carry the can' for them. Deference is ritually required of them, and they comply – but on strict conditions which are as well understood in the Officers' Mess as in the NCOs'. A ritual deference which masks contempt belongs in a gestural code as easily deciphered by the one party as by the other; and it hurts, as it is meant to.

I begin with these ruminations because I am persuaded by Bernard Bergonzi that, after my rather many attempts to explain my attachment to Pound, the nature of that attachment remains mysterious, if not contradictory.[2] If there is such a mystery, then I should try to confront it. And at the moment I am toying with the notion that what attracted me to Pound from the first, and attracts me still, is the voice of the NCO in his mess: a voice stroppy and irreverent, yet devoted to authority – not his own authority however, but one delegated to him by 'the Service'. That voice offends others by just so much as it appeals to me: the Officers' Mess hears it as insubordinate and bloody-minded; the barrack-room hears it as overbearing and pitiless. My own impression is that in Britain the antagonism to Pound falls into one or other of these categories. (I speak, it should be clear, of immediate sympathies and antipathies, at a level far below argument.) If I am right, the opposition will never melt away; for the squaddies and the officers between them will always outnumber the corporals and sergeants. And I may as well say at once that, after forty years championing Pound (though often exasperated by him), I see no signs of the antagonism to him easing. There have been certain tactical out-manoeuvrings: Pound is now a respectable subject of scholarly study – for as much as *that* matters! But the dislike of him, and of what he stands for, is as virulent now in Great Britain as it was in 1950. And there is no reason to think that will change: the NCOs must be kept in their place, and that place is in a minority.

Of course my analogy with a military hierarchy is fanciful, but it is not so wide of the mark as a vulgarly Marxist model that pits workers against bosses, or a political model that ranges the Left against the Right. (And I know, thank you very much, about the theoretical model that would see the sergeants' mess as *petty bourgeois*, between the proletariat and the ruling *bourgeoisie*.)

What complicated things in my case was that the Poundian practices I defended and argued for in theory, I could not make work in practice.

---

1   Denis Donoghue, *Warrenpoint* (London: Cape, 1991).
2   See Bernard Bergonzi, 'Pound and Donald Davie' (1983), in *The Myth of Modernism and Twentieth-Century Literature* (Brighton: Harvester, 1986).

My *Forests of Lithuania* (1959) was a redaction – call it that – of Mickiewicz's *Pan Tadeusz*. It was undertaken and carried through, quite consciously, on Poundian principles as to what translation of poetry involved, or might involve. When it was finished, I thought it no more than proper to acknowledge my debt in a versified Foreword that was conspicuously, if not very inventively, in one of the styles of Pound's *Cantos*. I called this piece 'Mickiewicz in England'; and since I've suppressed it from recent re-printings of *The Forests of Lithuania* I seize the opportunity to re-print it now:

> Don John of Chesterton was riding to the wars
> For Christendom and the Latin heritage
> When Monica Gardner spoke of me. *Le coq*
> *Gaulois* of Belloc crowed around the clock
> 'Too late, too late'; for Gorky held the stage
> And 'Never a patch of plot,' said James, enthralled.
> 'To draw blood,' in a story
> By Turgenev.
> > > Scythians invest
> Small perfect Europe, for whose sake
> All Souls' High Table hears expressed
> Dreams of 'Divide and rule'.
>
> Did Belloc baulk, did Pound protest
> When Saintsbury found Sienkiewicz unlicked?
> Who quoted Kochanowski, and to cap
> What Latin tag? Who cared
> That he was salvaged from Cyrillic script,
> The Ronsard of Czarnólas?
> > > > What orisons
> Rose, modishly baroque,
> > > > > > for our lady of Czestochowa?
> > > > > Who could see
> The Hun turn East? Who egged him on?
> Who raged at Chamberlain for a guarantee
> To Poland honoured?
> > > > > Europe's paladin,
> > > > > > the champion of the *civitas*,
> He killed Cock Robin.
>
> The man on the touchline sees most of the play
> But may not know the rules. The Antipodean
> Anti-Semite brilliantly alleges
> The best of Europe's all around the edges.
> The rest a ghetto, 'mittel-European'

His curse on Martin Buber.
                    In the white
Nights of the Neva, quays of Amsterdam
And lions of Venice violate a site
Stolen from quagmire and the Finn; an *urbs*
Not Augustinian yet not without
Pushkin's *urbanitas*.
                    Some work their passage
Home out of Kronstadt, through Crimean sonnets,
Or recognize in Florence with a start
The Piazza Demidoff. And Europe's heart
Is wherever community happens in any age.

Without exception, the readers of *The Forests of Lithuania* – even those who most welcomed my Poundian operations on the Polish original – deplored this Poundian 'Foreword'. Perhaps they were right; perhaps my imitation of a Poundian style was too laboured, even though, thus early, I castigated Pound's anti-semitism, impaling for that purpose the Australian Poundian Noel Stock (who has subsequently purged that offence). At any rate I had learned my lesson: overt Poundianism would never go down with a British audience – nor with an American one, at that time. My consolation was to know that *covert* Poundianism was all over the version that by and large readers approved. (And this, I may say, remains the case; because so few people have read *The Cantos*, one may steal from them quite shamelessly, without anyone noticing.)

However, the trouble went deeper. Whenever I tried to write in a Poundian style (and I tried often), I didn't like what I came up with. Perhaps I hadn't a keen enough ear for unmetred verse; perhaps my British sensibility rejected a graft from what was after all American. Explain it as you will: I couldn't to my satisfaction carry out in practice what I applauded in theory. It was my satisfaction, not that of my supposed or imagined public, that was balked. In the event, what saved and liberated me was the precedent of my fellow-European, Boris Pasternak. Perhaps a Russian NCO is more like a British NCO than either is like an American NCO – I dunno.

It's hard to think that these cogitations have much to interest or enlighten a child of the 1990s. Just to complicate matters for him or her a little further, it must be said that it was the non-European Ezra Pound who illuminated for this European just what Europe meant, had meant in the past and might mean in the future. 'The man on the touchline sees most of the play': so I wrote in my 'Mickiewicz in England', hitting at the Antipodean Noel Stock. But it holds true for the American Ezra Pound, and not derisively either. Australians and Americans, they *do* see most of the play – as Europeans, for instance Brits., don't and can't. Europe as a

cultural whole can be conceived in the mind, and experienced in actuality, only by those who come to it from outside. That visitor from
outside, so far as I was concerned, was Ezra Pound.

It helped that what he looked at was more often buildings, or ruins of
buildings, than it was manuscripts:

> Where was the wall of Eblis
> At Ventadour, there now are the bees,
> And in that court, wild grass for their pleasure
> That they carry back to the crevice
> Where loose stone hangs upon stone.

(Canto XXVII)

Who or what Eblis was, is of no account. (I have looked it up in the
handbooks more than once, and as often promptly forgotten it.) What
matters is that in my Barnsley boyhood I had seen that loose stone
hanging upon stone in for instance the ruins of Conisborough Castle,
near Doncaster. To this day it is true that the Europe which Pound allows
me to frequent is far more a realm of stone (not necessarily ruinous) than
it is a realm of words. Pound's Europe is a fabric, not figuratively but in
fact; he discovered it for himself, partly in libraries but more in walking-
tours. Thus the Pound I am most aware of venerating is the Pound who
made into a controlling emblem of *The Cantos* a building, the Tempio in
Rimini; the Pound who inherited through Adrian Stokes, elucidator of
the Rimini building, the mantle of John Ruskin.[3]

Only a few years ago I put Eblis into a poem of my own:

Except The Lord Build The House

> A song of the degrees,
> of the gradations,
> the steps to the temple...
>
> There is no need to insist;
> it is enough to name them.
>
> For Zion is a city
> uniform in itself,
> compact together.
>
> Why are you so strenuous, my soul?
> Vain to get up early,
> to sit up late,
> to bolt your bread in a hurry.

3   See Adrian Stokes, *Stones of Rimini* (London: Faber, 1934); and Donald Davie, 'Adrian
Stokes Revisited' (1983), in *Studies in Ezra Pound* (Manchester: Carcanet, 1991).

Short be your sleep and coarse your fare
in vain. The Lord shall turn
the key in the captivity of Zion,
and all go like a dream.

The grass grows over the ruins of Eblis,
nobody's hayfield;
you are loitering there, or studying
hard (you are a hard
loiterer) but no one
going by in the road calls out
'Good morning' or 'Good luck'.

No use of early rising:
as useless is thy watching.
No traveller bestows
a word of blessing on the grass,
nor minds it as he goes.

Climb the stair
manfully, and sing
a short song on each step of the stair:

It is not an arduous duty.
Eblis was hard, not Zion.[4]

No one will, or is meant to, recognize 'Eblis' as an allusion to Pound.
For of course, as with 'Mickiewicz in England', I've taken a special
private satisfaction in inserting Pound into a context where not the most
devoted Poundian would think to look for him – as there in Polish and
Russian literature, so here in the poetry of ancient Israel. My title gives
the plainest signpost to Psalm 127, in the Authorized Version:

Except the Lord build the house, they labour in vaine that build it:
except the Lord keepe the citie, the watchman waketh but in vaine.
   It is vaine for you to rise up early, to sit up late, to eate the bread of
sorrowes: for so he giveth his beloved sleepe.

I have been put out of countenance by discovering that nowadays the
plainest allusion to the Psalms of David stymies almost as many readers as
a glancing allusion to *The Cantos* of Pound. Where does one go in one's
writing, if the King James Bible has become a recondite source? One
answer, not a happy one, is that the pleasure one takes in writing has
become more than ever a private pleasure, and must be recognized as
such. Certainly private is the wry satisfaction I take in knowing that
Pound's presence in this poem isn't limited to the one word, Eblis. And

4   Donald Davie, *To Scorch or Freeze: Poems about the Sacred* (Manchester: Carcanet, 1988).

at the risk of showing off, I had better demonstrate this.

Though the title and the opening lines rest indeed on the Authorized Version (which subtitles this psalm, 'A song of degrees: for Solomon'), 'Short be your sleep and coarse your fare' is a straight steal from the eighteenth-century version of this psalm by Isaac Watts; and 'No use of early rising:/as useless is thy watching' comes from the Elizabethan version by the Countess of Pembroke. Lines 6 to 8 come from another psalm altogether (Psalm 122, v.3) and later lines draw on yet another, Psalm 129, as rendered by Watts:

> So corn that on the house-top stands
>   No hope of harvest gives;
> The reaper ne'er shall fill his hands,
>   Nor binder fold the sheaves.
>
> It springs and withers on the place:
>   No traveller bestows
> A word of blessing on the grass,
>   Nor minds it as he goes.

My poem in fact is as much a mosaic, or a florilegium ('an anthology or collection of choice extracts' – *Chambers' Dictionary*), as is any of Pound's *Rock-Drill* Cantos, and when I consciously composed this and similar poems in this way, I imagined I was working as he must have worked – less ambitiously indeed, but on the same principle.

I will not be denied a further small flourish. The verses from Psalm 129 that I have just quoted in Isaac Watts's admirable version had earlier been rendered by another translator thus:

> All that hate Zion
> shall be put to shame and turned back.
>
> They shall be like grass on house tops,
> which withereth before it come forth,
>
> Whereof the reaper filleth not his hand,
> nor the gleaner his lap.
>
> Neither have the goers-by said,
> The blessing of the Lord be upon you,
> we bless you in the name of the Lord.

Those last lines are evidently (and I assure you) what gave me, in my poem –

>   but no one
> going by in the road calls out
> 'Good morning' or 'Good luck'.

Who then was this translator? He was not King James's translator, nor the earlier Miles Coverdale who gave us the version in *The Book of Common Prayer*. He was Arthur Golding, in 1571. Yes, the same Arthur Golding whose version of Ovid's *Metamorphoses* into fourteeners was once rashly declared by Pound to be 'the most beautiful book in the language'. Golding, inspired translator of Ovid's pagan fables, was a Calvinist, and his version of the Psalms was done from John Calvin's Latin version. Now let anyone deny that my 'Except the Lord Build the House' is anything but a Poundian poem!

But of course this *will* be denied – by all of those (and they are very many) who cannot or will not detach art from ideology. How can my poem, which assumes and endorses Jewish monotheism, be judged 'Poundian', when Jewish (and Christian) monotheism was just what Pound in season and out of season rejected and derided? I have just tried to answer that question, and I rest my case.

'Why are you so strenuous, my soul?' Of course the Psalmist never said that.[5] He neither said, nor could have said, anything of the sort. The persons whom he addressed in his poems were beings external to himself: his God, his enemies, his true or false friends. But 'you' in my poems often signifies myself. Thus the 'you' in my poem who is called 'a hard loiterer' (an expression, I will admit, that I am proud of) signifies in the first place myself, in the second place Ezra Pound, the Pound who made a pilgrimage to Ventadour. Though in the poem this person is mocked (for expending on ruined monuments of historical time the attention that rationally should be directed to Eternity), the mockery is indulgent: if we are condemned while waiting for Eternity to waste most of our time, then frequenting old sites, looking respectfully at ruined castles and old churches – as my parents taught me to do – is a more respectable sort of time-wasting than most.

It is hard work, however – 'Eblis is hard, not Zion'. It is hard, not just in the labour exacted day after day by antiquarian serendipity, but in the consequences that you can be brought to book for. Loitering round the ruins of an old Norman fortress, or inside the architectural masterpiece of a *condottiere* like Malatesta, may be thought innocuous; but if your imagination is stirred, and you then articulate and trust your sentiments on such occasions, you can be in trouble. That was the trouble that Pound in 1945 discovered he was in, having (it must be said) invited it, even dared it. We respond to the daring; but another part of us – the NCO's part – counts up how many died to implement the commander's derring-do. Pound seems to have looked at World War II through the binoculars of an

5 In a letter to me, Davie calls this sentence a 'foolish blunder'. He had forgotten that the line quoted is based on another psalm, Psalm 42.14, which is not by the same author as Psalm 127. [Ed.]

incompetent field-marshal; those who suffered and died got changed into statistics on a staff officer's desk. When he was incarcerated outside Pisa, he at last met the sufferers; but it was all too late, and in any case they didn't move him to remorse (except as regards some women in his private life). In *The Pisan Cantos* the ideology is as abhorrent as ever; but the art — so most readers have thought — is more masterly and audacious than ever before or since.

To recognize this, to acknowledge it as even a possibility, is labelled 'aestheticism'. But the art in the Pisan Cantos isn't at all of the 'ivory tower' kind; odd and anomalous as it may seem — to many, unthinkable and impossible — much in these Cantos is deeply *humane*, for instance the way the poet respects and delights in the individuality of certain of his guards and fellow-felons. This indeed is the quality that raises these Cantos to a level — and a level of *art* — above those that had gone before. But the world of readers is divided between those who see this and those who won't see it, ever.

'The world of readers…' When I was young I was sure that there was such a world, one that I must storm and break into. Now, having I suppose successfully broken and entered, I think that that world, if it ever existed (as I think it did for Pound), had disintegrated before I came on the scene. Now what we have are Poundians, Larkinites, Gravesians, and so on — factions that no longer even war among themselves but feebly persist, indifferent to challenges that they don't even know about or else disdain to notice. If we ask how that disintegration came about, Pound is often cast as one villain in the piece. It's thus that he figures in one representative and influential account of what happened:

Who can forget Diaghilev, the greatest impresario of modernism, saying to Cocteau, the best known of all its sprites: '*Etonne-moi, Jean*'? As we entered middle age, we were to experience the fearful effects of this command to be original. The first effect was to separate the artist from the mass of society. The avant-garde outdistanced the army it was leading. On marched the artists. They were not marching to any known land, they were marching to discover new countries beyond the horizon of their fellow men and women. Desperate to follow them an elite corps broke away from the army to join them. The elite ended by being as isolated as the artists as they strove to keep pace with the change in styles. You come to love an artist only when you have struggled to understand his latest puzzling novelty: and love, not respect, is what an artist wants. What he does not want is the plaudits of democratic voters who if they had their way would vote art out of existence. Not only Eliot and Pound despised democracy. For D.H. Lawrence humdrum people didn't matter. They must never be given a clue about the direction art might take…[6]

The writer is that far from humdrum person, Noel Annan. And it's astonishing he should think that when we read Pound or Eliot or Lawrence, we do so in order to 'keep up'. There is one modish class of consumers who may read with that motive; but they soon fall away, and good riddance. How can one be thought to be 'keeping up' with Conisborough Castle or Ventadour? One is, if anything, casting back. Pound wasn't inviting me to unprecedented experiences, but on the contrary causing me to re-experience, with a new seriousness, experiences I had had already; and his formal innovations were designed to incite me to that. Nor was there ever an army on the march, which the artists got too far ahead of. The 'avant-garde' encapsulates a French metaphor that (typically) obfuscates more than it enlightens.

So the world of readers didn't disintegrate because writers like Pound perversely and gratuitously fractured it. The causes of the disintegration were certainly much more various than that, and more deep-seated. Some would say, perhaps portentously, that what we have seen – readers and writers of my generation – is the end of the age of print. Undoubtedly the printed word, as a medium of expression and communication, doesn't enjoy anything like the pre-eminence that Pound in his heyday could take for granted (though he was early aware of a challenge from radio). This means that any relationship between a writer of my generation, and a writer of his, has to be complicated. Certainly it can't be called, forthrightly, love; there is too much envy in it for that, and too much bitterness. But then, when Lord Annan declares 'You can come to love an artist only when you have struggled to understand his latest puzzling novelty', he astonishes me all over again. That sort of love, I think, belongs in 'Pound Studies'; it is the attachment of a commentator, an exegetical specialist, to the author he has made his speciality. Because I have myself contributed to Pound Studies, and have at times set up as an exegete, I must put it on record that my author's 'latest puzzling novelty' has often enraged me, and I have resented the labours that his latest antic has let me in for. This is true particularly of the late sequence of Cantos called *Thrones*, because all my quite assiduous labours on those many pages yielded me only Dead Sea fruit. I learned from them only what to avoid in my writing, nothing that I could applaud or profit from. (They were followed of course by the final *Drafts and Fragments*, and from them all of us can profit.)[7]

Since I seem to be coming clean, I have to confess to an appropriation of Pound that may be unforgivable. This is in the fourth part of a six-part poem that I wrote perhaps fifteen years ago, called 'A Garland for Ronsard'. The third and the last of these pieces are straightforward trans-

6   Noel Annan, *Our Age* (London: Fontana pbk rpt, 1991), p. 72.
7   See 'More on the Muddle of Thrones' (1990), in *Studies in Ezra Pound* (*op. cit.*).

lations of quite famous poems by Ronsard; and the first, second and fifth
pieces ought to be readily intelligible to anyone who has studied even
superficially the life and works of this great poet. (Who nowadays does so,
however? I'm wearied by the thought of seeking such people out, even
among the French.) The fourth piece in my 'garland' is quite different:

> At Ste Madeleine de Croixval,
> housebound with gout, four sonnets;
> October –
>   'dusty air...
> September's yellow gold that mingled fair
> With green and rose tint on each maple bough
> Sulks into deeper browns.'
>   He died in that
> same year at the other priory, St Cosme.

> Hélène, Cassandre, Yseult
> Is–hilda, Undine, 'O
> swallow, my sister' – look
> out for whom you
> fatuously endow, though
> posterity fail not desert perhaps.

> Frenetic and protean
> (One noted: double chin!)
> 'perched like a bird at dusk',
> huge eyes, thin shoulders; or
> the strapping one perched, shoes off
> at the foot of his bunk. They are
> no good, you know, these girls.

> What did he write?
> 'Myrrh and olibanum',
> gum-resin from incisions
> in South Arabia: *dendron*,
> cecily, chervil – and
> AMOR, the palindrome ROMA.
> Backward or forward it read
> the same: she-wolf.

> 'There is a mellow twilight 'neath the trees
> Soft and hallowed as is a thought of thee...'
> 'Whisper in the murmurous twilight where
> I met thee mid the roses of the past
> Where you gave your first kiss in the last...'

And which of them all did he, oh well,
'love'?
        The Lady Loba.

Here, nearly all the verses in quotation-marks are pinched from
Pound's boyish poems to his teenage sweetheart Hilda Doolittle ('H.D.');
and the only signpost I give to this derivation is the title I give to this sub-
section, 'End to Torment' – which is the title of H.D.'s late and in my
view quite untrustworthy memoir of her relationships with Pound, early
and late.[8] My piece incorporates her jealous impressions of the infatua-
tions of the aging Pound – with *La Martinelli*, and Marcella Spann. How
far these were real liaisons, how far H.D.'s fantasies, is a question that my
poem, simply because it's a poem, doesn't have to answer.

How can I justify this procedure? Obviously in terms of reader-
response I can't, since not one in a thousand readers can be expected to
discern what I am driving at, let alone identify my sources. But a poem is
not in the first place a communication; otherwise it would be limited by
what its foreseeable readership could be expected to cotton on to – an
expectation that *The Cantos* are at great pains to flout, first and last. My
perhaps unacceptable justification is twofold: first, I advance without
pruriency or any pretence to special information a hypothesis about
Pound's equal status with the virtually unassailable status of Pierre de
Ronsard, whose sexual career is as impenetrable by us (and ultimately as
irrelevant to us) as Pound's. Of course 'impenetrable' and 'unassailable'
are just two alternative red rags to the populist bull that will charge into
my china-shop; but that cannot be helped. Ultimately, I suppose, the
poem is about how an artist uses women at the same time as they use him.
(It's 'personal', then? Oh yes.)

These early and touchingly vulnerable poems by the young Pound are
known to us only in 'Hilda's book', now in the Houghton Library at
Harvard. And with this item – 'a small (13.7cm. x 10.5cm.) book, hand-
bound and sewn in vellum, of 57 leaves' – my narrative moves from
matters of literary 'influence' into lived, and located, experience. It was a
chance encounter on a train from London to the West Country, about
1980, which alerted me to Frank Wintle, director of programmes for
Television South West, operating from Plymouth. Frank, it emerged, had
applied himself to discover why and how 'Hilda's Book', in all its unique-
ness, had been recovered from the debris of a bombed house after a
Luftwaffe blitz on Plymouth and Devonport in 1941. The crucial link, he

---

8   *End to Torment: A Memoir of Ezra Pound by H.D.*, ed. Norman Holmes Pearson and
    Michael King, with the poems from 'Hilda's Book' by Ezra Pound (Manchester:
    Carcanet, 1980).

discovered, was Frances Gregg, who died in the bombing raid along with her octogenarian mother and her mentally retarded daughter. Their remains were identified by her son, Oliver Wilkinson, then a serving bluejacket in the Royal Navy, who survived to play a crucial and exceptionally dignified role in the film that Frank Wintle made. Frances Gregg, it turned out, was American, though she had lived outside her own country since she and her mother in 1911 had arrived along with H.D. from Philadelphia. Frances and Hilda and Ezra had been close, as teenage literary aspirants in and around the Philadelphia suburb of Wyncote, where Pound grew up, to which Frank Wintle at one stage summoned me to speak a few sentences to camera. Unbelievably *naïve* it now seems, the idea that because one of the trio had established a modest toe-hold in literary London, it was reasonable for his two companions to cast aside worldly security and follow him. And yet for one of them, H.D., the outrageous gamble in the end paid off. Frances Gregg, lacking perhaps the talent of H.D., certainly lacking the ambitious egotism that impelled her bisexual compatriot, in worldly terms got nowhere at all. She married an English novelist Louis Wilkinson, who in one of his novels gave a fictionalized vignette of the youthful Pound. After he left her — not without provocation, in the opinion of their son — Frances seems to have declined into a sort of penurious vagrancy which, in Oliver Wilkinson's view, she may have put paid to, almost suicidally, by moving to that one of the West Country cities that would certainly, sooner or later, be targeted by the Germans. It's morbidly appropriate that in Efford, Plymouth's memorial to its blitzed dead, she should be listed under her married name, Wilkinson.

It's difficult to derive from this protracted episode, thus unearthed, anything but sadness. And what is one more sadness, among the innumerably many caused by World War II? Yet Frances Gregg's wretchedness, though the war crowned it, wasn't caused by the war, but (one can't help thinking) by artistic Modernism. The modernists, Pound among them, set in their lives a furious and unforgiving pace that few of their companions and associates could keep up with. How many more were there who, like Frances Gregg, fell out of the hunt yet had been incapacitated for doing anything else that satisfied them? Pound seems to have been more aware of their fate, and more concerned about it, than the other modernists; he intervened at least once to prevent H.D. from manipulating Frances's life still more disastrously.

My visit to Wyncote was illuminating. It is still an attractive place, preserved almost in a time-capsule, pre-1914, though much more leafy and umbrageous now than when the poet's father, Homer Pound, set up house there. His house is virtually unchanged, and kept that way — as a sort of shrine — by the present occupant, who entertained Pound there in 1958. This admirable host, showing slides to me with the rest of the TV crew, provided the right context for Pound's belated disavowal of 'that stupid, suburban prejudice of anti-semitism'.[9]

That epithet, 'suburban', has been thought insufficiently breast-beating; but the slides we were shown, of newspaper clippings from Wyncote in the 1890s, show that as usual Pound was being merely exact – the exclusion of 'Israelites' from social institutions and occasions was at that time in that place quite explicit and unabashed. Of course this is not offered as any sort of excuse. But it does show that Pound's anti-semitism wasn't an infection that he picked up in Europe, but something he brought with him from America – and not from the Midwest either, but from the Eastern seaboard. This indigenous root of Pound's obsession is obscured by the portrayals of him on screen, including I'm afraid the one in the film, *Hilda's Book*. For these present him as a sort of Aleister Crowley figure, satanically cloaked, whereas the lamentable truth was far more 'folksy'. Dorothy Pound's dislike of Jews may have been that of the Officers' Mess, but her husband's wasn't.

Frank Wintle's film, though flawed, deserved better than to be shown only in a regional network. Though as a Poundian I guard against too easily succumbing, like the master, to conspiracy theories, I do find something sinister in the refusal by any of the national networks to take it on. It presents Pound in a human, not an ideological, context. And that is the last thing that Pound's enemies, and even some of his false friends, want or will tolerate. What it showed me, who like most literary people thought of TV as a menace, is that television has nurtured some people whose researches go beyond the best that literary researchers can come up with.

This piece has turned out more elegiac than I had been prepared for. But this is inevitable. Not only Pound's life, but mine in the shadow of his, is for many readers already ancient history. And yet 'in the shadow' is wrong. I should like my life in writing to be considered in the light of Pound's; and not Eliot nor Yeats, not Hardy nor Pasternak nor (least of all) Mandelstam, can be substituted for 'Pound' in that sentence. Why this should be, others may explain. My own best stab at it would have to use fuzzy and loaded words like 'heroic' and 'adventurous', even or particularly 'magnanimous'. If in my chosen trade I was looking for authority, he more than anyone embodied it.

9   Michael Reck, 'A Conversation between Ezra Pound and Allen Ginsberg', *Evergreen Review*, 57 (June 1968).

Sons of Ezra: British Poets and Ezra Pound, ed. Michael Alexander and James McGonigal (Amsterdam and Atlanta: Rodopi, 1995).

XXVI Ezra Pound in Pisa

Excellence is sparse.
I am made of a Japanese mind
Concerning excellence:
However sparred or fierce
The furzy elements,
Let them be but few
And spaciously dispersed,
And excellence appears.

Not beauty. As for beauty,
That is a special thing.
Excellence is what
A man who treads a path
In a prison-yard might string
Together, day by day,
From straws blown in his path
And bits of remembering.

Sun moves, and the shadow moves,
In spare and excellent order;
I too would once repair
Most afternoons to a pierced
Shadow on gravelly ground,
Write at a flaked, green-painted
Table, and scrape my chair
As sun and shade moved round.

The Listener, 18 January 1968; reprinted in *Essex Poems: 1963–1967* (London: Routledge and Kegan Paul, 1969).

Index

246 *Modernist Essays*